*Civil War in Guangxi*

# Civil War in Guangxi

*The Cultural Revolution on China's Southern Periphery*

ANDREW G. WALDER

STANFORD UNIVERSITY PRESS
*Stanford, California*

STANFORD UNIVERSITY PRESS
Stanford, California

Library of Congress Cataloging-in-Publication Data

Names: Walder, Andrew G. (Andrew George), 1953– author.
Title: Civil war in Guangxi : the Cultural Revolution on China's southern
    periphery / Andrew G. Walder.
Description: Stanford, California : Stanford University Press, [2023] |
    Includes bibliographical references and index.
Identifiers: LCCN 2022024759 (print) | LCCN 2022024760 (ebook) |
    ISBN 9781503634671 (cloth) | ISBN 9781503635227 (paperback) |
    ISBN 9781503635234 (epub)
Subjects: LCSH: Insurgency—China—Guangxi Zhuangzu Zizhiqu—History—
    20th century. | Massacres—China—Guangxi Zhuangzu Zizhiqu—History—
    20th century. | Political violence—China—Guangxi Zhuangzu Zizhiqu—
    History—20th century. | Guangxi Zhuangzu Zizhiqu (China)—Politics and
    government—20th century. | China—History—Cultural Revolution, 1966–1976.
Classification: LCC DS793.K6 W35 2023 (print) | LCC DS793.K6 (ebook) |
    DDC 951.2/805—dc23/eng/20220525
LC record available at https://lccn.loc.gov/2022024759
LC ebook record available at https://lccn.loc.gov/2022024760

Cover design: Lindy Kasler
Cover photo: (top) Surrendered fighters from the April 22 faction, Nanning, early August 1968; (bottom) Shutterstock
Typeset by Newgen North America in 10/15 Brill

*To the memory of*
*Roderick MacFarquhar*

Guangxi and China in 1966

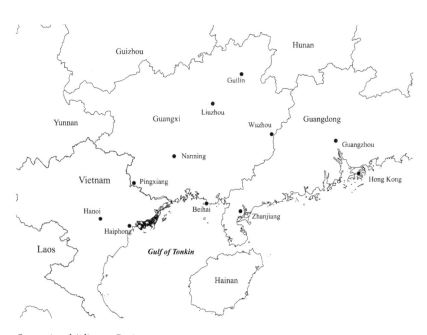

Guangxi and Adjacent Regions

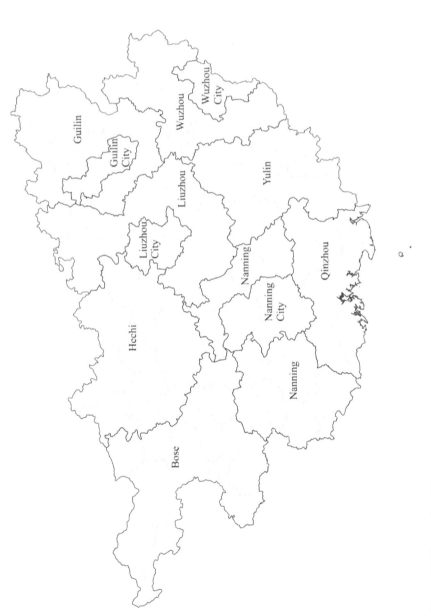

Guilin

Guilin
City

Wuzhou

Wuzhou
City

Liuzhou

Yulin

Liuzhou
City

Nanning

Qinzhou

Nanning
City

Hechi

Nanning

Bose

Guangxi Prefectures in 1966

Guangxi Cities and Counties in 1966

# CONTENTS

# ILLUSTRATIONS AND TABLES

## Maps

## Figures

Tables

# AUTHOR'S STATEMENT

In some ways, this book has been the most difficult of any I have written. It has been difficult because of its subject matter. The Cultural Revolution in Guangxi unleashed what was by far China's largest wave of deadly violence against innocent people—men, women, children, and the elderly—who were often killed in the most gruesome fashion. In years of writing about the conflicts of this sad period of Chinese history, I have become familiar with senseless factional violence, large death tolls in organized suppression campaigns, and the callous and even celebratory brutality with which alleged enemies of the people were beaten and tortured. What one encounters in Guangxi is a step beyond anything that I have encountered in my previous research—including my examination of Beijing's Red Guard movement in the book *Fractured Rebellion*, or my analysis of the nationwide collapse of civilian political structures and the subsequent spread of factional warfare in *Agents of Disorder*. In none of my prior work have I been forced to confront the killing not just of surrendered combatants but of noncombatants, the latter often dispatched in the most cruel and inhuman manner—beaten with clubs, knifed, disemboweled, buried alive, or thrown into pits. For the first time I have encountered widespread sexual violence against women after male household heads were killed, often committed by their murderers. I have not previously had to confront, and try to make sense of, reports of cannibalism—the eating of the organs and flesh of those recently killed. There were also waves of suicides by individuals who sought to escape a death that was even more difficult to contemplate. These were horrific events on a large scale. I have tried to turn my subjective reaction into a determination to focus on explanation—to sort out the evidence for a range of possible answers that have been offered by past authors, and other ideas that have yet to be considered. I treat these events as analytical puzzles, sifting through mounds of evidence—both descriptive accounts and statistical patterns—that might help to resolve them. I have a nagging sense that this analytical approach fails to fully convey the sheer horror of what happened in Guangxi. But there have long been accounts in both English and Chinese that dwell on these atrocities in gruesome detail.

In other ways, this book has been the easiest to write. It was facilitated by the existence of a large-scale systematic investigation mandated by China's central government in the early 1980s, which resulted in a classified eighteen-volume set of materials that described what happened in each of Guangxi's cities and counties, with a focus on documenting the scale of the death toll in the province and identifying the parties responsible. The voluminous materials compiled by the investigators, described in this book's appendix, went far beyond the purposes for which the investigations were mandated. Eight of the volumes were detailed chronologies of political events in each of the cities and counties, along with extensive statistical material on their impact. Another six volumes provided detailed description of individual episodes that went even more deeply into matters described in the chronologies. The material compiled in these documents was far more than what was needed for the purposes of the central government's investigation, and little of this material was analyzed by its compilers. What is most valuable about this information is that it bears on a wide range of questions that the investigators never considered. When combined with other information about cities and counties, it can be used to adjudicate a range of different explanations for the onset, duration, and severity of the violence. In no previous work have I been able to bring such a wide range of evidence to bear to adjudicate among alternative explanations for puzzling political events.

## ACKNOWLEDGMENTS

I did not do this work alone; many others have contributed. A handful of student research assistants from Chinese universities worked as interns over several summers, testing out provisional coding schemes for the data set employed in this book. Given the sensitive nature of the subject in today's China, I will not acknowledge them by name, but their contributions were invaluable. Several students who were enrolled in graduate programs at Stanford or elsewhere also made important contributions to the coding of material that entered the data set, or to other aspects of the research for this book. I am grateful to Yuqian Chen, Ziyao Tian, and Calista Wells. By far the most important contributions were made by Qianmin Hu. She led the final effort to devise and implement rules for coding complex events and worked closely with me in weekly meetings over two years to resolve questions about particularly difficult coding problems, and later to identify and reconcile errors in the completed data set. She also generated the maps that are included in this volume. James Chu wrote programs for coding events with multiple participants that identified activities that involved different combinations of participants, and I have relied on some of his work in this book.

I would like particularly to acknowledge the influence of Yang Su's previous work on collective killings in Guangxi and Guangdong. Yang is a former PhD student and coauthor who made vitally important contributions to my earlier research project, which drew upon data extracted from published local annals. His award-winning book on this subject drew upon a preliminary and partial version of the national data set that was later the foundation for my 2019 book, *Agents of Disorder*. Yang's analysis of intergroup violence in rural communities and the impact of historical migration patterns in Guangxi and Guangdong served to focus the questions that I pursue in this book. The more detailed materials at my disposal led me to different answers, but this does not diminish his scholarly contributions. Yang and several other colleagues have read and commented upon earlier fragments of this manuscript in ways that shaped the revised material included here. These colleagues include James Chu, Susan Olzak, Patrician Thornton, and Fei Yan.

I am also grateful to Daniel Leese of Freiburg University, the project director for the digital archive "The Maoist Legacy: Party Dictatorship, Transitional Justice and the Politics of Truth" (https://www.maoistlegacy.de). Daniel directed me to research generated by the project that helped me to understand how the Guangxi materials were compiled. He put me in touch with one of his former PhD students, Song Guoqing, whose dissertation is an in-depth examination of the compilation of the Guangxi materials, placing them squarely in the context of the politics of the era in which they were generated. Song has responded very generously to my requests for clarification on several points. Most of what I know about how these materials were compiled I have learned from his careful research.

Several others helped in various ways. Dong Guoqiang and Fei Yan steered me to relevant materials and helped me to understand matters that puzzled me. David Shambaugh responded quickly to queries about unit designations in the People's Liberation Army, and put me in touch with Kenneth Allen, who shared unpublished drafts on the subject that helped greatly to clarify this obscure subject. Norman Naimark responded generously to my requests for recommended reading on mass killings in other historical settings. Two anonymous readers for Stanford University Press provided suggestions for revision.

A data-intensive project such as this requires generous funding. I am grateful to the China Fund of the Freeman-Spogli Institute for International Studies at Stanford University for seed funding that permitted me to complete the preliminary work necessary for a successful research proposal. National Science Foundation Grant SBS-1753552, "Political Violence and State Repression," provided funding for this research from 2018 until it was completed in 2020. Stanford's Shorenstein Asia-Pacific Research Center provided supplementary funds for correcting errors in the final data set and devising programs for coding events that involved multiple actors.

This book includes previously published material in "Anatomy of a Regional Civil War: Guangxi, China, 1967–1968," *Social Science History* 46, no. 1 (Spring 2022), © Cambridge University Press. I am grateful to the publishers for permission to incorporate some of that work here.

Finally, I would like to acknowledge my debt to a late colleague and close friend, Roderick MacFarquhar, without whose inspiration and unstinting encouragement I would likely not have embarked on the series of studies about China's Cultural Revolution that has culminated in the present volume. I regret that I did not complete this volume in time for Rod to see this dedication.

*Civil War in Guangxi*

# Prologue

On July 16, 1968, the final battle for control of Guangxi's capital city of Nanning was about to begin. Rebel forces had overthrown civilian governments across the province at the outset of 1967, and in the succeeding months armed factions fought one another across the region, intensifying as the long stalemate wore on. Several thousand fighters from one of two rebel alliances—the Allied Command (*lianzhi*)—took up positions that sealed off a downtown district around Liberation Road. The mixed commercial and residential neighborhood was located on the northern bank of a sharp bend in the Yong River, a major shipping channel. It was bordered on the west and north by a tributary known as Chaoyang Creek, which curved around the district, creating a peninsula. Dug into the neighborhood, trapped behind defensive positions, were the leaders, supporters, and surviving combat brigades of the other alliance, the April 22 faction (*si.erer*, or "4.22"), who had refused to surrender and were making their last stand.[1]

As the Allied Command forces prepared for their assault, they launched a campaign to "cleanse the population" in areas of the city under their control. The "cleansing" sought to capture members of the April faction who had fled to the city from surrounding rural districts in recent months, as their faction was suppressed. All were treated as enemy combatants. Of the 283 individuals who were arrested in the initial sweep that day, 33 were summarily executed, and the rest went missing, their fate unknown. The killings foreshadowed the brutality of the battle to come.

The Allied Command, backed by People's Liberation Army (PLA) soldiers from the Guangxi Military District and rural militias from surrounding counties, began by hurling makeshift firebombs (glass bottles filled with gasoline) at buildings occupied by their enemies. April faction fighters responded with sniper fire and their own firebombs, and homes and shops were set ablaze. Firefighters who rushed to the scene were targeted by snipers, and three of them were killed. Allied faction forces on both sides of the Yong River bombarded boats used by the April faction to ferry supplies and reinforcements. They scored a direct hit on a freighter containing more than a thousand barrels of diesel and aviation fuel, setting the docks ablaze.

Rifle fire, firebombs, and destruction along the riverbanks failed to dislodge the defenders, so PLA troops joined the battle, bringing to bear heavy weaponry. In late July, the attacking forces used anti-aircraft machine guns, rocket-propelled grenades, and bazookas to dislodge the defenders. The strategy was highly effective when focused on individual buildings. On July 31, troops backed by an artillery unit turned their firepower onto an exhibition hall occupied by the April faction. From midafternoon into the night, they poured thousands of rounds from rifles and machine guns into the building, along with hundreds of artillery shells. The battered survivors surrendered the next morning. The assault left 23 dead and 57 wounded among the defenders; 470 were taken prisoner. The attackers suffered 6 dead and 52 wounded.

Similar weapons were then used indiscriminately to bombard the neighborhoods under April faction control. Despite the inevitable destruction, the bombardment continued, and reinforcements from the PLA and rural militias continued to join the battle. By the first days of August, shops and homes along twelve streets, covering thirty-three city blocks, were reduced to rubble, and fires blazed uncontrolled in the structures that remained standing. By August 5, after a siege of almost three weeks, April faction resistance had collapsed. The last few holdouts surrendered on August 8. The devastation to the Liberation Road district was total, and the April faction was crushed. Shops, homes, factories, government offices, and temples were destroyed. More than 10,000 families—50,000 residents—were left homeless.

The authorities would later document close to 1,600 deaths in the battle for the district and a handful of other sites in the city, a count that was admittedly incomplete. In the Liberation Road neighborhood, 680 corpses resulting from the fighting were eventually dumped into a coal pit, and a similar number were recovered from burned-out buildings. Another 72 were buried hastily along the banks of Chaoyang Creek; 52 were killed while trying to flee; and an unknown number of corpses floated off down the creek and into the Yong River. During the entire course of the battle of Nanning, only 60 Allied faction fighters were killed, along with 26 PLA soldiers.

The ordeal of the surviving defenders was just beginning. Close to 6,500 April faction fighters were taken prisoner, along with some 2,500 residents suspected of supporting them. The victors did not have a plan to process so many prisoners. The detainees were assembled under guard at several locations nearby, to be marched in groups to the government headquarters for investigation and sentencing. During one such procession Allied faction guards pulled twenty-six prisoners out of the ranks and summarily executed them.[2] Large numbers of the survivors were members of the April faction from rural counties who had moved into Nanning to seek protection or to reinforce their allies in the battle for the city. A total of close to 7,000 either had surrendered after the battle or had been captured during the "cleansing" of the city's population. They were expelled from Nanning and taken back to their home counties, which were no more forgiving: 2,324 were executed, and 246 were given long prison sentences.

*      *      *

The pacification of Nanning was one of two decisive urban battles that spelled the end of factional warfare in Guangxi. As the April faction was being crushed in the provincial capital, a much longer and more evenly matched battle was coming to a similar conclusion in Guilin.[3] This former provincial capital in the northeastern corner of Guangxi, a region renowned for the beauty of its steep limestone mountains, had long been the stronghold of the April faction. The Guilin branch of the April alliance, known locally as the Rebel Army (*zaofan dajun*), had seized power in January 1967 with the backing of a PLA regiment stationed there. Relying on continuing PLA support, the Rebel Army staged a massive arms seizure from military stockpiles in August 1967. Heavily armed with military weaponry, they drove their opponents out of the city and into the surrounding counties. Not until June 1968 would the Allied Command, backed by rural militias from surrounding counties, launch their offensive to take Guilin.

Unlike the final battle for Nanning, Guilin was a prolonged, two-month campaign. Both sides had advanced weaponry—automatic rifles, light and heavy machine guns, rocket launchers and mortars. Each side had infantry and artillery companies. Each had advisors from different units of the PLA. After a cease-fire in April 1968, followed quickly by the establishment of a new city government dominated by the Allied faction, the truce broke down and the two sides fortified strongholds in different districts. Drawing on instruction from their respective military backers, the two sides organized combat units. Still smaller and less well-armed than their opponents, the Allied Command called upon rural militias in the surrounding counties, under the direction of local People's Armed Departments (PADs), to send reinforcements. The first militia contingents entered Guilin on June 4, and battles between the two sides escalated. By the end of June, more than 8,000 militia fighters from twelve counties had entered the city. The rural militias, however, were only lightly armed. In one of the large battles that month, ninety-three were killed on the two sides, and the Rebel Army forced the militia to retreat to suburban counties.

After these initial engagements, the Allied Command realized that their weaponry was inadequate. At the end of June, they staged raids on a large PLA arms depot located at a rail terminus in Xing'an County, on the line running north from Guilin into Hunan Province. Eventually mobilizing more than 1,000 fighters, they made ten unsuccessful assaults on the depot before prevailing. They hauled off a large stockpile of arms and ammunition, including 60 cannon, more than 11,000 artillery shells, 12,000 hand grenades, and other military supplies.

The arms were distributed to militia units, and two weeks later they began a co-ordinated assault, advancing into Guilin from three directions. The two sides faced off on a long front, and intense fighting by infantry and artillery units continued from July 13 to 24. Enjoying a continued flow of reinforcements from rural militias, the Allied Command gradually gained the upper hand in a series of decisive battles from July 27 to August 3. They finally overwhelmed the Rebel Army forces, declaring victory on August 6.

During the battle for Guilin, the two sides mobilized more than 10,000 armed fighters. They possessed more than 13,000 rifles, 80 cannon, 19,000 cannon shells, 230,000 hand grenades, and 8.3 million rounds of ammunition. Over the most intense weeks of fighting, Guilin was paralyzed. Transportation was halted; factories, schools, and shops were closed; suburban farmers were unable to tend crops; and civilian noncombatants were terrorized. A partial count of casualties listed 406 deaths among urban combatants and noncombatants, and 198 from the militias drawn from the surrounding counties. It was common for prisoners to be summarily executed. Rural militia members who returned home after suffering casualties in Guilin exacted revenge on April faction adherents and others in order to "consolidate the rear area." Militia forces engaged in a wave of mass killings in rural counties across Guilin Prefecture, liquidating close to 8,500 noncombatants during June, July, and August.

The Rebel Army suffered violent retribution after their defeat. The authorities initiated a coordinated sweep of neighborhoods and workplaces, focusing on Rebel Army activists and fighters, along with their many supporters. Arrests and house searches claimed more than 10,000 victims; 7,000 were held at one point in the main detention center. Prisoners were subjected routinely to beatings, torture, and public humiliation. Some were stoned to death, others beaten to death in public rallies, and there were group executions by firing squad. By the end of the suppression campaign, 345 deaths were officially recorded: 160 beaten or shot to death; 94 killed during public rallies or processions; and 91 suicides.

\*     \*     \*

As the urban warfare in Nanning and Guilin reached its violent conclusion, rural counties across Guangxi were also in the midst of intensely violent upheavals, but of a very different kind. In almost all counties, factions aligned with the April coalition had been subdued months earlier by militia forces under the command of PADs. Yet a startling wave of violent persecutions intensified across Guangxi's rural regions just as the final battles in Nanning and Guilin were reaching a climax. The casualty counts dwarfed those in the major cities, however, and the persecutions did not focus exclusively on April faction forces and their supporters. They also targeted uninvolved individuals from politically stigmatized "class enemy" households, the surviving members of former propertied classes and those historically associated with the Nationalist Party and other opponents of the new regime, along with their offspring. Moreover, the death tolls were rarely generated by armed combat or retribution by victorious militias over their vanquished enemies. Instead, unarmed village residents were liquidated in large numbers, at times in the most gruesome manner.

This was a form of violence rarely seen in urban combat and its aftermath. The victims and their killers were residents of the same rural districts. Most disturbing to those who subsequently chronicled these events was the discovery that entire families were sometimes liquidated, including the elderly and small children, in acts that were at times accompanied by sexual violence, the mutilation and display of corpses, and even cannibalism.

Emblematic of this wave of rural violence was Binyang County, northeast of Nanning, whose closest border was only 25 miles from the city's near suburbs.[4] On July 24, as the fighting in Nanning was reaching its climax, the county authorities organized meetings of public security and militia offices in neighborhoods and villages, ordering them to draw up lists of class enemies and other political suspects. Commune and village militia officers were instructed to compile "dictatorship" lists—those in villages who were to be subjected to public trials and executions. Under the direction of these committees, waves of mass killings spread across villages. Over a ten-day period from the end of July to early August, 3,691 individuals were killed or committed suicide. Of these, 2,036 were members of stigmatized "class enemy" households, few of whom had dared to get involved in factional activities. There were 191 households in which more than one individual was killed; 176 children were orphaned; and in 14 extreme cases, everyone in the family was killed. A summary paragraph in an official investigation report reflects the sense of shock felt by those who chronicled these events two decades later:

> During the few days that the massacres reached a climax, there were corpses littered all over the county seat, to the point where vehicles could not pass on the streets. Families were scattered and broken up; some were dug up by the roots and completely eradicated; some were plundered by the killers so there was no home to which to return; wives were raped by their husband's murderers or forced to submit to them.[5]

Detailed accounts from Binyang and other counties describe events in hundreds of individual villages that illustrate the way these campaigns were conducted. Numbing accounts of savage cruelty have been highlighted in a range of publications over the years.[6] One example shows how these campaigns spread widely across rural regions. On July 29 the battalion commander of the Luojiang Commune militia returned from a meeting at the Binyang county seat and called for a meeting of the commune's leaders. They drew up a list of eight men from several villages for execution. On the next day the commanders of the village militia escorted the men to a mass rally attended by 200 to 300 residents, during which they were harangued in speeches that detailed the individuals' alleged crimes and called for the elimination of class enemies. At the end of the rally, members of the militia and other activists dragged the eight men to the outskirts of the village and clubbed them to death. Two days later, on August 2, the commune's leaders met again to discuss how to push their campaign against class enemies to an even higher level. The head of the district's recently established Revolutionary Committee gave a speech urging the commune to make more progress. He claimed that they had not done enough, and a commune of their size should "do [*gao*]" at least 100. The commune committee then hastily drew up a new list of six names for execution and ordered the militia commanders to bring them to the commune seat for another mass rally. At the end of the rally the individuals were dragged to the commune's tile kiln and clubbed to death on the spot.[7]

*     *     *

As the disastrous consequences of the Cultural Revolution were chronicled and publicized by the new leaders of the Chinese Communist Party in the late 1970s and well into the 1980s, Guangxi earned a reputation as the most violent region of China. There had been urban warfare in other cities that resulted in extensive devastation and large death tolls, but destruction on the scale of Nanning and Guilin was rare.[8] Violent retribution against defeated factional enemies was common elsewhere, but it rarely generated death tolls on the scale observed in Guangxi.[9] There were also mass killings of "class enemy" households in other regions, but these were isolated cases, restricted to one county or a small cluster of them. In no other province were such killings as widespread and intense as in Guangxi.[10]

And in no other region was sexual violence and cannibalism reported with such disturbing frequency.

The most credible estimate of the total number of people killed in political violence in China during this phase of the Cultural Revolution is in the range of 1.6 million.[11] A detailed series of investigations in Guangxi organized by the Beijing authorities during the 1980s documented a final count of 89,810.[12] With a population of 25 million in 1967, this would yield a death rate of 3.6 per thousand in Guangxi. China's total population at the time was close to 750 million: excluding Guangxi, the national death rate would be close to 2.1 per thousand. By this measure, Guangxi's death rate was 70 percent higher than that of the rest of the country. There is some uncertainty, however, about how the Guangxi investigations handled the thousands of people who "disappeared." A memoir by an official who participated in the investigations stated that there were 20,000 or so individuals recorded as "missing"—they disappeared during this violent period, but their deaths could not be documented.[13] If only half of this number is added to the official death toll, it would approach 100,000, which would be a death rate of close to 4.0 per thousand, almost double that for the rest of China.

Some regions in Guangxi suffered much more intense violence. In the most violent fifth of the cities and counties, the average death rate was 7.7 per thousand. In two counties more than 10 per thousand, or 1 percent, were killed.[14] The only other region of China where death rates are suspected of approaching these levels is Inner Mongolia, for which detailed evidence is scarce.[15]

A death rate of 3.6 to 4.0 per thousand would place Guangxi within the range of estimates for the notoriously brutal counterinsurgency campaign in Guatemala in the early 1980s or the widespread massacres of suspected communists and other leftists by the military junta in Indonesia in 1965 and 1966, both of which occurred over a much longer period of time.[16] Although events in Guangxi resembled civil wars in other settings, the death rates in Guangxi are a far cry from much longer conflicts between heavily armed combatants of the kind that has accompanied civil wars in collapsing nation-states. The death rate in Bosnia-Herzegovina after the fall of Yugoslavia in the 1990s was 25.5 per thousand. The civil war that accompanied the collapse of Syria in recent years has generated death tolls of similar magnitude.[17]

Although Guangxi's civil conflicts do not rank among the deadliest in recent world history, they generated a startlingly large death toll in a very short period. They did so without prolonged military campaigns between well-organized and well-equipped military units. The violence is especially puzzling, given the sudden formation of two civilian factions; their lack of an overt identification with class, ethnic, or national identities; and the fact that both sides claimed absolute loyalty to the central state as embodied in its Chairman, Mao Zedong. What made Guangxi so different from most other regions of China?

## CHAPTER 1

# Puzzles

Why was Guangxi's violence so much more intense than that of other regions of China? This straightforward question breaks down into several separate ones. The first concerns the origins and nature of the conflict between the Allied Command and April 22 factions, and the issues that motivated their mutual animosity. These groups did not previously exist, and began to form only in February 1967, in the wake of a mishandled rebel power seizure over the provincial government in the capital city of Nanning. The factions took full form in Nanning in April of that year and spread steadily across Guangxi's other cities and counties in the months to come. Who were these groups, how and why did they form, and what set them on an opposed course? How far did they spread across Guangxi, why did they spread, and how deeply did their conflicts extend into rural communities? It would seem essential, as a start, to closely examine the political divisions that were the ostensible motivations for the violence.

A second question is why so much of the violence was focused on politically stigmatized households, whose family status resembled caste distinctions handed down over generations. Why would violence against these households, largely uninvolved in factional conflicts, become so widespread? Was this development inadvertently spurred by the factional warfare carried out in the name of the Allied and April factions? These political categories, and the associated stigma, existed all across China. Why did these groups become such a focus of political violence in Guangxi?

A third question concerns the scope and intensity of the violence. Factional warfare was common across China during this period, and the restoration of political order exacted the highest death tolls of this period nationwide.[1] Politically stigmatized "enemy" households existed everywhere, and they were routinely persecuted. Yet the death tolls from factional warfare, its suppression, and the persecution of stigmatized households were far higher in Guangxi than elsewhere. What caused political violence to be more widespread and intense once it had gotten under way?

There are two broad approaches to these questions. The first is to characterize the political processes that generated high death rates—a focus on *what happened*, on how events unfolded into a deadly climax in 1968. What actors were responsible for killings, and *why* did events unfold the way they did? The second approach is to set aside narrative accounts and identify distinctive regional characteristics, defined by history, ethnic diversity, or economic and political structures, that may have intensified political violence to levels that surpassed those of other regions. To simplify, the first approach is to focus on political activities as a *process*, tracing them as a narrative flow of *events*; the second is to identify *static structures* or *variable characteristics* of the region that set it apart. In evaluating potential explanations, we need to keep another distinction in mind. Our problem is not to explain political violence in Guangxi, but to ask *why violence in Guangxi was so much more severe than elsewhere.* These two questions are not the same, and I will return to this distinction later in this book.

## Political Processes

There are three different claims about Guangxi's politics in the scholarship about this period, and all are relevant to one or more of the questions that I have posed. The first places a heavy emphasis on orders issued from Beijing on July 3, 1968, which called for the ruthless suppression of continuing factional resistance to the long-delayed reimposition of political order in Guangxi. The second characterizes factional conflict in China during this period as a struggle between conservatives with vested interests in the status quo and radicals who sought to challenge the existing system of power and privilege. From this perspective, Guangxi was a particularly violent example of how far the powerful were willing to go to defend their privileged positions. The third draws on sociological theories about intergroup violence as collective behavior, and it attributes the unusually high death tolls to the mobilization of community-level antagonisms toward politically stigmatized households in "reactionary" class categories.

*Beijing's "July 3 Orders"*
Official histories published in China provide detailed chronological narratives with a bare minimum of interpretive structure. They recount major events and describe in detail the formation of factions and subsequent conflicts, while providing little or no interpretation or analysis, never framing puzzles to which alternative explanations might apply.[2] The narratives implicitly condemn the violence—the primary reason for describing it in such detail. The explanation for the violent outcome places overwhelming emphasis on the impact of the "July 3 Orders" (*qi.san bugao*).[3] This was a harshly worded directive from Beijing in 1968 that mandated the restoration of order in Guangxi by force, designating rebel holdouts as class enemies and agents of foreign powers. In these accounts, the orders are condemned as extreme leftism, and the wave of killings that followed is framed as the consequence of an erroneous political line. From this perspective, the July 3 Orders are the primary feature that set Guangxi apart from other regions.

The July 3 Orders indeed triggered subsequent events and provided a political opportunity for Guangxi's military and security forces to apply overwhelming force against a stubborn insurgency. But an interpretation that places such singular emphasis on a directive from the nation's capital portrays the outcome as a foregone conclusion, the following of administrative orders by civilian and military authorities. The restoration of political order elsewhere in China during this same period also generated the highest observed death tolls.[4] This raises the question of why the July 3 Orders resulted in a much more deadly outcome in Guangxi. As we shall see in later chapters, mass killings in rural Guangxi began well before July, so the orders appear only to have accelerated processes that were already under way.

*Political Struggle between Conservatives and Radicals*
What political processes were unleashed by the July 3 Orders? Two very different interpretations have been applied to this question. The first is that the Allied Command faction represented forces that were aligned with the existing power structure, against a more radical April faction that sought to challenge it. This

interpretation is supported by the observation that the Allied faction was in a mu-
tually supportive relationship with the Guangxi Military District and local PADs.
Moreover, the stance that defined their political orientation was their declaration
of support for Wei Guoqing, Guangxi's longstanding top official, who in early 1967
was appointed to lead military control forces. Wei's highly unusual retention as
head of military control forces cut directly against the grain of the radical Maoist offensive against "revisionist" power holders in late 1966. The April faction, by
contrast, was adamantly opposed to Wei's appointment as head of the military
forces that served as an interim substitute for a collapsed civilian government, and
they fought long and hard to resist the imposition of order by units aligned with
the Guangxi Military District. From this perspective, violent conflict was a struggle over the reimposition of the existing order, with one side fighting to defend it,
while the other sought to overturn it.

This interpretation is a variant of the interest group interpretation of Cultural
Revolution factionalism known as the "radical-conservative hypothesis."[5] At the
core of this notion is the idea that individuals who enjoyed advantages in existing structures of power and privilege—in particular party members, households
headed by revolutionary veterans, party cadres, and the military—had an inher-
ently conservative orientation and would gravitate toward factions that sought to
defend these structures and reimpose order through repression. This interpretation is popular with émigré authors, often former participants in these conflicts,
who fought against the imposition of military control and saw themselves as the
true rebels against injustice and oppression.[6] It also appears as a central organizing
theme in critical histories of the Cultural Revolution penned by Chinese authors
who dissent from official interpretations. These accounts posit a struggle between
a "bureaucratic clique" and rebel forces, manipulated by Mao, which ultimately
resulted in the victory of the former.[7] One account of the Cultural Revolution in
Guilin portrays the struggles as a rebellion by a radical April faction against the
provincial power structure and their conservative defenders in the Allied faction.[8]

This interpretation is lent further plausibility by the rhetoric of the two
sides. The Allied Command eventually portrayed their opponents as counter-
revolutionary forces seeking to overturn the Communist Party and the political
order. The April faction portrayed themselves as a progressive force seeking to
overthrow reactionary elements defending the old regime. From this perspective,

the violence was an expression of the deeply rooted nature of the political forces in conflict over existing structures of power and privilege. The implied explanation for Guangxi's unusually high death tolls is that they illustrated the extreme violence to which the powerful were willing to resort in defense of their privileges, once authorized to do so by Beijing. This analysis views the political processes in Guangxi as identical to those elsewhere in China, with the July 3 Orders as a catalyst that removed constraints on extreme repression.

This line of analysis offers solutions to two of our puzzles—what political forces the two factions represented and why their conflict became unusually violent. It views the two factions as a reflection of latent political divisions that existed prior to this period, and that found organized expression in a period of disorder. And it attributes the violence to the enormity of the stakes involved and the willingness of the powerful to defend their privileged positions at any cost. This characterization of the conflict, however, does not address the widespread persecution of politically stigmatized households, or the ferocity of the violence unleashed against them. To approach these questions, we need to consider other ideas.

*Community-level Collective Behavior*
A very different portrayal of political processes in Guangxi directly addresses these shortcomings. It views the struggle between factions so often portrayed as radicals and conservatives as largely irrelevant to the generation of the unusual death tolls. In this account, factional struggle was restricted almost entirely to cities and towns, while all but a small percentage of deaths were in rural villages, where conflicts between the two factions did not penetrate. This analysis attributes the high death tolls to collective behavior in villages inadvertently touched off by claims in the July 3 Orders that the April faction was in collusion with historical class enemies. This framed stigmatized "class enemy" households as targets of retribution, and killings spun out of control in remote rural communities as an unintended consequence of official rhetoric during a campaign to suppress an urban insurgency.[9]

This explanation draws on theories about social processes that generate intergroup violence and genocide. In this case, the social categories that created group antagonisms were defined by political labels affixed to households at the time of the Communist seizure of power. The families headed by members of former propertied social classes (landlords, rich peasants), those affiliated with the Nationalist

regime, or those who fell afoul of early campaigns against real or suspected opponents of the Communist Party were collectively labeled as political enemies, and
frequently referred to as "four type elements" (*silei fenzi*). The "four types" were
"landlords, rich peasants, counter-revolutionaries, and bad elements"—labels
given to individuals and households when the new regime was established. With
the addition of "rightists" (*youpai fenzi*), individuals sanctioned in later political
campaigns in the 1950s, the stigmatized categories expanded to "five type elements" (*wulei fenzi*)—*di fu fan huai you*. The labels had the caste-like feature of
being inherited across generations. Individuals in these families were systematically discriminated against in job assignments on collective farms. During political
campaigns they were the first to suffer suspicion and punishment.[10]

According to this explanation, Guangxi's military authorities sought to discredit the April faction by charging that they were conspiring with former class
enemies who sought to overthrow Communist Party rule. The July 3 Orders explicitly embraced this portrayal of stubborn April faction resistance, implicating politically stigmatized households, which were labeled and stigmatized precisely for
their historical opposition to and presumably enduring animosity toward the new
regime. The campaign to suppress the April faction, in this account, inadvertently
unleashed collective violence in villages that focused on these households, particularly in rural regions where there were few if any members of the April faction.

High death tolls were therefore not due to actions by the Allied faction or
agents of the state, but instead were the product of mass killings in villages, where
popular antagonism toward these stigmatized groups was activated by the political rhetoric of the military authorities. The campaign to suppress the April faction incited residents of rural communities to engage in campaigns of extermination against their own neighbors, who were otherwise uninvolved in the political
battles of the towns. This explanation invites parallels with genocidal intergroup
violence in Rwanda in 1994; communal warfare among Hindus, Muslims, and Sikhs
in the Punjab, Bengal, and other regions spurred by the partition of India in 1947;
and ethnic cleansing by local militias in Bosnia-Herzegovina during the Yugoslav
wars of the 1990s.[11]

While state actors often facilitated the violence in these other settings, ordinary citizens participated actively in killing other members of their communities.
In Rwanda: "the violence was low-tech: many perpetrators used ordinary farm

tools, such as machetes, clubs, and hoes, to kill. The violence was public, face-to-face, crowd-enforced, and neighbor sometimes killed neighbor." "Perpetrators in rural areas were ordinary men. They were fathers, husbands, and farmers who had average levels of education and who had no prior history of violence . . . for the most part, Rwanda's genocide perpetrators . . . were regular citizens."[12] In Bosnia, "much of the Serb population took part in the genocide against Bosniaks [Muslim Bosnians], either directly or as bystanders." "Witnesses knew their attackers—their Serb neighbors—who participated in the looting, raping, torturing, and killing of Bosniak men and women."[13]

This proposed explanation, unlike the others, directly addresses the puzzling victimization of stigmatized households, placing it at the center of attention. It seeks to explain how a conflict between urban factions could have spilled over into rural regions where these conflicts seemed to be largely absent, mobilizing ordinary residents into acts of widespread violence against families that were apparently uninvolved in the larger struggles. It also implies that Guangxi's high death tolls were a product primarily of community-level collective behavior in rural regions, which generated violence that went far beyond what the authorities anticipated.

This line of analysis sets aside questions about the nature of factional conflicts, which are viewed as tangential to the rural killings. Instead, it directly addresses violence against stigmatized households. But it does not provide an equally compelling explanation of why the persecution of these households was so much more severe in Guangxi than elsewhere. There were stigmatized households everywhere in China, and there were similar outbreaks of mass killings of "enemy" households in other regions, although they were rare and isolated events.[14] Why would mass killings of this type elsewhere in China be limited to a small number of localities, whereas they spread like a tidal wave across Guangxi? One possibility is that Guangxi had distinctive features that may have served to escalate community-level conflicts to an unusual degree.

### Regional Distinctiveness

Guangxi differed from other provinces in a variety of ways that might plausibly be related to our questions. It had an unusually large population of ethnic minorities. Its historical pattern of migration generated successive rebellions against expanding Chinese empires over the centuries. The region exhibited intense intergroup conflicts and repeated rebellions after the incorporation of the region into early modern Chinese states. And it remained economically underdeveloped, with low rates of literacy, its villages poor and remote. All these features might have intensi-fied political violence, and some accounts explicitly suggest this.

*Ethnic Diversity*

The most obvious feature that sets Guangxi apart is its ethnically diverse popula-tion. Only 60 percent of the population in the mid-1960s were officially classified as Han Chinese, and just over one-third were Zhuang, China's largest ethnic minor-ity.[15] One of the last regions to be settled by the southward migration of Chinese-speakers, Guangxi was for centuries a battleground that bred periodic rebellion against expanding imperial states. During the Tang Dynasty (618–906) the region was "a loosely held colonial frontier where the tropics began."[16] Several centuries later, during the Ming Dynasty (1368–1644), it was still considered "the end of the realm of civilization": a mountainous, malaria-ridden region of breathtaking natu-ral beauty, filled with poisonous snakes and insects, howling monkeys, menacing leopards and tigers, and hostile natives.[17] According to one historian, writing in the 1960s, despite subsequent centuries during which successive Chinese states extended their rule, "the southernmost provinces of China are not truly Chinese even now. They are 'interior colonies' of non-Chinese peoples, exploited and op-pressed for more than two thousand years by Chinese settlers and the agents of their northern government. The most extreme case is Guangxi Province, recently recognized as the "Guangxi-Zhuang Autonomous Region."[18] This portrayal invites suspicion that the unusually intense violence of the late 1960s may have had his-torical roots.

The Zhuang, with whom Guangxi is now identified, are descended from Tai-speaking people that occupied the river valleys and coastal regions of Guangxi prior to the southward expansion of ancient Chinese empires. They lived in settled agricultural communities, grew rice in irrigated fields, cast bronze, wove silk, and by 300 BCE had an organized state known as Yue.[19] The first united Chinese em-pire, the Qin, conquered the region as it expanded south from 234 to 222 BCE. The Yue ruling elite fled south and organized another state in the territory of present-day Thailand, while large Tai-speaking populations remained in Guangxi.[20] The modern Tai language group is distributed across the southern borders of China, northern Vietnam, and adjacent regions in southeast Asia. Zhuang is considered a northern branch of the language commonly spoken in Thailand and Laos.[21]

The region remained only loosely within the boundaries of Chinese states as they expanded and contracted in the millennium after the initial Qin conquest. Several smaller kingdoms ruled by Zhuang chieftains rose and fell during this period. The last kingdom associated with the Zhuang had a formidable military, which mounted an extensive rebellion against Song Dynasty forces that finally defeated it in 1055.[22]

The Ming Dynasty was the era when permanent Chinese governance was finally extended into Guangxi. Soldiers and administrators fitfully extended imperial rule into the province, but they and Chinese-speaking settlers were greatly outnumbered by indigenous people. The reach of the state remained tenuous. Ming officials conferred official titles on native chiefs in exchange for their nominal submission to the Chinese state. This divided the region into a patchwork of native domains—more than forty in the year 1580, mainly in the southern and western reaches of Guangxi, where the native populations were increasingly concentrated after Chinese-speaking settlers pushed indigenous groups out of the northern and eastern regions of the province. This sparked repeated rebellions by the largest of these groups, the Zhuang, who had settled in the valleys, and the Yao, who lived primarily in the hills.[23] At several points during the Ming era large armies were raised to quell insurrections.[24] Despite the continuing flow of Chinese-speaking migrants, in the early 1700s only 20 percent of Guangxi's population were Chinese-speaking Han; half were still classified as Zhuang and the remainder primarily as Yao.[25] The chieftain system survived in various guises throughout the Qing Dynasty (1644–1912), and it had the effect of creating ethnic categories recognized by succeeding Chinese states.[26]

Well into the twentieth century, the Zhuang continued to speak a language distinct from the Cantonese and Mandarin dialects spoken by Han Chinese.[27] They are the largest of China's officially recognized "minority nationalities," and almost all of them live in Guangxi. In recognition of their status, Guangxi Province was belatedly designated as the Guangxi Zhuang Autonomous Region in 1958.[28] This made Guangxi the administrative equivalent of China's other "autonomous regions" set aside for large "minority nationalities"—Tibet, Inner Mongolia, Xinjiang (Muslim Uighurs), and Ningxia (Chinese-speaking Muslims).

The regional distribution of the Zhuang and other ethnic minorities in Guangxi during the 1960s reflects this legacy of historical migration, in which indigenous

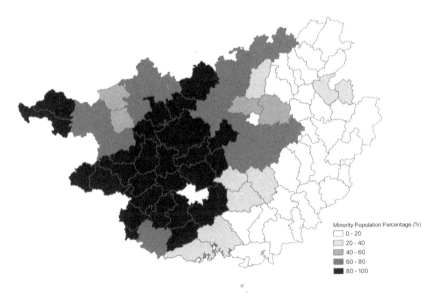

Minority Population Percentage (%)
☐ 0 - 20
▨ 20 - 40
▨ 40 - 60
▨ 60 - 80
■ 80 - 100

MAP 1.1.   Distribution of Ethnic Minorities across Guangxi's Cities and Counties

populations were pushed westward by flows of Han settlers from the north and east. If one draws a diagonal line from Guilin prefecture in the northeast to the coastal border with Vietnam in the southwest, the area above that line was where Guangxi's minority populations were concentrated, while the area below was primarily Han (see map 1.1). The only exceptions (the white patches in a sea of dark gray and black on the map) are the two cities of Nanning and Liuzhou. This reflects an additional feature of Guangxi's ethnic profile: minorities were heavily concentrated in rural districts, while the cities were overwhelmingly Han.

Some have argued that political violence in other Chinese regions during this period was the product of ethnic antagonism or ethno-nationalism. On China's northern borderlands, Inner Mongolia suffered a brutal political campaign that was explicitly designed to root out alleged disloyalty among ethnic Mongols, generating death rates that in some locations rivaled Guangxi's.[29] One analyst views this campaign against an alleged underground "Inner Mongolian People's Party" as a thinly disguised form of ethnic cleansing.[30] Tibet is another region where violence during this period has been interpreted through the lens of ethnicity and national identity. One remarkably bloody rebellion in Nyemo County (*Nimu xian*) has been interpreted as mobilization against Han Chinese oppression.[31]

These considerations suggest that political violence in Guangxi may have been intensified by ethnic antagonisms. As map 1.1 clearly indicates, the distribution of Han and ethnic minorities varies widely across the province. Some regions were almost entirely Han, while others were almost entirely minorities, and there is a wide range of variation in between. If ethnic antagonisms were responsible for Guangxi's elevated death tolls, the highest death rates within the province should be related to local ethnic composition and should be especially apparent in localities with mixed populations.

### Historical Migration Patterns and Subethnic Identities

A related characterization of Guangxi focuses on a different aspect of its history and demography. In his analysis of mass killings in Guangxi and neighboring Guangdong Province, Yang Su linked the region's history to events in the 1960s through the distinctive Han subgroup known as the Hakka.[32] "Hakka" is the Cantonese term for "guest people" (*kejia* in standard dialect). Culturally and linguistically distinct from Chinese migrants who settled in the valleys of Guangxi and Guangdong in earlier centuries, the Hakka arrived much later, settling in marginal hilly lands, and often becoming involved in battles with established groups over land and water rights.[33] The largest and most dramatic of these perennial battles were the Hakka-Punti wars that raged in coastal regions of southern Guangdong from 1855 to 1867.[34] The region along Guangxi's seacoast, now Qinzhou Prefecture, was part of Guangdong at the time.[35] The massive Taiping Rebellion (1850–67), which came close to overthrowing the Qing Dynasty, originated in Hakka communities in eastern Guangxi, and its founders and early leaders were Hakkas from the region. Counties that were the birthplace of that rebellion had high death tolls in the 1960s.[36]

Su identified this history of migration and conflict as a major cause of the region's violence. It created strong group identities and a "frontier mentality," expressed in intensified clan solidarities that survived the land reform and other changes of the 1950s.[37] He reasoned that these intense clan-based ties, combined with traditions of collective self-defense, served to intensify rural conflict in the region. Retaining their traditions of collective self-defense, Hakka communities experienced more intense political violence when conflicts broke out in the 1960s.[38] In support of the argument, Su offered evidence that counties with large

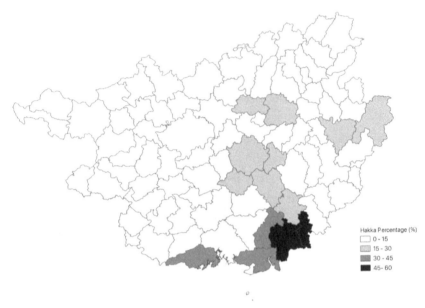

MAP 1.2.  Distribution of Hakka across Guangxi's Cities and Counties

populations of Hakka in Guangxi and Guangdong had higher death tolls than counties where Hakka were absent.[39]

Su's argument about the important role of the Hakka subgroup was developed in an analysis that considered Guangxi together with the neighboring province of Guangdong, which overlaps with the historical Hakka heartland, where the group was concentrated in a border region with Fujian and Jiangxi. There were fifteen counties in Guangdong that historically were almost entirely Hakka-speaking, and one-third of Guangdong's population were Hakka.[40] In Guangxi, by contrast, there were only two counties with a slight Hakka majority, and Hakka constituted only 9 percent of the population.[41] Map 1.2 indicates that Guangxi's Hakka were concentrated in the predominantly Han regions of eastern Guangxi, close to the border with Guangdong, or in the coastal counties that historically were part of Guangdong Province. This reflects the later migration of Hakka into regions where Han migrants had already settled.

The small size of Guangxi's Hakka population suggests that they may not have been present in sufficient numbers to have had a large impact on province-wide death rates. But past research has suggested that the regions where Hakka were concentrated should have had higher death rates, and therefore this may have helped, along with other forms of group antagonism, to elevate provincial totals to unusually high levels.

*Economic Backwardness and Geographic Remoteness*

A third and more general feature of Guangxi was its pronounced backwardness. It was one of the least urbanized and industrialized regions in China in the 1960s. Its cities were small. The largest, the provincial capital of Nanning, had a population of only 457,000, while China's provincial capitals at the time averaged more than 1.5 million in population. The other five cities averaged only 188,000 residents. Nanning's population was smaller even than those of seventeen of Guangxi's rural counties.

Educational levels were very low. There were only 7,120 university students in Guangxi in 1966. Each of the two largest campuses in Beijing had more students.[42] In a province of 25 million, there were only 28,556 students enrolled in high school in 1966. With more than 317,000 students in junior high, the odds of advancing were very slim.[43] Low educational levels ensured that Zhuang and other minority languages would survive as a marker of group identity.

Guangxi's mountainous terrain left many villages remote and isolated, reinforcing perceptions of the region's backwardness. Some who have chronicled these events viewed reports of cannibalism as marks of the region's extreme backwardness, while others suggested that these practices were throwbacks to archaic Chinese traditions that survived on the outer fringes of historical empires.[44] Poor roads and the resulting remoteness of so many of Guangxi's villages limited the reach of the Communist Party and its administrative apparatus. This is thought to be an important reason why violent attacks on stigmatized households spiraled out of control in many rural communities.[45]

## Evaluating the Alternatives

Was Guangxi's unusually intense violence the straightforward result of ruthless orders from Beijing? Was it an illustration of the deadly extremes to which bureaucratic insiders were willing to go in defending their privileged positions? Was it an example of the kind of collective violence that has bred genocidal attacks against stigmatized outgroups in other settings? Did Guangxi's ethnically and linguistically diverse population, economic backwardness, or geographic remoteness intensify the violence? Which, if any, of these potential explanations are credible, and are there alternatives that have yet to be considered?

In this book I will closely examine each of these potential explanations for Guangxi's unusually high death tolls—both the characterization of political processes and the possible impact of its regional distinctiveness. In doing so I will draw on new sources of evidence that have only recently become available outside of China. These materials provide far more narrative and statistical detail about the conflicts of this period than can be found in the published provincial and local annals and other sources that have been the primary foundation for prior research. They provide a much clearer view of the origins and development of the two major factions, the course of the conflicts between them, and the events across time and place that eventually generated such high death tolls. They also provide a basis for examining the possible impact of distinctive local characteristics.

The new materials come from an extraordinary series of investigations conducted by central government authorities in the early 1980s, a period when the post-Mao leadership was determined to expose the violence and injustices of the Cultural Revolution. After it became clear that Guangxi officials, many of whom were implicated in the violence, were covering up the death tolls and the parties responsible, the Central Committee of the Chinese Communist Party dispatched two waves of investigators to the province in the early 1980s. They bypassed provincial authorities and fanned out across cities and counties, where they examined local party and government archives, and interviewed hundreds of provincial and local officials, ordinary citizens, and inmates of prisons and labor camps. After this initial foray revealed evidence of a coverup, a second investigation team of higher-ranking officials was sent to the province in 1983 and 1984, and carried out an even larger and more thorough investigation. More than 100 officials sent from Beijing organized teams that employed close to 100,000 investigators over four years to compile documentation on every county and city in the province.[46]

The result was an eighteen-volume set of paperbound books, encased in blue plastic covers, issued in 1987 and 1988 and classified as "organization-level secrets" (*ji mi*). Ranging from 394 to 854 pages, these volumes clarified the scope of violent events that had long been covered up, and they identified the actors involved. The chronologies trace daily developments from May 1966 to late 1976, with a primary focus on 1967 and 1968. They cover these events separately for each of Guangxi's cities and counties, and for a wide range of government agencies, party offices, and universities, often providing statistical detail about the scope and impact of the conflicts.[47]

The wide coverage and greatly enhanced detail in these materials permit a much clearer focus on the development, spread, and evolution of factional conflict and related violence, far surpassing what is available in other sources. Prior research on the conflicts of this period has relied on data sets that were compiled by coding information contained in published local histories. The first publication to analyze these local histories drew on data from more than 1,500 county histories.[48] A second drew on this preliminary work and compiled a more detailed data set from 187 counties in 3 provinces, including Guangxi, in the first detailed analysis of mass killings.[49] A full national data set that completed this effort permitted an analysis that draws on 2,246 local histories, covering 97 percent of all local jurisdictions.[50]

The detail in the unpublished investigation reports far surpasses that of published local histories. Abbreviated and redacted materials from these investigations subsequently were reflected in published local annals for Guangxi's cities and counties, but the true scope and nature of these events was obscured in published accounts. Chronologies published in the local annals from Guangxi, which were based in part on the investigation materials, devoted an average of 5.8 pages (defined as 500 Chinese characters per page) to describing events from mid-1966 to the end of 1971. The chronologies provided in these investigation reports devote an average of 37 pages to events from mid-1966 to the end of 1969. The published histories chronicle 560 political events in Guangxi, an average of 6.5 per jurisdiction. The investigation materials contain descriptions of 4,938 events, an average of 57 per jurisdiction—almost nine times more than the published accounts. These materials provide much more detailed political narratives at the provincial and local level, and they are a rich source for the construction of a data set that will permit us to evaluate several explanations for Guangxi's unusual violence. The appendix at the end of this book provides further detail about these materials, their potential biases, and the procedures used in coding the events described in them into a data set that informs much of the analysis that follows.

## A Preview

These materials yield a portrayal of political processes in Guangxi that is surprisingly different from the ones characterized above. Instead of a struggle between conservative forces aligned with existing power structures against rebel outsiders, we see a split among political elites from top to bottom, the result of a widespread rebellion by the party-state's own cadres that overthrew incumbent leaders at each level of government. Different fragments of the old provincial leadership each headed separate rebel coalitions in Nanning that reached down into all of Guangxi's cities and counties. The insurgency sustained by the April faction is more accurately portrayed as opposition to local military networks that had aligned themselves with one fragment of the former power structure, rather than as an insurgency by marginal groups predisposed to challenge the political and economic status quo.

Another new dimension revealed by these materials is that the rural hinterland was not isolated from the factional struggles of cities and towns. Instead, these conflicts reached across the province and entered deeply, if unevenly, into rural communities. The wave of killings was not due to collective activity by ordinary rural residents that spiraled out of control, but was instead part of an organized, top-down campaign designed to stamp out stubborn factional resistance across the province. These village campaigns were organized and implemented by rural militia under the command of military and security networks. They focused on the losing April faction where it had been active, but they swept up stigmatized households as alleged co-conspirators. This process has much in common with the organized massacres of hundreds of thousands of communists and other leftists coordinated by the Indonesian army during 1965, or with brutal counter-insurgency campaigns observed in Guatemala and many other settings.[51]

What is distinctive about this portrayal is how political processes were structured by the network of military and security forces under the command of the Guangxi Military District. The unusual decision to place Guangxi's longstanding leader, Wei Guoqing, in command of military control forces became the opening wedge that spurred the initial formation of the Allied Command and the April 22 factions. The armed forces under the Guangxi Military District stretched down through Military Subdistricts in the prefectures and the PADs at the county level and armed People's Militias in small towns and rural communities. This military network remained intact despite provincial and local power seizures that overthrew civilian governments. It was under the command of Wei Guoqing and became overlaid onto the factional divisions across Guangxi. The Allied faction became so closely aligned with these military networks that its fighting groups became indistinguishable from officially organized rural militias. The April faction, from Nanning down to each of the cities and counties, was defined by its opposition to political decisions made by local military officers. The province-wide factional conflicts therefore had an organizational structure that extended deeply into rural regions. This gave factional conflict in Guangxi a province-wide character that stretched outward in ways that were not common in other provinces.

Another unusual feature of Guangxi's conflicts was the deep involvement of elite actors in Beijing in the formation and perpetuation of conflict between the two sides. The April 22 faction was the creation of radical figures in Beijing's Central Cultural Revolution Group (CCRG), who during February and March 1967 became alarmed about the suppression of rebels by military forces across China, which led them to worry that army commanders were hostile to the rebellion that they had supported as the agent of China's political transformation. The appointment of Wei Guoqing to head military control forces in late March struck them as a reversal of the main thrust of the Cultural Revolution. Wei, after all, had been Guangxi's top leader for the previous decade, and he had himself been the primary target of *all* rebel groups that mobilized to challenge the provincial establishment in prior months. Envoys from the CCRG, consulting repeatedly with their superiors in Beijing, worked behind the scenes to encourage rebel opposition to Wei Guoqing, hoping to have him replaced by a civilian leader more sympathetic to the rebel campaign. They actively recruited other top officials and rebel leaders into a coalition that became the April 22 faction. These actors in Beijing continued to support and protect the April faction for almost a year.

Given Wei's centrality to the factional conflicts, there is one distinctive characteristic of Guangxi that is defined not by static characteristics due to demography and history, but by evolving geopolitical events. Guangxi bordered Vietnam, and these years were precisely the ones when the American war effort escalated to previously unimagined levels, and when the US bombing campaign was extended to areas not far from China's borders. Guangxi was the staging area for the shipment of armaments and other military supplies, and for air and ground defenses near China's border. This made political stability in Guangxi a particularly high priority in Beijing, but it also had direct implications for Wei's appointment to head military control forces and for his retention despite initially unanimous rebel opposition. Wei had strong ties with Vietnam's leaders, due to his long residence there as China's top military advisor in their successful war against French forces in the previous decade. Wei was appointed as Guangxi's leader after repatriating from Vietnam, and he continued to be a symbol of the close ties between China and Vietnam's Communist leaders as the war escalated. As we shall see, his role in support of Vietnam in the struggle against American imperialism was explicitly mentioned by Beijing officials when he was appointed to head military control forces, and in subsequent efforts to convince his opponents to stand down. As it turns out, one of the most important distinctive features of Guangxi was its geopolitical and strategic significance. In a roundabout sense, the victims of Guangxi's violence were collateral damage of the war in Vietnam.

While the data extracted from the investigation reports serve to document political processes as they unfolded over time and place, they also permit a systematic evaluation of several potential explanations that link intense violence to other regional features that make Guangxi distinctive. When they are combined with data from other sources about each of the cities and counties, it is possible to analyze the relationship of these features to local death rates. Death rates varied widely within Guangxi. If certain regional characteristics are responsible for Guangxi's unusually high death rates—ethnic diversity, level of urbanization, the presence of the Hakka subgroups, or geographical remoteness—then the localities with certain characteristics should have higher death rates. In this way we can leverage intraprovincial variation to systematically examine the impact of Guangxi's distinctive features. As we shall see, the ethnic and subethnic profiles of a locality have no discernible impact on death rates, but geographic and political remoteness has a surprisingly strong impact that is the opposite of what we would expect based on past research.

\*   \*   \*

Each of the following chapters will develop a different dimension of this analysis and address a distinct puzzle. The initial chapters trace the formation of factions and their conflicts. Chapters 2 through 4 provide a narrative account of the initial formation of the Allied Command and April 22 factions in Nanning, the spread of these affiliations across virtually all other cities and counties in Guangxi, the initial skirmishes between the two sides during 1967, and the surprisingly limited extent of violence during a period when representatives of the two factions were engaged in high-level negotiations in Beijing. These chapters, based on narrative accounts culled from the investigation reports, provide evidence for a portrayal of the political cleavages as a split within Guangxi's civilian power structures that radiated down into rural regions through military networks. Any understanding of Guangxi's violence must be premised on a clear account of how political cleavages formed and generated political conflicts that eventually led to extreme violence.

Chapter 2 traces the steps through which the Allied Command and April 22 factions emerged in the wake of a bungled rebel power seizure in the provincial capital of Nanning. It emphasizes the disorganized nature of rebel activity and the rivalries among disparate rebel groups, and the way that political actors in Beijing encouraged and exacerbated the unfolding political divisions in Guangxi. Especially important were maneuverings behind the scenes by younger members of Beijing's CCRG, who urged rebel opposition to the appointment of Wei Guoqing as head of regional military control forces. This pushed the disparate array of rebel groups, all of which had targeted and abused Wei Guoqing in recent months, into a difficult choice: declare support for the appointment of Wei, or support efforts to have him replaced. Each of these choices involved potential peril for those who chose the losing side, digging them into positions they subsequently were compelled to defend.

Chapter 3 addresses the question of how factional divisions spread across Guangxi, and why they became linked with Nanning's Allied and April factions. Despite the variety of patterns through which local civilian governments collapsed, and the wide range of choices made by military units in adjudicating disputes among rebel groups, factional conflicts of varied intensity jelled in virtually every city and county, with military control forces as the central axis of factional alignments. As a result, the military hierarchy that extended down into localities defined the lines of factional alignment. The Allied Command generally became the civilian auxiliary of local PLA units and PADs, while rebels opposed to the initial decisions of military forces eventually aligned themselves with the April faction.

Military forces in the region, however, were not unified and consistent in their political stances. Regular PLA combat divisions were not under the command of the Guangxi Military District. They were only charged with "supporting the left" in their localities, which did not necessarily mean supporting Wei Guoqing. This was especially consequential in the city of Guilin, where mainline PLA units that reported to the Guangzhou Military Region supported the city's large April faction, turning Guilin into that faction's stronghold.

Chapter 4 explains how it was possible for the April faction, despite its opposition to Guangxi's military hierarchy, to survive and spread during 1967. It describes the impact of new orders that forbade military units from suppressing dissident rebels, and the influence of ongoing negotiations in Beijing between representatives of the Allied Command and April 22 factions, which gave the latter's cause legitimacy and protection. Throughout the period from May to November 1967, when leaders of the two factions were negotiating in Beijing, there was remarkably little violence in Guangxi, unlike in other Chinese regions. Each side developed an increasingly large following, became more organized, and engaged in heated rhetoric and local confrontations that rarely involved deadly violence. In August 1967 there were clear signals that the April faction had Beijing's favor, only for that to be withdrawn suddenly the following month by a shift in Mao Zedong's stance. This undercut the April faction in ways that were not immediately clear, and which its leaders appear not to have recognized until it was too late.

Subsequent chapters focus on the escalation of violence during 1968 and its causes. Chapters 5 through 7 build narrative accounts of the origins and spread of intensified factional warfare and mass killings by rural militias, providing descriptive statistics culled from these narratives about the distribution of violence across time and place, the actors responsible for the killings, and the identities of the victims. This culminates in Chapter 8 with a statistical analysis that tests the implications of the narrative accounts and descriptive analyses in the preceding chapters.

Chapter 5 turns our attention to the escalating violence that began shortly after November 1967, as the cease-fire and power-sharing agreements reached in Beijing broke down. Beijing's ostensible resolution to the stubborn "Guangxi Problem" collapsed as local militia under the command of PADs in rural regions initiated the violent suppression of local April faction forces in anticipation of a final settlement. It was only at this point that extreme violence began to spread across

Guangxi, as the militarized wing of the Allied faction in rural regions sought a final solution that would favor them in local struggles. This, in turn, spurred the rearming and militarization of the April faction and the formation of larger and better fighting forces, especially in Nanning and Guilin, with the tacit protection of PLA units in those locales. Far from being solved by six months' negotiations in Beijing and a final agreement coordinated by Zhou Enlai and blessed by Mao Zedong, the "Guangxi Problem" escalated to levels of violence not previously seen.

Chapter 6 examines the unfolding of mass killings across Guangxi, offering statistical evidence extracted from narrative accounts about the identity of the killers and the killed, and the timing and location of the killings. In contrast to prior accounts based on published annals, it shows that factional conflict was by no means restricted to urban districts, and in fact penetrated widely if unevenly into rural communities. This shaped the pattern of killings in response to the July 3 Orders, when Beijing for the first time gave explicit support for military forces to use any means necessary to suppress continued armed opposition and expressed this support in language that put politically stigmatized households directly at risk. Finally unleashing the full power of military suppression on a region that had proven so enduringly resistant to agreements brokered by Beijing, the Guangxi Military District mobilized for a top-down suppression campaign that generated the death tolls for which Guangxi would become infamous. Statistical evidence demonstrates that village militias were the primary actors in the indiscriminate killings, and that April faction adherents and members of stigmatized "class enemy" households were both targeted in large numbers.

Chapter 7 shows that all but a tiny percentage of the deaths were generated in rural counties. The high death rates were concentrated geographically, with only 20 out of 86 jurisdictions generating half the provincial total. This chapter provides narrative accounts from a selection of the most violent counties, examining in some detail the bureaucratic mechanisms through which county and district authorities pressured village leaders and rural militia to draw up death lists and accelerate rural killings. It also describes examples of sexual violence and predation, and the cannibalism of the corpses of victims, portraying them as crimes of opportunity that were closely linked to organized killings by rural militia.

Chapter 8, finally, turns to the possible impact of ethnic diversity and other distinctive features of Guangxi. If political violence was intensified by distinctive features of the province, death rates should have been higher in subregions that most fully reflected these characteristics. As we shall see, examining the relationship between a range of local population and regional characteristics and death rates yields no support for conjectures that group antagonisms generated higher levels of deadly violence. However, these same analyses reveal a much larger impact of geographic remoteness and the reach of the party-state that is counter to what past studies have claimed. Location in a remote border region or in a locality with fewer government officials lowered death rates by a large margin—indicating that deadly violence was more severe where the reach of the state was stronger. There is also a strong relationship with the unfolding of political events: localities where the April 22 faction was able to hold out the longest and delay the formation of a new local government until July 1968 suffered death rates that finally pushed Guangxi's overall averages far above other regions of China.

## CHAPTER 2

# Origins

The split between the Allied Command and April 22 factions originated in the provincial capital of Nanning. It emerged in the wake of an overthrow of the provincial government by a coalition of rebel groups, and subsequent intervention by military units to stabilize new structures of power. This was a familiar pattern across China in early 1967.[1] The factions were the product of a highly fragmented rebel movement, a rushed and disorganized January power seizure, and inconsistent and contradictory political interventions by different political actors in a fractious national leadership in Beijing.

Past analysts attributed political orientations to rebel factions based on what was readily observable on the surface: the rhetoric of the two sides, and the fact that one side resisted the provincial military district and Guangxi's longstanding top official, while the other side supported both. While one can plausibly label the former faction "radical" and the latter "conservative," one cannot infer that rebels selected factional affiliations based on prior political orientations that were a product of their relative positions in existing structures of power and privilege. The political orientations of rebels were the product of choices made in the wake of the collapse of existing structures of power, where it was highly uncertain which choice would lead to favorable political outcomes for anyone, and where signals from the ultimate arbiters of success or failure in Beijing were ambiguous, mixed, and unpredictable. Factional identities and political orientations were the product

of a series of choices made over time in a path-dependent fashion as circumstances evolved and the choices facing rebel groups shifted. To understand how
factions were constructed over the course of complicated political interactions, it
is essential to trace in detail the sequences of events through which they emerged.
This yields evidence for an interpretation that portrays rebel factions as a split in
existing power structures rather than as a contest between supporters of the powerful versus radical challengers.

The ultimate point of contention between the factions was whether to accept the
appointment of Wei Guoqing, Guangxi's long-serving leader, to head military control forces imposed on the province in March 1967. On the surface, this would hardly
seem to be the kind of issue that would unleash the catastrophic violence that later
engulfed the province. However, a faction's stance toward Wei Guoqing signaled a
position on a more immediately consequential matter—rebel groups' relationship
with local military units that intervened to "support the left." In almost all localities, rebel groups declared their support for Wei if their claims to have seized power
were accepted by local military officers. Rebel groups whose claims were denied or
ignored by the local military signaled their opposition to Wei and their allegiance to
Guangxi's second-ranking party official, Wu Jinnan. To understand this development,
we need to trace the steps by which these divisions first emerged, and how they became entangled with shifting currents at the apex of the political hierarchy in Beijing.

Permitting a top provincial leader like Wei Guoqing to continue in power
was almost unheard of at this point in the Cultural Revolution.[2] The decision was
deeply controversial among local rebels, virtually all of whom had focused on Wei
as the primary target of their rebellion in the final weeks of 1966. Wei's surprise
appointment forced rebel groups into difficult choices. Many dropped their adamant opposition to Wei after being persuaded by military commanders that he
had the firm support of Beijing, and ultimately of Mao Zedong. Wei's retention reflected geopolitical and national security issues that were uniquely compelling in
Guangxi, and these ran directly counter to the radical thrust of the rebel campaign
that overthrew provincial officials across China in early 1967.

## Wei Guoqing and Vietnam

The unusual decision to place Wei in charge of the interim military government
was a product of a personal history that made him a symbol of China's support for

the Vietnamese Communist movement. As a PLA general he spent five years in Vietnam in the early 1950s, working closely with the Communist insurgents who would become the leaders of North Vietnam. His subsequent appointment to lead the province bordering Vietnam was due to this relationship. Were it not for the fact that the events described in this book occurred at the height of the American escalation of the war, Wei Guoqing might well have been judged expendable by Mao. But China's support for Vietnam, and Mao's insistence that they fight to victory rather than negotiate with American imperialists, was a key plank in the radical ideology that inspired the Cultural Revolution.

Wei Guoqing, an ethnic Zhuang, joined the Red Army in Guangxi in 1929, and later joined the Communist Party in 1931 after his unit abandoned Guangxi for the Jiangxi Soviet that was headed by Mao Zedong. A regimental commander during the Long March of the mid-1930s, he served as a divisional commander during several decisive battles in the civil war against the Nationalists. After the Communist victory in China, he served as the head of the Chinese Military Support Group to the Viet Minh during their insurgency against the French. Wei went to Vietnam in 1950 and remained until 1955, serving as the general military advisor representing China in all military and political decision-making. In October 1953 he returned to Beijing to report on the situation in Indochina to the Central Committee and met with Mao.[3] He is credited with military advice that led to key victories, in particular the strategy that led to the surrender of French forces at Dien Bien Phu. After that victory, he attended the 1954 Geneva conference on Indochina as part of the Chinese delegation headed by Zhou Enlai.[4]

Wei returned to China in 1955 and took up a post across the border as governor of Guangxi Province. He continued in the equivalent position as the chairman of the Guangxi Zhuang Autonomous Region when the province was renamed in 1958. In 1961 he added the more important role of first party secretary.[5] His presence in Nanning, only 200 miles from Hanoi, kept him close to the newly created government of North Vietnam as its leaders prepared their military campaign to unify the country.

Wei's Vietnam experience was surely a major reason why he was assigned to the province on Vietnam's border. Another reason was that Wei was an ethnic Zhuang from Donglan County, which from 1927 to 1930 was part of Guangxi's only rural

Communist base area.[6] In 1966, despite its status as an autonomous region for the Zhuang nationality, there still were only three Zhuang among its top sixteen party officials.[7] Wei had unique qualifications: he simultaneously signaled China's close relationship with North Vietnam and its leaders, its strong commitment to waging war against American imperialism, and the CCP's symbolic recognition of Guangxi as the Zhuang homeland. In addition, his contributions to the Viet Minh's successful war against the French gave him an almost unique status as one of China's few true heroes in the global struggle against colonialism and imperialism.

These considerations were intensified by the timing of the US escalation of its military involvement. The first American combat units landed in Vietnam in March 1965, and by the end of that year there were 184,000 in the South. As the Cultural Revolution gathered momentum during the last half of 1966, the military buildup accelerated. By the end of 1966 US forces stood at 385,000, and reached 448,000 by June 1967, the period during which the events described in this chapter took place.[8]

More directly relevant to Guangxi was the parallel escalation of the American bombing campaign against the North. Systematic attacks on bridges, power plants, airfields, railway yards, and fuel storage sites in North Vietnam began in 1965. In 1966 the target area expanded for the first time to a northeastern sector that included Hanoi and Haiphong, close to the Guangxi border. More than 148,000 bombing raids were flown over the North during 1966.[9] There were regular violations of Chinese air space by American military aircraft. From 1965 to 1968, there were 155 such violations, and 12 aircraft were shot down by Chinese air defenses.[10]

China's leaders were alarmed about the prospect of direct American involvement in Vietnam. In 1963 and 1964 Mao increased military assistance and adopted an increasingly militant stance. Aggressive support for Vietnam's struggle against America was an integral part of the radicalization that led both to the split from the Soviet Union and the Cultural Revolution itself.[11] In August 1964, the headquarters of the PLA's 7th Air Force Division was relocated from Guangdong Province to Nanning to take charge of activity over Guangxi and the Gulf of Tonkin, and two new airports were built to serve four air divisions that were moved toward the border. The PLA's 47th Army Corps was also sent into Guangxi in 1964 for border defense. Guangxi became the rear base for air support and the transport of engineering and anti-aircraft units into Vietnam. It was also the primary route for shipping military supplies through a railway network under the Liuzhou Railway Bureau through the border town of Pingxiang.[12]

Mao used the escalation of the war to further radicalize China's domestic political atmosphere. A nationwide campaign to "Resist America and Aid Vietnam" displayed China's commitment to Vietnam's struggle against imperialism. This was a core element of the revolutionary ideology that inspired the Cultural Revolution. During this period China urged Vietnam to fight on to total victory and refuse to negotiate over the withdrawal of American forces.[13] Support for Vietnam dictated that political and military disruptions in Guangxi be kept within bounds. In Guangxi, however, this imperative ran headlong into the nationwide campaign against "revisionist" officials that toppled provincial leaders across China in a wave that crested early in 1967.

These two imperatives collided in the person of Wei Guoqing. Like provincial leaders everywhere else in China, Wei became the target of a large rebel insurgency that demanded his overthrow. Would he be sacrificed to a rebel movement that sought to topple him along with other provincial officials as alleged "revisionists" antagonistic to Mao's political line? Or should he remain to ensure stability and continuity in the region crucial to China's military assistance and border defense, as an old friend of North Vietnam's leaders and a symbol of the commitments Beijing had made both to Vietnam and the Zhuang minority?

## Wei Guoqing and Guangxi's Rebel Movement

Wei's close relationship with the Vietnamese Communists and his historic contributions to their war against the French meant nothing to Guangxi's rebel movement as it peaked in late 1966. From their perspective, Wei had long been Guangxi's top power holder, part of a revisionist party establishment across China. He made a series of moves to resist the rebel campaign during its first months, of the kind that had been roundly condemned by Beijing when committed by other national and provincial leaders, who lost their posts as a direct consequence.

As Guangxi's top official during the first few months of the Cultural Revolution, Wei led the response to the growing Red Guard movement. In June he appointed Wu Jinnan, who at the time was Guangxi's third-ranking party official, as chairman of Guangxi's Cultural Revolution Committee, making him the one responsible for the party's direction of the unfolding campaign.[14] Both men were targeted by the rebel movement as it escalated at the end of 1966, but oddly they became figureheads for opposed rebel factions in April 1967.

Wei's troubles began with his response to an unusually disruptive group of college rebels in the city of Guilin in early August 1966. Students at Guangxi Normal College had challenged the "work team" sent into their school to investigate political disloyalty in June and July, and they were punished in retaliation. The investigators were withdrawn from the school on August 5 after Mao denounced work teams in Beijing as an illegitimate effort to suppress the student movement and oppose the Cultural Revolution. Two days later the school's leaders organized Scarlet Guards, who were loyal to them, to confront the unruly students. A fight ensued, wounding more than ten of the student rebels.[15]

The Communist Party's 11th Plenum was under way in Beijing at the time, and during these sessions Mao made clear that he wholeheartedly supported rebellious students who had confronted work teams, and he denounced the officials who had dispatched them.[16] This spurred rebellious students in Guilin and Nanning to protest what they called Guilin's "August 7 Incident." The students from Guangxi Normal sent a petition delegation to Beijing, and they demanded that Guilin's leaders be punished.[17]

As an alternate member of the Central Committee, Wei Guoqing was in Beijing for the 11th Plenum meetings. Given Mao's clearly expressed support in those meetings for the student rebellion, Wei was compelled to intervene to resolve the conflicts back home. He ordered Guangxi's other top officials to meet him in Guilin, and he flew there to discuss a response. They quickly decided to fire Guilin's party secretary and the deputy party secretary, a move intended to placate the rebellious students.[18]

After this purge was announced, militant students seized the deputy party secretary and humiliated him publicly, parading him in the city streets wearing a dunce cap. This was the first time that any ranking official in the province, and possibly anywhere in China, had been abused in this fashion. They were unable to capture Guilin's first party secretary, who fled to the city of Wuzhou.[19] Outraged by the students' actions, Wei condemned them as politically reactionary, the work of "rightists" who were disloyal to the Communist Party and socialism. He mobilized students and teachers to go to Guangxi Normal to confront the unruly students, and he ordered the public security bureau to prevent a recurrence.[20]

This was precisely the wrong move. Wei's action exposed him to potential condemnation from both student rebels and Beijing. Condemning student militants as "rightists" was one of the worst offenses that officials could make at the time. On August 18, the same day that Wei denounced Guilin's student rebels, Mao Zedong held the first of his massive Tiananmen Square rallies to express his wholehearted support for the student rebellion, despite the violence it had already unleashed in the nation's capital.[21] Wei's denunciation of the Guilin students was precisely the kind of stance that was condemned as suppression of the student movement. Any goodwill that Wei's sacking of Guilin's leaders might have earned from the rebel students dissipated immediately. His move further energized the students, leading to the formation of one of the largest and most adamantly anti-Wei factions, later a major force in the April 22 alliance.

It is likely that this situation was viewed with concern in Beijing. Within days Wei was removed as Guangxi's first party secretary, but the change was framed as a promotion, not as punishment. On August 24 Wei became the second party secretary of the Central Committee's Central-South Bureau. He was replaced as Guangxi's party boss by his second in command, Qiao Xiaoguang. Wu Jinnan became Guangxi's second-ranking party secretary. Wei remained in Nanning and continued to work in the Guangxi Party Headquarters.[22]

The timing of this "promotion" was unusual. Given later developments, it may have been an effort by figures in Beijing, most likely Zhou Enlai with Mao's agreement, to prevent Wei from committing further errors and shield him from rebel animosities. If this was the intent, the move failed completely. Wei's problems intensified when the students from Guangxi Normal staged a hunger strike at the headquarters of the Guilin Party Committee, demanding a further investigation and punishment of those responsible for the "August 7 Incident." Initially numbering some 1,000, over several days it grew to more than 3,000 rebel activists.[23] The hunger strikers sent a delegation of two dozen to Nanning to lodge a protest at the headquarters of the Guangxi Party Committee. The students were blocked at the compound's entrance by the Scarlet Guards of the headquarters, and a standoff followed with much shouting and shoving. News of the confrontation spread, and more than 2,000 students from local colleges and high schools streamed to the site to support the Guilin students, and staged a large hunger strike.[24]

In the first days of the protest a female student became delirious from dehydration and heat exhaustion. Wei Guoqing, trying to demonstrate sympathy, left the party headquarters and walked into the crowd to encourage her to drink and eat. As he reached to feel her forehead, the student slapped his hand away and another student grabbed Wei's hat and threw it on the ground. Before long, rumors spread across Guangxi via wall posters and handbills that the militant students had beaten Wei Guoqing so severely that he had been hospitalized. The hunger strikers remained at the site, demanding that Wei come out and show that he was unharmed, but he declined. The protest eventually dissipated as students left on travels to Beijing and other places. Wei did not publicly refute the rumors about his beating and hospitalization until mid-October.[25] This became another rebel grievance against him.

After the protest at the party headquarters, Wu Jinnan, the official in charge of Guangxi's Cultural Revolution Committee, bore the brunt of rebel anger. Students at Nanning's universities demanded that he appear for mass struggle sessions. In early October, a Nanning student rebel group known as the Red Headquarters (*hong zong*) seized him for several mass struggle sessions (this alliance would nonetheless later join the pro-Wu rebel faction). Wu, distraught from the abuse, resigned as head of the province's Cultural Revolution Committee. This did nothing to shield him from the wrath of rebels.[26]

At the national party conference held in Beijing from October 9 to 28 to "clarify thinking" about the Cultural Revolution, Mao and his radical associates turned their fire against what they called the "bourgeois reactionary line"—efforts by local officials to contain and blunt the student rebellion. It now became clear that the only hope for local officials to survive was to acknowledge their errors fully and apologize to rebels for their past actions.[27] The Nanning rebel movement inevitably focused its fire on Wu Jinnan's superiors, Wei Guoqing and the official who replaced him as Guangxi's top official in late August, Qiao Xiaoguang.

The dam broke in early December: Wei issued a written self-criticism for his responsibility for Guangxi's bourgeois reactionary line, and on December 8, rebels held a mass rally of 150,000 to denounce him and other leaders. The rebels were unable to locate Wei and force him to the session because he had taken refuge at the Guilin Air Force Base hospital. Instead, Qiao Xiaoguang presented a self-criticism on behalf of Wei and the Guangxi Party Committee, with Wu Jinnan and other leaders in attendance.[28]

After this, the rebel campaign focused increasingly on Wei Guoqing. On January 7, 1967, rebels in the editorial offices of *Guangxi Daily* took control of the printing presses and issued a news sheet that declared the closure of the newspaper because it had carried out an erroneous political line over the past decade under Wei. On January 10 rebels dragged Wei from his hospital room and held him hostage in a dormitory on the campus of Guangxi Normal College. They assembled a collection of other top provincial and city leaders for a series of three mass denunciation rallies on successive days. The targeted officials wore placards and tall hats and were forced to kneel on the stage. After each session they were placed on the back of open trucks and paraded through the streets of Guilin, pelted with stones, and spat upon by the crowds. Wei was the primary attraction, placed prominently on the first truck.[29]

Powerless to defend themselves and unable to exercise authority, the Guangxi Party Committee collapsed. A rebel power seizure in Shanghai during the first week of January was publicized nationwide and praised by Mao in a congratulatory telegram carried in the national media on January 12. It was clear that rebels elsewhere were encouraged to follow suit. Led by rebel cadres in the Guangxi party offices, cadres inside the administration were in widespread rebellion against their superiors.[30] On January 21 Guangxi's leaders issued a statement of support for the city's largest rebel alliance, which had seized control over *Guangxi Daily,* and invited them to seize power.[31]

### The Guangxi Power Seizure and Its Aftermath

On January 22, *People's Daily* issued an editorial that urged rebels to seize power immediately over their workplaces and regional governments, a call repeated in radio broadcasts nationwide. Simultaneous power seizures over the Guangxi provincial and Nanning municipal governments took place on the very next day. The power seizure was orchestrated by a coalition of twenty-six rebel groups that had formed only one week before, on January 15. On that day an alliance of rebel cadres who worked in the provincial party and government headquarters joined forces with the city's largest alliance of rebel workers, the Workers' General Headquarters (*Guangxi gongzong*), and together with some two dozen smaller rebel groups of students and workers, they formed an alliance known as the Great Rebel Army (*zaofan dajun*).[32]

The groups that formed the Rebel Army had held a series of large mass rallies over the previous six weeks to denounce virtually all the top provincial and municipal party leaders. They included the largest of the rebel alliances in Nanning, and the ones that were the earliest to challenge top officials. Party officials had long been prohibited from deploying security and military forces against their tormentors, and after the October Party Conference in Beijing they could no longer rely on Scarlet Guards to shield them. In recent weeks they had been reduced to making abject public apologies at mass rallies, during which they submitted to humiliating mistreatment. As power seizures spread across China, officials in Nanning resigned themselves to cooperating with the Workers' Headquarters and the Rebel Army. At a meeting with the city's top officials on January 21, Guangxi's leaders called for cooperation with the Workers' Headquarters as it assumed control of party and government offices.[33]

The power seizure was organized hastily on January 22, in a meeting convened by student rebels stationed in Nanning as representatives of Beijing's Third Red Guard Headquarters, the rebel faction backed by Mao and the Central Cultural Revolution Group (CCRG).[34] A power seizure committee was formed, with the Workers' Headquarters as the "core." The next day they seized control of Guangxi's Party Committee and key offices. Rebels within each of the party and government departments separately overthrew their leaders and took control of their own offices.[35] The Rebel Army then asked the Guangxi Military District to send teams of soldiers to key departments and enterprises to back up their claims to authority. The troops arrived over the next several days. The Rebel Army proceeded with mass public struggle sessions against close to 100 provincial and city leaders.[36]

### The Collapse of the Power Seizure

Despite the support of local PLA forces, the Rebel Army coalition soon began to fall apart. As they held mass struggle sessions against deposed party leaders, the Rebel Army also attacked rival rebels, charging that they were "conservative," and demanding that they be shut down. This created discord among local rebels, and some groups in the Rebel Army coalition objected to the suppression of other rebels. Despite the arrival of PLA teams to back up power seizures in government offices, routine work was effectively paralyzed. In early February representatives from Beijing's Third Red Guard Headquarters issued handbills criticizing the Workers' Headquarters for divisive attacks on other rebels and administrative ineptitude.[37]

These criticisms reflected the views of an envoy from the CCRG in Beijing. His backstage efforts to help consolidate the Rebel Army power seizure only made matters worse, and eventually led directly to the split that developed into the April 22–Allied Command rivalry. The envoy, Wang Li, arrived in Nanning on February 2 and began consultations with local rebel leaders and military officers.[38] He met with the leaders of a group of rebel cadres and the students from Beijing's Third Headquarters and told them that the power seizure had failed because it had not enlisted senior party leaders to declare their support. He counseled the rebels to encourage ranking officials to "stand forward" for the Revolution, which meant that they should be willing to denounce their superiors in the Guangxi leadership and cooperate with the rebels in administering the province.[39] His next suggestion was that a "second power seizure" was needed. This set in motion a series of events that led to the collapse of the Rebel Army and its power seizure.[40]

In a further meeting with rebel leaders in early February, Wang suggested the names of party leaders who might be acceptable as candidates to "stand forward" and denounce Wei Guoqing and Qiao Xiaoguang. He convened several meetings along with student rebel leaders and senior provincial officials, including Wu Jin-nan and He Ximing, who was deputy governor and third-ranking party secretary.[41] The officials expressed reluctance to denounce Wei Guoqing, but they were assured that anyone who carried out the bourgeois reactionary line could be overthrown.[42]

As they realized that their Beijing sponsors were critical of their performance, the Workers' Headquarters backpedaled. But they fought back against the harshest criticisms, announcing several new initiatives. They withdrew the supervisory groups of worker rebels from government offices, and they requested that the Guangxi Military District take control. Public debates held as part of an "open door rectification" aired disagreements without resolving them, and split the Rebel Army coalition, generating deep divisions among the rebels in Nanning.[43]

The setbacks for the Workers' Headquarters emboldened rivals who had not been part of their coalition. On February 1, an alliance of workers that had formed in early December, but had not joined the larger Workers' Headquarters, mobilized dozens of smaller rebel groups to a mass rally of some 40,000 on the city's main square to announce the formation of the "Proletarian Alliance" (*wu lian*). It attracted defectors from the Rebel Army and eventually became one of the two main rebel factions, the Allied Command. Two days later, yet another rebel alliance announced its formation in a mass rally of some 30,000. The alliance was led by former Scarlet Guards who had earlier defended party authorities before turning against them. This group became known as the "Red Alliance" (*hong lian*). They were denounced by the other rebel groups, who viewed their newfound radicalism as a "fake rebellion."[44] Whether or not the rebellion was "fake," both new rebel alliances proceeded to demonstrate their revolutionary credentials by holding violent mass struggle sessions against the Guangxi leadership, including Wei Guoqing and Qiao Xiaoguang.[45]

By mid-February the Guangxi Military District withdrew their support for the Rebel Army. At a meeting of military officers, the head of the Military District stated that the Rebel Army had not prepared adequately for exercising power, and they were now retreating from their responsibilities and engaging in needless conflict with other rebels.[46]

As military support ebbed, Wang Li sought to shore up support for the Workers' Headquarters and their rebel allies, a move that increasingly put him at cross-purposes with the army officers. His work behind the scenes yielded a "February 19 Proclamation" by twelve provincial leaders: seven members of the Guangxi Party Committee, and five heads or vice heads of provincial departments. The most senior of the signatories was He Ximing, the third-ranking official in the party hierarchy. The proclamation, authored by rebel cadres in the Guangxi Propaganda Department along with Wang Li, called for "smashing" the old Guangxi Party Committee and overthrowing Wei Guoqing and Qiao Xiaoguang.[47]

As these moves were under way, the Workers' Headquarters' rivals moved against them. On February 22 the Proletarian Alliance sent a convoy of more than fifty trucks loaded with a thousand activists to the offices of the Workers' Headquarters and several of their branches, ransacking the premises, beating up the occupants, and taking nine of them briefly into custody, including the organization's leader.[48] The Military District organized a mass rally on March 1 for disgruntled members of the Rebel Army coalition and others to air their criticisms of the Workers' Headquarters. Some of the disaffected rebels advocated "smashing" the organization. The Workers' Headquarters offices were sealed up and their leader, Xiong Yijun, was escorted to the Bureau of Public Security and detained.[49]

Other rebels objected to the suppression of the Workers' Headquarters. On March 11 and 12 large delegations marched to the Guangxi Military District headquarters to object to efforts to undermine the group. On the second of these days the Workers' Headquarters and its remaining allies mobilized more than 40,000 activists to a mass rally to denounce Wei Guoqing and Qiao Xiaoguang. They resolved to establish a "New Workers' Headquarters" to replace the old organization and drew up a petition for a delegation to present to Beijing.[50]

## Toward Military Control

Seven weeks after the power seizure, conflicts between rebel factions were intensifying with no solution in sight. In early March, authorities in Beijing concluded that Guangxi, like many other provinces in China with similarly failed power seizures, should be put under military control. As the transshipment point for military supplies for Vietnam and the rear area for air defenses, Guangxi could not be left without a functioning government. Wei Guoqing was selected to head the Guangxi Military District as a provisional order was imposed. Wei was informed of Beijing's decision in a phone call from Zhou Enlai on March 13, during which Zhou emphasized Guangxi's role in support of Vietnam: "The Guangxi region is on the front lines of assisting Vietnam to resist America; military control must be implemented, and Wei Guoqing must step forward as head of the military control committee." Wei was flown to Beijing for consultations the next day.[51]

As Zhou Enlai was preparing to consult with Wei about his new role, Wang Li was working to undermine him. A dossier of accusations compiled by local rebels charged Wei with a long series of moves against local rebels, and even played the nationality card, charging falsely that he had incited minority localism.[52] They realized in mid-March that the local Military District backed Wei, and sought reassurance from Wang Li that their accusations would not backfire on them. Wang told them that he would return to Beijing and consult with his superiors, but they should continue to compile incriminating materials and should feel free to publicly denounce both Wei and the commanders of the Military District.[53] It is highly unlikely that the rebels would have continued their resistance without these back-channel signals of support from Beijing.

The decision to place Wei Guoqing in charge of the Military Control Committee became public on March 21. Military commanders held meetings with local rebels presenting what they said was the viewpoint of "the Center": Wei was a "good comrade" and had made "important contributions in supporting Vietnam"; he might have made mistakes, but they were of secondary importance. Several rebel groups reversed their longstanding opposition to Wei, but the officers were less successful with student rebels, very few of whom were willing to accept Wei.[54]

While military commanders were advocating for Wei in Nanning, Wang Li was in Beijing actively seeking to undermine him. On March 25 he presented the accusations compiled against Wei in a meeting with three younger radicals of the CCRG: Wang Li, Guan Feng, and Qi Benyu. He told them that the local rebels were adamantly opposed to Wei and complained that local military commanders were still supporting him, despite all his misdeeds. The three CCRG radicals praised Wang for his work and encouraged his efforts to undermine Wei.[55]

Wang Li's efforts were welcomed in the capital because they were aligned with growing concerns, shared by Mao, that military units dispatched to "support the left" across China were in many cases indiscriminately suppressing rebel groups, or were supporting one wing of a local rebel movement while suppressing another. These concerns were heightened by confrontations in meetings in Beijing during which prominent military commanders angrily confronted senior members of the CCRG about the destruction wrought by the rebel movement and in particular the abuse of veteran party leaders.[56] During this period Mao became convinced that certain figures in the army were opposed to the rebel campaign. He purged the military figures involved in the February meeting, labeling it a "February Adverse Current" by conservative PLA commanders. In early April new orders to army units prohibited them from arresting rebels and banning their organizations. From this time forward they were forbidden to use force against any rebel group unless that decision was cleared in Beijing.[57] Wang Li's maneuvers behind the scenes against Wei Guoqing were aligned with political trends in Beijing at that point in time, and this is undoubtedly why he and his superiors in Beijing, and the Nanning rebels with whom he collaborated, thought that their efforts might succeed.

### The Formation of the April and Allied Factions

In Nanning, the pressure applied by military commanders to convince local rebels to support Wei Guoqing forced rebels into a difficult choice. *All* of them had targeted Wei as the architect of Guangxi's "bourgeois reactionary line." They had all subjected him to violent struggle sessions in their efforts to display revolutionary credentials. They had all assumed that Wei, like almost every other top provincial official in China, would be deposed. Now they had to decide whether to reverse their earlier stand and accept that local military commanders genuinely represented the viewpoints of Beijing, and ultimately Mao himself. Their choices, pro or con, would sharply define Guangxi's emerging factions.

Two groups were predisposed to reject Wei. The Workers' Headquarters had already fallen out with local military forces, and it was their power seizure that had been challenged and undermined by their cultivation of rival rebel groups. They had welcomed military intervention at the time of their power seizure, but now they realized that Wei Guoqing, their primary target for several months, was to be put in charge of military control. They called this a "counter-revolutionary restoration." The Military District had ensured their hostility when it arrested the Workers' Headquarters leader, Xiong Yijun, and banned the organization and its proposed successor, the "New" Workers' Headquarters, in early March.[58] A second group consisted of rebel leaders who had worked together with Wang Li, believing that this back channel to the CCRG provided them with inside information about the obscure views of Mao himself. Wang Li encouraged their resistance, hinting strongly at support from the highest levels. This group included the dozen or so provincial leaders, headed by Wu Jinnan, who had "stood forward" against Wei Guoqing.

These cross-pressures split Guangxi officialdom. The members of the Guangxi Party Committee, 64 officials in all, were pressured to take a stand for or against Wei. The rebel cadres in party and government organs who had participated in the original power seizure were also faced with a choice, which split the former power structure of Guangxi and the politically active staff in the administrative offices. Near the end of March, a group of 51 middle- and higher-ranking party officials, along with 150 small rebel groups in the administrative offices, publicly declared their support for Wei Guoqing. The worker rebels in the Proletarian Alliance, a rival of the Workers' Headquarters, also declared their support for Wei, as did two alliances of worker rebels who had defected from the Rebel Army coalition.[59]

Opposed to Wei were forty-five rebel groups, including rebels in the party organs who had remained close to the Workers' Headquarters, along with university and high school rebels and the large group of Guilin students who had clashed with Wei back in August, seizing him at Guilin's Air Force hospital in January and subjecting him to a series of humiliating struggle sessions.[60] The two sides organized mass rallies, pledging their support for or opposition to Wei, and violent clashes between them multiplied in late March and into April. During the first few weeks under military control, the antagonism between the Military District and the rebels led by the Workers' Headquarters deepened. The Military Control Committee did nothing to discourage attacks on them.[61]

The Military Control Committee's clear tilt against the Workers' Headquarters, however, ran afoul of the new orders issued to the PLA in early April. Local commanders were now forbidden to suppress any rebel faction simply because it opposed them, and they were no longer empowered to judge whether a local rebel group was "reactionary" or to ban their organizations and arrest their leaders. The new orders, accompanied by criticisms of recalcitrant military commanders, energized rebel opposition to Wei Guoqing, because it seemed to signal that Beijing was sympathetic to their cause.

The new orders weakened the authority of military units in dealing with dissident rebels, but they did nothing to resolve the disputes about Wei Guoqing. During the third week of April Wang Li left Nanning for consultations with his superiors in the CCRG. He had consistently encouraged local rebels to resist Wei's appointment, but he was now unsure of the "Center's attitude" toward Wei and sought clarification from his superior, the senior Wang Li. He was told that the "Center" (essentially, Mao), was protecting Wei—at least for the time being. But during these discussions the senior Wang Li made many critical comments about the political stances of some military commanders and disagreements about Wei among different PLA units in Guangxi. These comments, and the implicit encouragement of resistance, were relayed to Nanning and elsewhere in Guangxi, leading to a stalemate between the two camps.[62]

The anti-Wei opposition coalesced after a mass rally on April 19, attended by several provincial leaders: Wu Jinnan, He Ximing, and Huo Fan, who immediately prior to the power seizure were respectively the province's second-, third-, and sixth-ranking party officials.[63] All three of them spoke at the rally to declare their support for the anti-Wei rebels, effectively creating a permanent split in the Guangxi power elite. Wu Jinnan and the others relied upon the new orders to military control forces to criticize Wei for favoring one rebel group while suppressing another, behavior now clearly forbidden by Beijing.

On April 22 the anti-Wei rebels held a massive rally to announce the formation of a new alliance. They marched to the offices of *Guangxi Daily* to present a long list of demands to Military District authorities, initiating a sit-down protest and later breaking into the building.[64] A delegation from the group traveled to Beijing to present their accusations against Wei to the CCRG.[65] These anti-Wei forces became the faction known as the Guangxi April 22 Headquarters (*Guangxi 4.22 zhihuibu*), or April 22 for short.

The upheavals in Nanning soon escalated to levels not previously seen. Massive rallies for and against Wei Guoqing were staged by large rebel alliances, and clashes between the two sides multiplied, becoming more violent.[66] In light of the intensifying local conflicts, with no obvious resolution in sight, on April 30 Beijing ordered the Guangxi Military District to send delegations from the two factions to Beijing for consultations. By May 3 representatives from both sides arrived in the capital. Wang Li, Beijing's emissary to Nanning, met with the members of the April 22 delegation shortly after their arrival. While acknowledging that the "Center" continued to protect Wei Guoqing, he urged them to keep up their resistance. Wang held out the possibility that the "Center's" attitude might change: "Originally the Center thought the Wei Guoqing problem was simple and planned to support him, but after reading your materials, they realized that he had all kinds of problems, and won't necessarily protect him, it will depend on the attitude of the rebel faction." Wang also urged them to show their determination in street fighting, and not to shy away from more violent tactics that the local military forces were now forbidden to counter. Wang also met with Wu Jinnan, encouraging him and his colleagues to submit denunciations of Wei that he would hand over to his superiors in the CCRG.[67]

The Beijing consultations spurred the pro-Wei rebels back in Nanning to form their own alliance. On May 11 they formed an alliance of all the pro-Wei groups known as the "Nanning Region Proletarian Revolutionary Allied Command," which later grew into a province-wide alliance known by the abbreviated name Allied Command (*lianzhi*).[68] They cooperated with the Guangxi Military District in the months to come, as the clashes with April 22 forces became larger and more frequent. Delegations from the two increasingly coherent political factions would remain in Beijing for consultations and negotiations until November, with neither side able to gain the upper hand.

## Interpreting the Political Cleavage

What created this split in Nanning's rebel movement? One interpretation, offered by the April faction, is that the Allied Command, aligned with the Guangxi Military District and pledged to Guangxi's long-serving top official, represented a "conservative" political orientation in defense of the status quo. By contrast, the April 22 faction was a "radical" insurgency that opposed the forces of order represented by the military and by the province's long-serving top official. From this perspective, the "conservative" Allied faction sought to curtail the disorders and transformative potential of the rebel movement, while the "radical" April faction sought to push the rebellion through to its end. This was certainly the way that radical members of the CCRG viewed the conflicts, and this view was embraced by the April 22 faction. Both argued that the Military Control Committee under Wei Guoqing represented a "counter-revolutionary restoration" at odds with the radical thrust of the Cultural Revolution. Scholarly analyses of these conflicts have incorporated these representations into their analyses of the causes of factional divisions.[69]

From a broad structural perspective, viewing these conflicts from a distance, this interpretation has a certain plausibility. But if we look more closely at how actors were pulled into factions by decisions they made in reaction to unfolding and contingent events, the story suggests a different interpretation altogether.

Let us begin with the decision to support Wei Guoqing, which was the original point of cleavage between the Allied and April factions. Did this signal an underlying preference for the existing order? The first problem with this idea is that *all* the rebel factions, including the ones later aligned with Wei, targeted him as the primary agent of Guangxi's "bourgeois reactionary line." Even former Scarlet Guards, the archetypal "conservative" defenders of the existing order in the first months of the Cultural Revolution, eventually turned against him and in early February 1967 declared their solidarity with the rebel camp.[70] The rebels who decided to support Wei at the urging of the officers of the Guangxi Military District did so only later, and they did so because the military officers had begun to move against their rivals in the Workers' Headquarters, giving them an opening to replace them. These supporters included rebel groups that were not part of the rebel coalition that seized power, and several of the rebel groups that *were* included in the power seizure, but later withdrew. From a narrow strategic perspective, support for Wei Guoqing gave a rebel group the backing of military forces, and the upper hand against rival rebels. From a normative perspective, this decision also reflected a motivation to act in accord with what they understood to be a legitimate course of action in line with the somewhat obscure intentions of Mao Zedong.

If we look at the alternatives available to Nanning rebels in March, it hardly represents a rejection of the political status quo. Anti-Wei rebels firmly embraced Guangxi's second-ranking official, Wu Jinnan, and a collection of other top provincial officials who stood up to denounce Wei Guoqing, and by extension the missteps by his Military Control Committee in handling local rebel rivalries. Wu Jinnan, like Wei Guoqing, was a Red Army veteran with a long revolutionary pedigree. A native of Guangdong Province, he joined the Communist Party in 1927 and like Wei was a military officer in the Jiangxi Soviet in the early 1930s. He was a Long March veteran and held military posts in Yan'an and anti-Japanese base areas. After 1949 he held civilian leadership positions at the prefecture level in Guangdong Province before his promotion as a deputy party secretary of Guangxi Province in 1954.[71] As we have seen, he was initially in charge of Guangxi's Cultural Revolution Committee and was targeted for denunciation by the same rebel coalitions that later came to support him.

This choice, moreover, cannot be said to reflect an inherent rebel distaste for allegedly "conservative" military forces. The Workers' Headquarters initially welcomed the intervention of army units, sought their support, and cooperated with them in the initial weeks. They became hostile only after the military withdrew their support and sought to assemble a new rebel coalition that excluded them. Upon closer examination, the cleavages that motivated the factional conflicts in Guangxi were the result of splits within the existing power structure, with rebel workers, students, and cadres drawn into the ensuing struggles.

Did the actions of the military control forces in Nanning reflect an inherent military bias toward preserving the status quo ante? Recall that the military units immediately declared their support for the Rebel Army coalition and its power seizure. They withdrew their support only later, after the Workers' Headquarters mishandled the transfer of power and pursued divisive vendettas against rival rebel groups. This charge did not originate with the armed forces—it originated in complaints from rival rebels excluded from the Rebel Army, and it was shared by rebel groups included in the Rebel Army, and who would soon defect. This critical stance toward the Guangxi power seizure was also shared by the CCRG's emissary, Wang Li, and by representatives of the Third Headquarters rebels from Beijing. The anti-Wei rebels persevered in their struggle because of the backstage support promised by the CCRG's emissary, who along with his superiors was waging an underground campaign against Wei, gambling that Mao's support for him would fade if rebel resistance continued.

The ranking officials who lined up for and against Wei Guoqing no longer held their former positions. Those who supported Wei would be retained as advisors to assist military officers in conducting the business of government, but the others remained in limbo. Officials pledged to Wu Jinnan were essentially banished from collaborating, and many of them had to move into compounds guarded by the April faction to ensure their personal safety. The deposed civilian officials, which-ever side they chose, could only hope that their side in the factional conflicts would eventually prevail—or at least that an enforceable compromise resulted—and that they would somehow survive the ordeal without suffering severe penalties. The imposition of military control, in other words, represented the militarization of China's government, ratifying the destruction of the old order.

When we examine closely the events out of which factional alignments emerged, it is hard to credit an interpretation that portrays the actors as groups with inherent, stable, and pre-existing orientations to the status quo that played out in some coherent and predictable fashion as events unfolded. The process looks very different when examined as a flow of events. Factional alignments emerged as different actors made decisions in fluid situations, where it was uncertain what the outcomes of one's choices would be, and where it was ambiguous what was the politically correct course of action in the minds of those who sponsored this upheaval in Beijing. As we shall see, a major part of the problem was that the key actors in Beijing had not yet made up their minds and would not do so for some time to come.

There is another consideration, which complicates this question further. The Allied Command and April 22 factions originated in Nanning, but they spread across the other five cities and eighty counties in Guangxi to create province-wide alliances. No matter how we characterize the split in Nanning, there were scores of separate local jurisdictions where rebel groups vied with one another, moved to seize power (or did not do so), had varied relationships with local military units that tried to assume government administration, and chose eventually to affiliate with either the April or Allied factions. The province-wide factions were composite constructions of local rebel alliances that took a variety of routes to their eventual position in Guangxi's political conflicts. It is to the spread of factional divisions, and the formation of province-wide Allied and April alliances, that we now turn.

## CHAPTER 3

# Spread

In the two months between the collapse of the provincial government and the appointment of Wei Guoqing, power seizures and military interventions occurred across all of Guangxi's five other cities, eight prefectures, and eighty counties. They rarely replicated the sequence of events that unfolded in Nanning. Where they occurred, power seizures took a variety of forms. Military officers intervened after a brief delay to support rebel power seizures almost everywhere, but they improvised in reaction to local developments, leading to an array of different outcomes. These events occurred rapidly across Guangxi prior to the imposition of military control in late March, and by early May rebel factions were already forming in almost all of Guangxi's cities and counties.

There was no compelling reason why rebels outside of the largest cities should have preferred either Wei Guoqing or Wu Jinnan. Both Wei and Wu had long served in positions at the apex of Guangxi's power structure.[1] Both had been prominent targets of the large rebel campaign in Nanning. The withdrawal of military support for Nanning's power seizure had no direct implication for rebels who had seized power in other cities and rural counties. Yet rebels across Guangxi, even in remote regions, nonetheless split into factions and eventually joined one of two large coalitions, pledging their support for either Wei Guoqing or Wu Jinnan. Why did this occur? By tracing through the spread of factions, we can clarify their foundations and understand more clearly the politics that generated province-wide violence.

### The Wave of Power Seizures

The first step toward the emergence of antagonistic factions in most localities was a rebel power seizure. Nanning's January 23 power seizure was conducted hastily, spurred by urgent messages emanating from Beijing via *People's Daily* and *Red Flag* editorials read out on national radio broadcasts.[2] The Nanning events were part of a national wave touched off by the January 22 exhortations from Beijing. The wave spread rapidly across China in a distinctly top-down pattern. Power seizures at the provincial level spurred imitations in prefectures and prefecture-level cities, and power seizures at the prefecture level spurred similar actions in counties and county-level cities. By the end of January, only nine days after the initial call for rebels to seize power, half of all cities and counties in China had already experienced power seizures, and by the end of February, 70 percent. By the end of March, rebels had deposed local leaders in all but 20 percent of China's cities and counties.[3]

This rapid, top-down pattern was replicated within Guangxi. Power seizures spread rapidly to other cities and prefectures after Nanning's, but none occurred beforehand. Rebels seized power in one prefecture (Hechi) on the same day, and another five cities and prefectures the day after.[4] By January 26, only three days after Nanning, the party and government committees in *all* the cities and prefectures had been overthrown.[5] Only one county out of eighty may have had a power seizure prior to that of its prefecture.[6] Local governments were overthrown in fifty cities and counties by the end of January, and another thirteen by the end of February, by which point the party and government leaders of just under three-quarters of cities and counties had been overthrown.

The rapid spread of power seizures across Guangxi reflected a pattern documented across China, where they reached far into regions where there was hardly any rebel activity beforehand.[7] The large coalitions of workers and students that were so disruptive in Nanning were rare outside of the largest cities. Coalitions of this type had formed in three of Guangxi's four major cities by November 1966: Guilin in September, Wuzhou in October, and Nanning in November. Of the eighty-two jurisdictions at the county level, only three had rebel coalitions by November 1966; by December this number increased only to twelve, or 18 percent overall.

Large rebel movements were rare in the rural counties because the groups that energized the early rebel movements in the cities were largely absent in the

TABLE 3.1.   Guangxi Population Groups, Average Numbers by Jurisdiction Type, 1966

| Jurisdiction | University Students | High School Students | Salaried Workers | Administrative Cadres | N |
|---|---|---|---|---|---|
| Prefecture-level Cities | 1,780 | 2,098 | 64,369 | 6,186 | 4 |
| County-level Cities | 0 | 362 | 6,958 | 1,315 | 2 |
| Counties | 0 | 243 | 5,538 | 2,160 | 80 |
| Total Number in Province | 7,120 | 28,556 | 714,432 | 200,174 | 86 |

Source: Published statistical yearbooks (*tongji nianjian*), local annals (*difang zhi*), and histories of local Communist Party organizations (*zuzhishi ziliao*).

counties. County-level jurisdictions—small cities and rural counties—had no university students, few high school students, and very small salaried workforces outside of agriculture (see table 3.1). There were an average of only 243 high school students in Guangxi's counties, and a salaried labor force of only 5,538.[8] There were only slightly larger numbers in the small county-level cities. These populations were too small to seriously challenge party and government authorities.

The rarity of significant rebel challenges to county governments and small cities prior to 1967 makes the rapid spread of power seizures something of a puzzle. Why did power seizures spread so fast and so far, given the near absence of significant student and worker rebel campaigns? Who were the rebels who carried them out? In Nanning, rebels within the provincial and city administration were a major force in the Rebel Army coalition. In local jurisdictions with few students and workers, the role of cadres was magnified. Cadres in party and government agencies worked in close collaboration with one another, had a strong capacity to mobilize, and were deeply affected by these political trends. Their jobs were potentially in jeopardy, and political charges could have even worse consequences. There were an average of 2,160 cadres in Guangxi's counties. The ratio of cadres to other salaried employees was much higher than in larger cities—there were an average of 10 cadres for every 100 salaried workers in the large cities, but 62 for every 100 in counties (calculated from table 3.1). Sixteen counties had more cadres than salaried workers in manufacturing and services.

Why would cadres overthrow their superiors? After all, they were the most privileged group, and had a strong interest in retaining their positions and in defending local power structures. This seems counter-intuitive, but on closer examination it is not difficult to understand. It had been clear since November 1966 that

Mao and his radical supporters were encouraging rebels to challenge "revisionist" power holders. We have already seen that rebel groups were active participants in the Nanning power seizure. In the counties, cadre rebellions advanced much more rapidly than those by students and workers. By December 1966 cadre rebel groups were reported in 43 percent of all county-level jurisdictions, but only 18 percent had rebel organizations of students and workers. By January 1967 cadre rebels had appeared in 90 percent of all counties.[9]

Most power seizures were carried out by cadres and staff who worked in county administrative offices. This explains the rapid, top-down pattern of their spread. Once rebels in the provincial capital seized power in Nanning, this immediately incited cadres at lower levels to act in concert. There was already an array of cadre rebels in county administrations, most of them organized within individual offices and departments.[10] They were spurred to imitate actions at the higher level, if for no other reason than to avoid any suggestion that they were loyal followers of party leaders who would soon be overthrown, which would subject them to retribution as well. Narrative accounts of these power seizures describe county-level cadres that observed power seizures in their prefecture capital while attending meetings there, and who rushed back home to urge their colleagues to act quickly in imitation as soon as possible.[11] The fact that there were typically many separate cadre rebel groups, usually formed within separate departments, introduced an element of competition, further spurring cadre rebels to seize power before others did so.

Although power seizures spread rapidly, they rarely conformed to the pattern in the provincial capital. The most important feature that distinguishes local power seizures was who carried them out. The power seizure in Nanning was carried out by a broad coalition of rebels from three different groups: university students, who initiated the early challenges to local leaders; industrial workers, far more numerous than students and whose rebellion was much more disruptive; and rebel cadres within party and government organs, who ultimately made it impossible for local leaders to govern. This type of power seizure—by a broad coalition of all three groups—in fact was rare and largely limited to cities, for reasons I have already indicated.

Descriptions of power seizures contained in the investigation reports permit us to clarify how this process unfolded. Power seizures over the entire local government, where they occurred, took three different forms, as summarized in table 3.2.

TABLE 3.2.  Power Seizure Types, by Level of Jurisdiction

| Jurisdiction | (1) Broad Coalition | (2) Cadre-led alliance | (3) Cadres alone | (4) Government Departments | (5) None | N |
|---|---|---|---|---|---|---|
| Province | 1 | 0 | 0 | 0 | 0 | 1 |
| Prefecture-level Cities | 4 | 0 | 0 | 0 | 0 | 4 |
| Prefectures | 0 | 4 | 2 | 2 | 0 | 8 |
| County-level Cities | 0 | 0 | 1 | 1 | 0 | 2 |
| Counties | 6 | 12 | 39 | 11 | 9 | 77 |
| Total | 11 | 16 | 42 | 14 | 9 | 92 |

Note: There were 3 power seizures in counties whose type could not be determined.

The first (shown in column 1) were power seizures carried out, as in Nanning, by a coalition of students, workers, and cadres. In the second (column 2), rebel cadres organized a power seizure and invited students or workers to join with them. In the third (column 3), cadres who worked in the party and government offices overthrew their superiors and seized power unilaterally, without involvement by others. There were two circumstances in which rebels did not seize power. In the first (column 4), cadres overthrew their bosses in individual departments, but did not claim power over the entire government. In the second (column 5), no power seizures of any kind were reported.

Outside of the larger cities, power seizures by broad coalitions were rare. Almost everywhere else, cadres played a dominant if not exclusive role. In half of the eight prefectures, cadre rebels seized power while inviting other groups to participate. In the others, rebel cadres seized power unilaterally or were content to seize control only in their own departments. Rebel cadres were even more dominant at the county level. In forty of eighty-two cases at the county level, cadres seized power unilaterally. In twelve other cases, they organized power seizures and invited students or workers to join. Only six counties had power seizures by broad coalitions. In twenty counties there was no power seizure, and in just over half of these, cadres seized power over their own departments, effectively nullifying the authority of county leaders without removing them.

## The Formation of Local Factions

The April 22 and Allied Command factions were fully formed in Nanning by the end of April 1967. Both sides received a kind of official legitimacy when their representatives were invited to Beijing to adjudicate their disagreements. The discussions continued for six months, until the delegates were sent home in November with a tentative agreement to prepare for a new government—a "Revolutionary Committee." As the meetings dragged on, rebel factions spread across Guangxi's five other cities and eighty counties, aligning with the Allied Command or April coalitions. By the time the Beijing negotiations concluded, almost every city and county had rebel factions aligned with a province-wide coalition.

As in Nanning, factions originated in disputes among rebels who previously had sought to overthrow local authorities. Initially, the disputes were between rebels who had seized power and other rebels who were excluded from the act. Even setting aside rivalries among rebel leaders, the speed with which power seizures were carried out made it almost impossible to include all rebels. These exclusions bred disputes and antagonisms. Disagreements also broke out within power seizure coalitions, as some rebels defected and moved into opposition. These were the seeds of the later factions, but these nascent divisions were crystallized and hardened only when military units intervened to "support the left," an act that forced them to take sides in rebel disputes. This inserted military forces into the middle of the developing conflicts and added a new dimension to emerging factionalism—rebels who supported the decisions of military commanders and those who dissented from them. This pattern, so evident in Nanning, unfolded in a variety of ways in other cities and counties, even where there were no power seizures.

Military intervention followed soon after power seizures and spread into places where rebels did not seize power. Figure 3.1 traces the spread of power seizures relative to military intervention. Rebel power seizures that overthrew local Party Committees, traced by the solid line, spread rapidly, and crested in February, eventually leveling off at sixty-six counties and cities. The dashed line indicates the first time that PLA or PAD officers are mentioned in local narratives as intervening in local political disputes or establishing control over selected government agencies. Military intervention reached all but three counties by April 1967. Even where there had been no power seizure, political authority had already collapsed due to internal rebellions by cadres and staff within administrative agencies. The dotted line indicates the establishment of a Production Management Committee under PLA or PAD direction, which was the next step in consolidating military control. By April 1967 these committees had been established in all but six counties. In the forty-nine

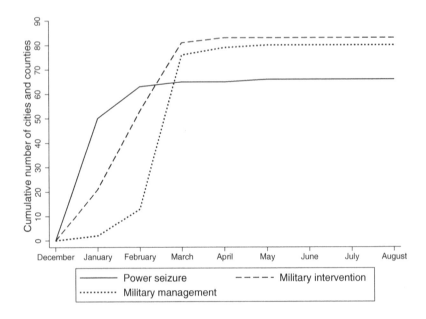

FIGURE 3.1.   The Spread of Power Seizures and Military Intervention, 1967

localities where the exact dates for a power seizure and military intervention are known, the latter followed an average of nineteen days after a power seizure.

## The Structure of Military Intervention

The process that culminated in province-wide factions began when the PLA was directed to assist rebel power seizures, near the end of January 1967. On January 28, six days after Beijing urged rebels to seize power, the Central Military Commission directed the PLA to "support the revolutionary left" in power seizures.[12] The interventions were facilitated by the structure of China's regional military forces. The PLA had regional forces organized into jurisdictions that largely mirrored the civilian governmental hierarchy. Each province defined a Military District; prefectures were coterminous with Military Subdistricts; and county-level units had PADs. The commanders and political commissars of these regional and local military units were integrated into the civilian leadership structures as members of the Communist Party Committee, in most cases also as members of the executive team known as its Standing Committee.[13] Orders for the PLA to "support the left" activated military units at each of these levels. As in Nanning, local rebels eagerly sought military support, which conferred legitimacy on their actions and was crucial in backing up their claims. The decisions of military officers were decisive turning points in local politics.

Regional PLA forces were the units primarily responsible for military intervention. They were distinct from another branch of China's armed forces: main force combat units, which at the time were organized into thirty-six numbered Army Corps. Unlike the regional forces, the PLA's Army Corps were not tied to government jurisdictions and their commanders were not integrated into civilian governments. They were under the command of one of thirteen broad military regions: Guangxi was under the Guangzhou Military Region, which was headquartered in neighboring Guangdong Province. The regional forces were smaller than these Army Corps, permanently stationed in local garrisons, and lightly armed. The main force Army Corps had armored divisions, artillery and engineering units, and air and naval forces. Not attached to any regional government, they could be moved around the country.[14] The PLA 47th Army Corps and several air force divisions were moved into Guangxi in 1964 in response to the escalating war in Vietnam. At various times during this period, they assisted the regional forces under the military district as needed.

When Wei Guoqing was appointed to lead military control forces in Guangxi, he assumed political command over the Guangxi Military District. The Military District commanded the lightly armed divisions in local garrisons in the cities, but the most important force that they commanded were the PADs in the smaller cities and counties. These were the lowest rung of the provincial military hierarchy. They did not command regular troops, but instead recruited, trained, and directed People's Militias (*min bing*) that were the only permanent armed presence in rural counties. The militia forces were organized in small cities and county seats, and had branches that extended into rural towns and villages.

The heads of the county PAD were serving PLA officers under the command of the Military Subdistrict, and they also held leading posts in local Party Committees. The PLA's orders to "support the revolutionary left" effectively made PAD officers the only local party leaders who were immune to overthrow in rebel power seizures. They became referees in disputes among competing rebel groups, and their support was eagerly sought by rebels who had seized power or who aspired to do so.

## The Consequences of Military Intervention

When military units intervened, they had two tasks—political and administrative. Their political task was to support rebels who had seized power. Their administrative task was to ensure the continued functioning of banks, post offices, telephone and telegraph bureaus, railway networks, and crucially important government departments. China's economy at the time was managed entirely by bureaucratic allocation, a fact that would magnify the economic damage of political disruptions far beyond what one would expect in a market economy. While this administrative responsibility might seem to be apolitical and uncontroversial, military units were forced to intervene in local politics to build a coalition of rebel groups that would cooperate with one another and with military authority. As in Nanning, this drew military units into the middle of rebel disputes.

Army officers had to forge working relationships with rebels to carry out their assigned task, and in doing so they favored some groups at the expense of others. Rebels whose claims were not supported by military forces adopted a critical or openly antagonistic stance toward them. Their opposition was not to military intervention per se, but to the decisions made by military commanders. In Nanning, rebels opposed to the decisions of the Military District seized on the appointment of Wei Guoqing to discredit prior decisions by military commanders that had undermined them and strengthened their rivals. They did not object to military control—they were very much in favor of it when they initially had military backing. They objected to the decisions made by local commanders and wanted them replaced by officers more sympathetic to their claims, or at least willing to adopt a more evenhanded stance. In Nanning this was encouraged by the emissary from the CCRG, but it inevitably occurred in other localities where, as in Nanning, rebels had already formed antagonistic rivalries. Army units could not carry out their tasks without intervening in these disputes.

Military units were forced into a series of choices. In many localities, one group of rebels had seized power, but the act was disputed by rivals who were excluded. In these cases, military units were forced to take sides—either approving a power seizure or supporting its opponents. Given the variety of forms taken by local power seizures, and the absence of power seizures in twenty counties, military officers were faced with an array of different circumstances, forcing them to improvise.

At the county level, most power seizures were carried out by cadre rebels whose acts were often contested by rival groups of cadre rebels, or by rebels outside of party and government offices. In these cases, the PAD had to adjudicate the conflicting claims of different rebel groups. In other cases, as in Nanning, military units approved a rebel power seizure and established administrative structures to support it, but the rebel alliance proved inadequate to the task and subsequently split, again forcing military units to take sides or organize a new coalition. In a third variant, military units intervened in counties where rebel groups were active but had yet to organize a power seizure that deposed the civilian government. In these cases, the PAD counseled rebel groups, urged them to act, or directly orchestrated rebel alliances—a level of involvement that could make them the virtual sponsor of the power seizure itself. In counties where there were few active rebels, the PAD simply thrust aside civilian party officials, effectively seizing power themselves, while recruiting rebel leaders to join them.

Although military officers in each jurisdiction were integrated into Party Committees, this did not mean, as some rebels would later claim, that the military intervened in a conservative attempt to shield existing power holders. Their intervention implied the opposite: virtually all civilian leaders were overthrown, and government functions would continue under a form of martial law. Subsequent disputes between rebel factions that supported and opposed military control obscures the fact that these events essentially militarized local government. Civilian officials were thrust aside, and military officers formed ad-hoc committees to carry out government functions, relying on cadre rebels and a few of the deposed local leaders. For the subsequent development of province-wide factions, the most important implication of the structure of military forces is that after March 1967 the forces under the Military Districts, subdistricts, and PAD were in a hierarchy headed by Wei Guoqing. This structured the province-wide conflicts between the Allied Command and April 22 factions. At the grassroots level, the Allied Command were rebels who aligned themselves with the PAD, and they worked together with the PAD's militia forces, which reached deeply into small towns and villages. This gave them an overwhelming advantage in rural regions.

Figure 3.2 traces the spread of factions across Guangxi. The solid line indicates the first time that rebel factions were reported. The first disputes appeared in a handful of localities in January; by July they had appeared in eighty of the eighty-six cities and counties. These local factions, which originated primarily for reasons

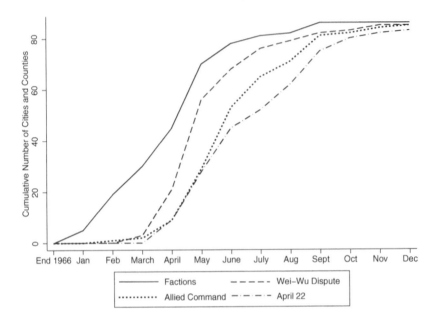

FIGURE 3.2. The Spread of Rebel Factions, 1967

unconnected to events in Nanning, gradually aligned with the rebel coalitions in the provincial capital. The first step was a public declaration of a stance in the dispute over Wei Guoqing's appointment. There were twenty such declarations by April, fifty-six by May, and by August local rebels in seventy-nine cities and counties had taken a stand. The final step was when local rebels adopted the names April 22 or Allied Command, formalizing their links with province-wide coalitions. The respective name changes are traced by the final two lines in the figure. By the time the Beijing negotiations between the two factions concluded in November 1967, almost every locality had factions aligned with the province-wide coalitions.

## The Emergence of Factions in Cities
Guangxi's four largest cities—Nanning, Guilin, Wuzhou, and Liuzhou—had the rank of a prefecture, which put them directly under the provincial government, with a rank equal to that of the eight rural prefectures. While there were separate but simultaneous power seizures over the provincial and city governments in Nanning, this was not the case in the other three large cities, where political

developments were considerably less complicated. In the important case of Guilin, the power seizure and military intervention unfolded in a radically different way than in Nanning, and this had major implications for Guangxi's politics.

## Guilin

Guangxi's third-largest city had a total population of 270,000 and a salaried work-force of 42,000. It was the only city in the province other than Nanning that had a significant number of university students—close to 3,000, most of them at Guangxi Normal College, a hotbed of early radical student activity. Unlike Nanning, Guilin's rebel power seizure was successful. It was coordinated with a main force PLA unit drawn from the 47th Army Corps, stationed in the city and responsible for "support the left" work. The largest rebel groups were integrated into new structures of power with full military support. There was an even more consequential difference from Nanning: these rebels were adamantly opposed to Wei Guoqing, and they were to become a major source of strength for Guangxi's April 22 faction.

Guilin's large and militant student movement challenged Wei Guoqing even before the rebels in Nanning did. Wei's sudden "promotion" out of the Guangxi leadership followed his missteps when dealing with militant Guilin students in early August 1966. Guilin's power seizure, led by these same students and carried out by a broad coalition with workers and cadre rebels, occurred the day after Nanning's, on January 24. The responsible PLA unit supported the power seizure and continued to support the rebels and defend them, even though the rebels declared their unalterable opposition to Wei Guoqing after his appointment in late March. Guilin survived as a bastion of the April 22 faction until the very end of these conflicts, culminating in the 1968 battles described in the prologue to this book.

The rebel students from Guangxi Normal College were the first and most militant of Guangxi's student rebels. They were instrumental in the formation of two large rebel alliances of workers and students in September. In mid-December the two groups joined with other rebels to form a single rebel coalition. Shortly after the mass struggle sessions in Guilin in mid-January, during which they humiliated and physically abused Wei Guoqing and other leaders, the rebel coalition planned to seize power. Along with rebel cadres from the city administration and students representing Beijing's Third Red Guard Headquarters, they declared a power seizure over Guilin on January 24.[15]

Subsequent events diverged from those in Nanning. On February 5, PLA Regiment 6955, a detachment from the 47th Army Corps, intervened to support the power seizure, and met with the rebel leaders to create a new administrative structure.[16] This new, army-sponsored alliance was named, after the power seizure coalition in Nanning, the Great Rebel Army (*zaofan dajun*). Soldiers from Regiment 6955 staged an armed parade through the city's streets, declaring their support. Working together with the rebels, the PLA detachment set up a Production Management Center in early March.[17] Up to this point, Guilin had a smooth working relationship between rebels and the PLA. However, after the controversy emerged over Wei Guoqing in Nanning, different military units in the city took different stances. After the April 22 declaration by Wu Jinnan and other party leaders, the Guilin rebels pledged support for him and joined the growing anti-Wei movement, placing them at odds with the Guangxi Military District.

As a main force combat unit under the Guangzhou Military Region, the 47th Army Corps was stationed in Guangxi in 1964 as a border defense unit in response to the escalating war in Vietnam. When Wei was placed in charge of military control forces in Guangxi, he had direct command over the Guangxi Military District, but not the 47th Army detachment assigned to Guilin. From the perspective of the commanders of PLA Unit 6955, they had correctly supported a power seizure by the city's leading rebels, fully in accord with Beijing's directives. Their orders were to "support the left," not Wei Guoqing. The controversy over Wei was a political issue, emerging almost two months after the Guilin power seizure. In their view they were not required to repudiate their prior actions. The commanders of Unit 6955 eventually issued a public statement of support for Wei in June, briefly alarming the Guilin rebels, but it soon became clear that the unit leaders did not intend to withdraw their support for the rebels.[18]

Local opposition to Guilin's Rebel Army did not emerge until May, when rebels who were excluded from the power seizure made a bid for military backing by declaring their support for Wei Guoqing. PLA units under the Guangxi Military District—the Guilin Military Subdistrict and the PADs in the counties under Guilin Prefecture—supported these pro-Wei rebels, putting them at cross-purposes with the 47th Army's Unit 6955. The opposition also received public declarations of support from several units under the PLA's 7th Air Force stationed in Guilin.[19] A June effort by the PLA units to reconcile the two groups was rejected by both factions and dropped.[20] The 47th Army regiment continued to support the Guilin mainstay of the April 22 faction with joint rallies and armed military parades in August and September.[21] Guilin remained a stronghold of the April faction until the very end.

## Liuzhou

A major rail terminus near the center of the province and a key transshipment point for the delivery of military supplies for Vietnam, Liuzhou had a total population of 353,000 and a salaried workforce of 68,000. The Liuzhou Railway Bureau, headquartered in the city, was a major employer, and more than 60,000 troops were stationed in the city to patrol the railway lines and guard storage depots. These forces played a dominant role in the city's rebel conflicts.

In early January 1967 an alliance of nineteen rebel groups seized power over *Liuzhou Daily*, sealed off the editorial offices, and announced that they had taken control of the party's newspaper. Several days later, fifty-eight rebel organizations in the city released a statement welcoming the action. In response to the January 22 calls from Beijing for rebels to seize power, two separate groups of cadres in the party and government organs of the city and prefecture prepared for a power seizure. Initially unaware of one another's preparations, one group moved first and declared a power seizure on January 25 after receiving prior approval from the commanders of the Liuzhou Military Subdistrict. Rebels who were preempted by this sudden move vehemently disputed the power seizure and the Military Subdistrict's support for it. The local military banned some of the more militant groups and arrested their leaders.[22]

In early February, despite disputes over the legitimacy of the rushed power seizure, the commander of the Military Subdistrict met with local troops to declare his firm support for it (which he had approved in advance) and directed the troops to march through the city streets in support, followed by a huge rally of troops on the main city square. Mass rallies by thousands of troops in support of the power seizure continued until early April, at which point the new orders for the military forced a pullback of aggressive displays of force in support of one set of rebels against another.[23] The shift in the military's orders, in combination with developments in Nanning that resulted in the formation of the April 22 coalition, spurred the reemergence of suppressed rebel groups that had earlier protested their exclusion from the original power seizure. In late April debates about the legitimacy of that power seizure spread, and two rebel alliances declared their formation in June. The much larger of the two assembled 70,000 followers in a rally on the city's main square. They declared their support for Wei Guoqing, aligned themselves with the Allied faction, and pledged to "overthrow" Wu Jinnan, whom they called a "political swindler." A smaller alliance of ten rebel groups declared their support for Wu and aligned themselves with Nanjing's April faction. They accused the Military Subdistrict of supporting one faction and suppressing the other in violation of the new April orders to the PLA. With the local military no longer empowered to suppress dissenting rebels, representatives from the two sides were invited to join the Beijing negotiations.[24]

*Wuzhou*

On Guangxi's eastern border with Guangdong, this small city on the West River (which flows across the provincial border to join the South China Sea through the Pearl River delta) had a total population of 146,000 and a salaried workforce of 39,500. On January 12, local rebels raided a welcoming ceremony for a military delegation, seized Wuzhou's party secretary, and dragged him through the streets. On two subsequent occasions they forcibly paraded him through the streets wearing a dunce cap. Two of these rebel groups formed a committee to prepare for a power seizure. On January 24, one day after the provincial power seizure, they took over the city offices at the head of an alliance of more than forty rebel groups, gathering the city's leaders to tell them that they were to work under rebel supervision.[25]

Several days later, the Wuzhou Military Subdistrict and PAD declared their support and paraded troops through the city streets to celebrate the power seizure. Problems began in mid-February, however, when the Military Subdistrict began to investigate the political backgrounds of some of the individual rebel groups in the power seizure alliance. To distance themselves from these problematic groups, some of the original organizers withdrew. At the end of February, they announced the formation of a new rebel alliance known as the Great Preparatory Committee (*da chouwei*). It brought together some 160 rebel groups and more than 16,000 members, including rebel cadres and several Wuzhou leaders who had publicly denounced the city's party secretary shortly after the power seizure. The Preparatory Committee denounced the earlier power seizure as "conservative." The Military Subdistrict withdrew support for the original power seizure and sided with the new alliance. In response, the rebels who had carried out the first power seizure declared that military commanders did not have the power to decide which rebel groups were legitimate.[26]

The local military tightened their grip during March. They banned six rebel groups as "reactionary" and labeled their leaders as counter-revolutionaries. The Preparatory Committee staged harsh struggle sessions against the former city leaders, focusing on the former first party secretary. One of them committed suicide. In late March, the Wuzhou Military Subdistrict and the Preparatory Committee pledged support for Wei Guoqing immediately after he was appointed to head military control forces. The rebels who had led the original power seizure reacted by pledging their support for Wu Jinnan. Shortly afterward, the Military Subdistrict was forced to release the rebel leaders it had arrested and reverse its recent bans on several rebel groups. This locked factional alignments into place, and several months later the two sides formally aligned with the Allied and April coalitions.[27]

## Beihai and Pingxiang

There were two other cities in Guangxi, both much smaller and ranked at the county level.[28] The larger of the two, Beihai, was a seaport on the Gulf of Tonkin with a population of 116,000, 11,500 salaried workers, and a total of only 584 high school students.[29] Historically part of Guangdong Province, along with almost all of Qinzhou prefecture, the city became a permanent part of Guangxi only in 1965.[30] Not until late December did the first student wall poster attacking the city's leaders appear. Two days later, Beihai's party secretary issued a self-criticism, unleashing a belated mobilization by small rebel groups in workplaces and government offices. The most consequential rebel mobilization occurred among the more than 2,100 cadres and staff in the city's administration. On the last day of 1966 an alliance of sixteen small rebel groups in city offices led attacks on the Party Committee, which culminated in a mass struggle session against the party's leaders, attended by 10,000 activists, on January 19.

Despite this activity there was no attempt to seize power over Beihai. Rebels seized power over several city departments but did not act to take control of the city itself. This created a power vacuum that the PAD filled in mid-March when they set up a Production Command Department to manage the economy. After the controversy emerged over the appointment of Wei Guoqing, the Beihai PAD

initiated a campaign to pressure all rebels to pledge support for Wei Guoqing, sending representatives into workplaces and government offices to carry the message.
It is not clear whether the effort backfired or was simply ineffective, but it forced
local rebels to confront this question for the first time. This inadvertently hastened
the formation of two wings of a previously disorganized local rebel movement,
which took opposite sides in the province-wide split. From that point forward Beihai was drawn into the broader provincial conflicts.

Pingxiang, a small border town where the main highway and rail links crossed
the border into North Vietnam, had a total population of only 29,000, with 2,400
salaried workers and only 140 high school students.[31] Given its location and strategic importance, there were large contingents of border troops stationed in and
around the town. There is no mention of student or worker rebel activity at any
point. Pingxiang's party leaders were overthrown by cadres who worked in the city
administration. In January 1967, a rebel group in the Party Committee offices pulled
together an alliance of eighty-one small rebel groups in the city administration and
held a series of struggle sessions against the city's top officials over several days.

The subsequent power seizure was a joint effort by rebel cadres and the PAD.
A Power Seizure Committee stripped the city's three top officials of their posts.
The PAD head spoke at the founding rally in support and denounced the deposed
officials. The power seizure was essentially an internal coup by rebels in the city's
administration, with the full support of the PAD. After the controversy over Wei
Guoqing broke out in April, some rebels sided with Wei, while others sided with
Wu Jinnan, but both sides agreed about the overthrow of party leaders and the actions of the PAD. There was little overt conflict between these groups in the months
to come.

## The Emergence of Factions in Counties

The reasons for the formation of local factions linked to province-wide divisions
were as varied in the counties as they were in the cities, but there were many more
counties, and much wider variation in their political developments during the first
months of 1967. Only a handful of the counties had power seizures by broad coalitions that included student and worker rebels, as in the largest cities. Cadres
who worked in the party and government headquarters were the main force in
most power seizures. In some cases, cadre rebels included representative groups

of students or workers, but in most cases, they seized power without any reference to outside rebel groups. There were also twenty counties where no rebels claimed power over the entire government. In roughly half of them, rebel cadres simply took over their own government departments, and in the other half, they did not even do this. Nonetheless, in virtually all counties, regardless of their experience during the wave of power seizures, there eventually emerged two rebel factions that aligned themselves either with the Allied Command or April 22.

In county-level jurisdictions intervention by outside PLA units was rare. In most cases the local PAD intervened. The PAD's political commissar or PAD head was a member of the local Party Committee, and in many cases also served on its elite Standing Committee. They were part of a military hierarchy under the command of a prefecture-level Military Subdistrict, and their interventions in local conflicts were crucial in defining local factions. To convey a concrete sense of the varied relationships between these military actors and local rebels, I will provide brief illustrations of their interactions for each of the four types of power seizures summarized in table 3.2, and for counties where there were no power seizures.

### Power Seizures by Broad Coalitions

CANGWU. There were only six counties where there were power seizures by a coalition that included students, workers, and cadre rebels. The January 27 power seizure in Cangwu County, in the Wuzhou suburbs, was one of them.[32] Two leaders of the alliance were a high school student and a construction worker, and half of the leaders were ordinary cadres in the county headquarters. The PAD sent two officers to monitor their power seizure.

The act was quickly challenged by a separate alliance of rebel cadres from the county headquarters. They had wanted to join in the power seizure but had been refused. These rebels argued that Beijing's policy was that personnel within each unit should overthrow their own leaders. They argued that workers and students should seize power only over their factories and schools, not the county offices. In response, the power seizure alliance argued that Cangwu County was the relevant unit, not its separate administrative offices. After debates and confrontations between the two groups, the cadre rebels appealed to the PAD, who refused to back their argument and firmly supported the power seizure coalition, ruling that the county government belonged to the entire population of the county—not to the

130 cadres who worked in the government headquarters. In fact, the PAD ruled, cadres in the government might be considered "power holders" and not "masses."

This ruling did not deter the disgruntled rebel cadres, who continued to insist on their right to seize power. They argued that they were not "power holders," but ordinary office staff, and that the power seizure had stripped them of their rights to rebel against their bosses. The cadres formed an alliance across the party and government offices, and they recruited previously uninvolved students and workers into a rival alliance. The two coalitions competed with one another to recruit members and show their revolutionary credentials by holding mass struggle sessions that targeted leading cadres from the county, districts, and other organizations. This effectively paralyzed government administration.

The PAD continued to support the original power seizure and helped them by convincing rebels to defect from their rivals. After the dispute over Wei Guoqing emerged, the PAD declared its support for Wei and persuaded the rebels who had seized power to support him as well. The opposition, unable to prevail against opponents who had PAD support, aligned with anti-Wei forces in nearby Wuzhou. The original power seizure coalition, broadly representative of rebels across the county, aligned with Allied Command. The opposition alliance, led by cadres and staff in the county government, aligned with April 22.

BINYANG. The power seizure in this county, whose later wave of mass killings was described in the prologue, was in many ways the creation of the PAD.[33] An alliance of rebels led by Red Guards from the county high school held a rally on January 25. As they met to formalize arrangements for their power seizure, individual rebels in the alliance began to argue with one another over who would control the seals of office. As the meeting fell into disarray, the PAD head went to the assembly hall and negotiated the formation of a power seizure alliance whose leaders included two representatives from the PAD, several ordinary cadres in the county government and party offices, one worker, and eight student Red Guards. After this power seizure, rebels in all government departments, enterprises, districts, communes, and production brigades seized power from their leading cadres, forcing them from their posts.

Shortly afterward, PLA troops from Unit 6949, a regiment in the 47th Army Corps, formed a Military Control Committee to support the power seizure arranged by the PAD. It was composed of officers from both the PLA and the PAD, numbering some sixty members in all. They placed key government departments under military control to ensure continuity of government administration. In March, the committee formed a Production Management Office, led by the PAD head, which included several deputy heads of the former county government.

The moves by military units to exert control over government functions led to dissent among some of the original groups in the power seizure alliance. Near the end of March, Red Guards from Binyang High School expressed opposition to the control exercised by the PAD. The content of their objections was not specified, and it may simply have been a reaction against overbearing military authority. This caused a split among rebels who had originally taken part in the power seizure. Debates over the PAD's role broke out, along with increasingly violent confrontations, and two factions formed.

This controversy had raged for just over a month when, in early May, the PAD pushed local rebels to declare support for Wei Guoqing. The rebels who supported the PAD fell into line, while the PAD's opponents pledged support for Wu Jin-nan. Both factions were broad and diverse rebel alliances. The pro-Wei group was headed by a worker and a student, and its leadership contained students, workers, and ordinary cadres in the government offices. The leaders of the anti-Wei group, which aligned with April 22, had a similarly broad representation of students, workers, and ordinary cadres. It was headed by two students from Binyang High School, where its headquarters were located. By the end of May, the two groups formed separate rebel organizations with ties to the emerging provincial factions.

### Cadre-Led Alliances

FUSUI. There were only twelve counties where cadres seized power after assembling a coalition of worker and student rebels. Fusui, in the near suburbs of Nanning, was one of them. It was a hotbed of rebel activity throughout January.[34] More than eighty rebel groups formed in schools, factories, mines, and rural communes, including twenty-two in the county and government headquarters. Leading cadres at all levels, and in most government departments, were seized and subjected to struggle sessions. In late January, as it became apparent that the county was becoming ungovernable, the PAD contacted the leaders of the main rebel groups to organize a power seizure. Rebels in the county headquarters coordinated the effort. The Power Seizure Committee was headed by a cadre on the staff of the county Organization Department; the vice heads were a former head of the Rural Work Department, a cadre from the county Planning Commission, and a deputy political commissar of the PAD. All the other rebel leaders on the committee were ordinary staff of government departments, technicians, manual workers, teachers, and students. The committee declared a power seizure on February 1, and the county leaders were stripped of their authority at a public rally two days later, presided over by the head of the PAD. This touched off a wave of power seizures in districts all over the county, with widespread abuse of deposed officials.

Factional divisions did not appear in Fusui until the PAD moved to consolidate its authority and formalize military control. In late March the PAD head organized a meeting of rebel leaders at the county headquarters and complained that there had been no vetting of those selected for the original Power Seizure Committee: just about anyone who headed a rebel group could join. He argued that the Power Seizure Committee should be disbanded and a new one appointed. Several rebel leaders at the meeting agreed and immediately withdrew from the committee. The result of the meeting was the formation of a "Liaison Group" with a broad rebel representation and a similar profile to the original Power Seizure Committee. The PAD then set up a Production Headquarters that included some recently deposed heads and deputy heads of various county offices, under the direction of the PAD. All the remaining leading cadres were assigned to a "study class" where they were forced to confess their crimes and denounce their former colleagues. Violent persecutions of party and government leaders and educated staff by rebels spread across the county, with the PAD's approval.

The PAD had the situation firmly under control, integrating the activities of local rebel groups across the county. The controversy over Wei Guoqing undermined efforts to forge unity among the county's many rebels. In the wake of the appearance of the April 22 alliance in Nanning, the PAD pledged its support for Wei, as they were obligated to do as part of the Guangxi Military District. This had few consequences until late May, when a group of April faction activists from nearby Nanning arrived, calling for the overthrow of Wei Guoqing. They argued that support for Wei identified rebel groups as "conservatives" and that only support for Wu Jinnan could be considered "revolutionary." These arguments persuaded a minority of local rebels, who began to put up wall posters, distribute handbills, and provoke debates.

The issue gained traction when rebels who had been part of the original power seizure coalition repudiated the PAD's decision to disband it. They declared that many local leaders who had been condemned during the subsequent purges should have their reputations and jobs restored. This made the nascent local April 22 faction an advocate for those who had lost out in the wake of the PAD's decisions since March, and it also turned the new faction into a lifeline for the many cadres who were being brutalized by the persecutions sponsored by the PAD. In late May the dissidents pulled together a new alliance as a branch of April 22. Each side began to seize buildings and public installations as bases of operation, cursing their opponents over loudspeakers, and engaging in periodic street brawls. The rebels who remained loyal to the PAD organized themselves as a branch of the Allied Command in early June. Armed confrontations followed as each side attacked the bases of their opponents.

QINZHOU. In this county factional divisions occurred at the very point of the power seizure.[35] As the administrative seat of the prefecture with the same name, Qinzhou was the location of administrative offices for both the county and prefecture, and it also was the headquarters of the Qinzhou Military Subdistrict. Cadre rebels were active in the offices of both the prefecture and county, and on January 24 they formed a power seizure alliance that included high school Red Guards and other rebel groups. Their power seizure was actively encouraged by local military officers. At a late January rally, officers from the PLA garrison and an air force division stationed in the prefecture gave speeches that urged local rebels to seize power.

On February 7 the rebels finally declared a power seizure over the county. Their declaration was immediately opposed by cadres in county administrative offices, who demanded a debate on the matter. Despite the earlier calls by PLA officers for an immediate power seizure, the political commissar of the county PAD dispatched troops to the scene to mediate, arguing against the declared power seizure, and the two sides argued violently. The status of the power seizure was ambiguous from this point forward—the rebels had seized power, but the PAD and PLA had different views about the action.

The PAD's refusal to support the power seizure was due to a major force within the rebel coalition that was formed to protest persecutions carried out during the recent Socialist Education Campaign. The group had more than 400 members and was led by several cadres in the county offices who had been removed from office in the campaign. They mobilized other victims in the county seat and rural communes, both deposed officials and ordinary citizens persecuted for allegedly reactionary parentage.

The PAD reacted differently than its counterparts in Fusui, where the PAD approved the power seizure but subsequently ejected objectionable rebels. The Qinzhou PAD instead withheld prior approval of the power seizure and first went after objectionable rebels who were contesting the verdicts of the Socialist Education Campaign. These rebels threatened the PAD and the county Public Security Bureau, both of which were central actors in punishing the victims. They banned the rebel alliance in late February, reportedly for harboring rebels with "counterrevolutionary" parentage and for contacts with a former labor camp inmate. In early March they banned another rebel group allegedly headed by individuals whose fathers had fled China after serving in Japanese puppet forces.

These charges against allegedly "impure class elements" in the rebel movement served to justify the PAD's next move—essentially a PAD power seizure. On March 4 the PAD established a headquarters to promote production, with branches at all levels headed by PAD officers. They held struggle sessions to repudiate 141 former county and commune officials who were accused of taking the "capitalist road." The PAD essentially substituted itself for the rebel movement as the agent that destroyed the old power structure.

These moves generated broad dissent against the PAD. The controversy over Wei Guoqing provided an opportunity to establish a new coalition. Leaders in the original power seizure alliance, including cadres and others victimized in the Socialist Education Campaign, formed a large coalition, the "April 22 Headquarters," which coordinated with dissenters across the county, demanding the withdrawal of charges against rebel groups and obstructing the PAD's ability to govern the county. In response, the PAD doubled down on its charges that counterrevolutionaries were behind the opposition, and with the support of the Military Subdistrict orchestrated a campaign to denounce Wu Jinnan as a traitor. This became the foundation for the Allied Command faction, setting the two groups on a collision course.

*Unilateral Cadre Power Seizures*

LINGYUN. By far the most common type of power seizures were those carried out unilaterally by cadres—forty in all. Lingyun, in Bose Prefecture, was one of them. In late January rebels in the county headquarters met to form a Power Seizure Committee.[36] All of them were ordinary staff in the county's administrative departments. In their discussions, they disagreed about how to treat the county's party secretary. Some argued that he should be attacked and repudiated. Others, noting that he was the son of a revolutionary martyr, argued that he did not merit harsh treatment. The disagreements delayed the power seizure by several days.

Noting that the cadre rebels were slow to act, the PAD's political commissar sent officers to exercise control over the county offices, Public Security Bureau, and bank. On February 2, there was still no power seizure, so the PAD official, the eighth-ranking official in the county, personally chaired a separate meeting to plan a power seizure, drawing on a different group of cadre rebels. He argued that the other cadres were too slow to act, and that if they did not move quickly, rebels from outside the county offices might take over. Their power seizure was carried out under the PAD's direction a few days later, drawing on this alternate coalition of cadre rebels. The leading cadres of the county and its various departments were deposed, including the county party secretary, and the PAD staged a show of support, with armed militias and a PLA detachment parading through the streets to celebrate.

In late March the PAD's political commissar organized a "Red Revolutionary Committee" under his direction, composed of a dozen PAD personnel, cadre rebels, worker and student representatives, and a few former leading cadres. He held a series of struggle sessions against the former county leaders, focusing particularly on the former party secretary. Many of the rebels from the county party organs still sympathized with their former party secretary; they argued that he had been in his post for only one year and had not made serious errors. They refused to accept the extreme charges leveled against him and denounced efforts to frame him with false charges. The PAD's political commissar counter-attacked by mobilizing cadres in the government departments to oppose the dissenters, and he intensified the charges against the former party secretary. He further charged that his opponents were anti-army reactionaries, and that the county's deposed party secretary was manipulating them in a counter-revolutionary plot. The two sides coalesced into coherent factions and hurled charges against one another with wall posters and loudspeakers, leading to beatings, the capture of prisoners, and armed confrontations. The PAD aligned its forces with Wei Guoqing and the Allied Command. Their opponents, who defended the former party secretary from extreme charges, aligned with the April faction.[37]

TIANDONG. This power seizure, like so many, was carried out in haste, a major reason for the factional divisions.[38] During the last half of January rebel groups in the county administration seized power over their own departments. The largest such group was an alliance of more than 100 cadres. Their leaders attended a mass meeting at the prefecture seat to denounce the party secretary of Bose Prefecture. The rally turned into a power seizure, and when the delegates returned to Tiandong, they rushed to seize power over the county without participation by workers and other outside groups. They observed that the power seizure in Nanning had failed because "every seal of office had two people controlling it and every key . . . whatever needed to be done required two separate mass organizations to approve." They should act unilaterally to avoid administrative chaos. They voted to seize power immediately. Confronted by the group on January 26, the county leadership handed over power.

The sudden power seizure caught many other rebels in the county by surprise, including a rebel alliance of some thirty-five cadres in the county government. They denounced the power seizure as illegitimate, pointing out that it had not received PAD support. They conducted a wall poster campaign over the next two weeks, during which the PAD still did not declare a stand. The Power Seizure Committee admitted its error, apologized, and disbanded. Its opponents formed a second and more broadly representative Power Seizure Committee representing some thirty-two different mass organizations, and declared a second power seizure on February 21. The PAD supported the act and formed a Production Command Office together with officers from PLA Units 6908 and 6948, which were stationed in the county.[39]

This appeared to settle local differences for more than a month, until the April controversy in Nanning over Wei Guoqing's appointment. The PAD demanded that all cadres in the administrative offices declare their support for Wei, organizing a campaign of rallies and parades. Debates nonetheless broke out over the stance taken by Wu Jinnan and the April 22 faction, and the PAD began to arrest those who spoke out in support of them, lodging false charges that those arrested were descended from "reactionary" households. This generated a backlash and increased support for April 22. Finally, in August, the Tiandong branch of the April 22 faction declared its formation. Its members included cadres in the county seat, workers, technicians, and high school students. The group was strengthened when the PLA Units 6908 and 6948 in the county, responding to remarks made by Zhou Enlai on August 28 (see chapter 4), issued a proclamation of support for April 22.

LINGUI. Cadre rebels were active in this Guilin suburb at an early date.[40] During November the Scarlet Guards, formed earlier to defend the county's leaders from rebel attacks, disbanded. As rebel groups spread rapidly inside the county headquarters, former Scarlet Guards changed sides and turned on their former leaders. In the twenty-nine departments in the county government, there were more than fifty rebel "fighting groups." The recent Socialist Education Campaign, which had punished a large percentage of local cadres for alleged political infractions, became a major subject of debate. The cadre rebels split into two factions, one headed by former Scarlet Guards who had turned on their superiors, but who earlier had been active in prosecuting the Socialist Education Campaign. A second was led by cadres who had not joined the Scarlet Guards, and they attracted those who had been victimized in the recent campaign.

Near the end of January, the first rebel alliance formed a Power Seizure Committee, with the approval of the PAD's political commissar, who had worked closely with the head of the alliance during the Socialist Education Campaign. They quickly convinced the county leaders to hand over power. When the second rebel alliance learned of the power seizure, they denounced it as a "fake" power seizure orchestrated by the PAD and protested the exclusion of the dozens of rebel groups in their alliance. Within days the PAD openly declared its support for the power seizure and implemented military control. This set the two sides on a collision course that led the PAD-approved rebels into the Allied faction and their opponents into the April faction.

### No Power Seizure

There were twenty counties where rebels never overthrew the local government. In roughly half of these cases, rebels are described as seizing power within their own administrative departments without attempting to seize power over the county.

The descriptions of events in these counties follow a similar pattern: an active but disorganized rebel movement disrupts government departments, but no cross-department rebel alliances appear. It is possible that there eventually would have been attempts at a power seizure in these places, but the opportunity was missed when military units moved to assert their authority.

FENGSHAN. Three large rebel groups emerged in this county on the western border of Hechi Prefecture. They did not form a single alliance to seize power, but instead seized power in separate county agencies. This effectively undermined the authority of the county's leaders, and administrative work fell into disarray. They did not split into factions until after the PAD stepped into the breach in the first days of March, declaring that it would be the highest authority in the county until a Revolutionary Committee was formed later.

Shortly afterward, the PAD banned two of the large rebel organizations as reactionary, creating a deep cleavage that reverberated across the county. The first of these formed inside the county administration in mid-January. It was founded by a Red Army veteran who had recently retired from his post as head of the county's Bureau of Civil Affairs, along with several other Red Army veterans who still worked in county and district offices. Their group became known as the "Old Revolutionaries" (*ge lao*).[41] A second, the Mao Thought Red Guards, was founded by cadres in the county propaganda and organization departments. With the blessing of the PAD, these two groups held mass meetings to denounce the county's party secretary.

The seeds for factional divisions were sown in early February with the appearance of a third rebel group known as the Battle Brigade (*zhandou bingtuan*), founded by a group of ten cadres who worked in county and district offices. Together with the Old Revolutionaries, they elevated their attack onto higher officials, focusing on two former county leaders who now occupied higher positions at the prefecture. These rebels raised an explosive political issue—the "extreme left" actions that had created and then deliberately intensified a famine in the county during the Great Leap Forward six years earlier. The targeted officials—one was Fengshan's party secretary at the time, and the other his deputy in charge of agriculture—were seized at their prefecture offices and dragged back to Fengshan for denunciation meetings. After abusive rallies at the county seat, the two were paraded around the county's rural districts wearing tall hats and were abused at public struggle sessions that were organized in the communes that had suffered the highest death tolls during the famine.[42]

The actions of these two officials had left a deep scar in Fengshan, and attacks on them elicited widespread support. Like many rural officials during the Great Leap Forward, they had grossly exaggerated the grain harvest of 1959, reporting a number that was 52 percent higher than the actual harvest. County officials pushed production brigades to turn over grain to the state based on these false production figures, and soon there was insufficient grain for the residents. As hunger spread in 1960 and local officials found it difficult to fulfill inflated procurement pledges, they began a coercive campaign against "hiding grain" (*fan manchan*). They covered up evidence of incipient famine and attacked as "rightists" the doctors and rural officials who insisted that there was no hidden grain left in villages. Determined to extract grain and meet sales obligations based on falsified output, they dispatched work teams that brutally abused farmers to compel them to reveal nonexistent hidden grain. As a direct result, 7,013 people died, a devastating number in a county that had only 90,000 residents.[43]

The Old Revolutionaries and the Battle Brigade, not surprisingly, attracted officials in the county seat and rural districts who had tried to resist the campaign against "hiding grain" and had been condemned as "rightists" as a result. The Mao Thought Red Guards in the county administration objected to the attacks on the former county officials, which they portrayed as attempts by "right wing elements" to overturn their verdicts. They charged that the political orientation of the attackers was based on personal spite and revenge. This was an attack on the Great Leap Forward, Mao's signature initiative. Mao himself had pushed the campaign against "hiding grain."[44] Raising this issue could be viewed as criticism of Mao. The PAD agreed with the Mao Thought Red Guards, reported the two groups to their superiors as "counter-revolutionary" organizations, and banned them on April 15.[45]

The banning as "counter-revolutionary" of a rebel group founded by former Red Army veterans, who were speaking out against abuses that had devastated the county only six years before, created a groundswell of opposition and led directly to the formation of two violently opposed rebel factions. The Mao Thought Red Guards aligned themselves with the PAD, pledged support to Wei Guoqing, and by September formed a large alliance affiliated with the Allied Command. Supporters of the Old Revolutionaries and the Battle Brigade demanded a withdrawal of the charges against them and a restoration of their status as legitimate rebels. Their campaign for support attracted Red Army veterans and ordinary farmers in rural districts, in addition to cadres in the county and district offices. On July 29 they formed a large rebel alliance that incorporated the core of the two original rebel groups and expanded their influence across the county. In October they formally affiliated with the April 22 faction.[46]

\* \* \*

What pattern emerges from this wide variety of local events? Whatever the form a rebel power seizure took, and whether one occurred, the result in all localities was the militarization of local government. Party Committees and government officials were tossed aside and in almost all cases subjected to harrowing persecutions. Officers of the PAD and in some cases the PLA assumed power while permitting rebel activity to continue, especially the persecution of former officials. Factions subsequently developed between rebels who received the support of military officers, and rebels who did not, and who moved into the opposition.

Out of the variety of ways that local splits developed, one broad pattern is clear. Local military actors thrust aside civilian government and took over the reins of power, forming alliances with some rebel groups (or sponsoring their formation) and developing conflicts with others. The ubiquity of military intervention, due to the regional structure of China's military forces, ensured that this pattern spread to every corner of Guangxi. It also grafted the Allied Command onto the structure of the PAD and its rural militias, which gave it an overwhelming advantage both organizationally and militarily. The Allied Command would eventually wield this advantage to the tragic detriment of April faction adherents, and many others across the province, in ways that would make Guangxi the bloodiest of China's regions during this violent period.

## CHAPTER 4

# Stalemate

In early May 1967 representatives from the two Guangxi rebel factions, along with local military commanders, were called to Beijing to negotiate. The meetings continued into November, doing little to reconcile the two sides. In the end they were forced onto a provisional "Preparatory Committee" for a new provincial government and sent back to Nanning. Although the two sides had roughly equal representation, officers from the Military District held the ranking positions, and they had long supported the Allied faction. Wei Guoqing was placed in charge, denying the April faction's primary demand.

This was a decisive defeat for the April faction. Yet for most of this period they had the initiative and appeared to have Beijing's favor. Especially in the summer, it appeared that the April faction would emerge victorious. This six-month period was essentially a standoff back in Guangxi. The April faction made inroads in major cities, while both factions spread their loose alliances across the province. Beijing's close monitoring of events in Guangxi and the ongoing negotiations in the capital ensured that each side actively mobilized to assert its claims.

Guangxi, in fact, was unusually free of deadly violence during this period. The summer of 1967 saw armed factional warfare spread across China, generating some of the highest death tolls of the entire period. Yet this violence largely bypassed Guangxi. With only a few exceptions, even the largest clashes resulted in very few deaths. Narrative descriptions in the investigation materials report only

1,652 deaths in the province during 1967. The comparable total for 1968 was 42,507.[1] If one suspects that there were distinctive features of Guangxi that would make political violence there more intense than elsewhere in China, the fact that the province was initially *much less* violent deserves closer examination.

A possible reason for Guangxi's initially low death tolls is the prominence of the Beijing negotiations themselves, and the strong signals of support for the April 22 faction from the CCRG. During the first year of the Cultural Revolution, the views of the more radical figures on the CCRG usually presaged Mao's eventual position, and they were clearly supportive of April 22. Nanning's April faction, as we have already seen, was in many ways the creation of radical figures on the CCRG—Wang Li and Qi Benyu in particular. They continued to push against the imposition of military control across China, because they interpreted the actions of many regional commanders as efforts to suppress the rebels who spearheaded their campaign against revisionist party leaders. This led to tight restrictions on the use of military force against dissident rebels like April 22. This effectively restrained the Allied Command and their military sponsors, who otherwise had a large advantage in any armed conflict. For the time being, they did not press their advantage.

## The Beijing Sessions

The rebel delegations assembled in Beijing in early May. Most delegates appear to have remained there continuously for several months. The most important of their sessions were the ones chaired by Zhou Enlai, who met with them a total of eight times, the first time on June 1 and the last on November 23.[2] Immediately before the first session, Zhou met with members of the CCRG about the "Guangxi Problem" before walking into the session with the delegates.[3] Zhou also met separately on several occasions with one or the other of the delegations. Partial records of these long meetings are available from transcribed recordings provided by each of three major parties—the two civilian factions and the military delegation. These transcripts were publicized in Guangxi as part of the central authorities' drive to reconcile the two factions, but each of the parties issued their own transcripts. The versions provided by the civilian factions contain omissions and use phrases that are designed to place their group in a more favorable light, but the transcripts are largely consistent with one another about the content of the meetings.

Almost all the meetings included both Wei Guoqing and Wu Jinnan, along with a handful of other provincial leaders aligned with each of them. It appears from the content of the discussions that these officials remained in Beijing throughout the entire period. In part, this was surely to ensure their personal safety—both Wei and Wu were targets of kidnapping efforts by hostile rebel factions in Nanning. This also meant, however, that the provincial leaders supported by each faction were absent from Guangxi and played little if any role in the unfolding conflicts there. The meetings also included a revolving roster of military representatives: commanders and political commissars from the Guangxi Military District, and in later sessions their superiors in the Guangzhou Military Region.

The rebel delegations were primarily from Nanning and Guilin, where opposition to Wei Guoqing was strongest. They included twelve rebel leaders from each side and three senior officials affiliated with each.[4] The delegates were housed in two hotels in the capital's Western District. The military officers and provincial officials were lodged at the Jingxi Hotel (*Jingxi binguan,* or Capital West Hotel), a few miles west of Tiananmen Square. Run by the military, it regularly housed delegates to leadership conferences.[5] The rebel delegates were lodged at the Xiyuan Hotel (*Xiyuan lüshe,* Western Garden Hotel), several miles north. The hotel locations meant a short ride to the audiences with Zhou, held in various conference rooms in the Great Hall of the People.

The sessions typically ran for several hours, usually beginning shortly before midnight and running on through the night. The transcripts primarily contain statements made by Zhou, and they are too short to be a full account of a meeting that lasted several hours. The discussions often focused on detailed points of conflict between the factions. Zhou showed a deep familiarity with developments in Guangxi. He questioned delegates about specific events, about the reasons for their opposition to Wei Guoqing or their accusations against Wu Jinnan. Zhou warned, cajoled, and often expressed exasperation and anger at the unwillingness or inability of the two rebel factions to set aside their differences.

Zhou's primary objective was to reconcile the two factions, while the rebel delegates saw the meetings as an opportunity to justify their stances and lodge accusations against their opponents. Especially in the first few sessions, Zhou repeatedly shuts down rebels who try to press their point of view and lodge accusations against their rivals, and he redirects the conversation to the question of finding common ground.[6] Zhou is eventually able to refocus the discussions, and in separate sessions apparently held without his direct participation, he was able to pressure the rebel delegates into several cease-fire agreements. They were publicized by military forces in Guangxi and by each of the rebel factions in news sheets and handbills. These compromises, agreed to by rebel leaders in Beijing, had little impact back in Guangxi.

There were two crucial flaws in this effort to reconcile the factions. The first was that neither was a unitary organization with a clear command structure. Both were alliances of convenience, loose collections of rebel groups whose conflicts involved intensely local issues, and which aligned with one another only according to whether local PLA or PAD commanders sided with them in local conflicts. The second flaw was that agreements reached in Beijing did not provide a credible mechanism for enforcement at the level of cities and counties, a problem that was replicated at lower levels, for example, in strategically important units like the Liuzhou Railway Bureau. The only mechanism for enforcing agreements was the local PLA and PAD units whose previous actions were precisely the reason why rebel factions had become entrenched in the first place. In sum, delegates had no way to enforce the commitments they made under pressure in Beijing. The only potential parties to enforce settlements between local rebel groups were the PLA and PAD units that were themselves involved in the conflicts.

Zhou and other officials came to realize the futility of their efforts by the end of the summer. In September they decided to take a different approach. But in the meantime, in venting his frustration over the futility of the negotiations, Zhou repeatedly expressed the reasons why Beijing had all along insisted that Wei Guoqing *had to* remain in charge of Guangxi, and why Beijing was paying such close attention to events in such a distant region. Both had to do with the rapidly escalating war across the border in Vietnam.

Large-scale factional warfare was not necessary in order for Guangxi to become a chokepoint that throttled the supply lines into Vietnam. An early example, one that preoccupied Zhou in several of the early Beijing meetings, was the disruption of the railway system over a seemingly trivial factional dispute. In his second meeting with the delegations, on June 14, Zhou opened by saying that he was setting aside the disputes between the two sides for a discussion of "urgent matters," namely, the "disruption of international traffic" in Guangxi's railway system. He mentioned specifically support for Vietnam as well as foreign trade with Hong Kong. During the discussions the problem became clear: rail traffic had been paralyzed for five days due to actions by Allied Command affiliates at a key railway junction near the town of Litang, in Binyang County, roughly halfway between Liuzhou and Nanning.[7] At Litang the sole north-south railway line through Guangxi branched in two directions. One turned southwest and passed through Nanning on its way to Pingxiang on the border with Vietnam. The other turned southeast and continued through Yulin Prefecture to the southwest corner of Guangdong Province and the port city of Zhanjiang. Zhou expressed concern with both, but he was especially exercised by the blockage of the line to Vietnam.[8]

The origin of the problem was the takeover of *Guangxi Daily* by the April faction in Nanning, after which they quickly turned the provincial party newspaper into an organ that spread their point of view. This was the most important early controversy between the two factions, as it involved an attack on military control forces that had taken control of the newspaper. An express train from Pingxiang to Beijing picked up copies of the paper in Nanning and continued its journey north to Liuzhou and Guilin, when it was stopped near Litang by Allied Command activists, who wanted to prevent the distribution of this "illegal" publication. The activists boarded the train and beat up the engineer to the point where he could no longer continue. Other engineers refused to take over unless the offenders were turned in. After eighteen hours the train was prepared to continue, but rebel activists sat on the tracks to prevent the train's further journey, and moved a locomotive to block a switch point, preventing movement through the station in both directions.[9] During this five-day period, southward trains bound for Vietnam were blocked all along the railway network and were unable to continue with their shipments of military supplies and support personnel.

At the June 14 meeting Zhou demanded that delegates order their colleagues to permit trains to pass. He convened another meeting the next day and asked why there had been no resolution, and the delegates from the two sides accused one another of lying about the incident and spreading false rumors. Zhou was unable to get to the bottom of things, and ended the meeting by warning Wu Jinnan, as the putative head of the April faction, not to interfere in Guangxi's railway system. "Wu Jinnan, I warn you in the strongest possible terms, if you continue to interfere in the railways, interfering in military matters, you'll be put into custody." Zhou added, "Guangxi is at the front lines, a key war district. If something happens, we must send troops; enemy planes are constantly overhead, taking photographs. We can't have chaos down below."[10]

While the blockage at Litang was apparently resolved shortly thereafter, Zhou continued without success to get the two sides to curtail their local conflicts, and the fighting escalated in August, despite repeated promises made by delegates in Beijing to stand down. By late summer, Zhou had lost all patience, and expressed his frustration and anger as he opened the August 24 meeting with the delegations:

Allied Command, your actions just get more and more outrageous, always attacking others, there's no limit! April 22 blocks shipments of military supplies for the support of Vietnam. And so much of this you've kept! You really didn't know that this was for Vietnam? April 22's behavior is totally wrong. Turn it all back in, obey orders. If you want to defend yourselves, rely on the Military District! And you (pointing to the Allied Command delegates) are seizing all their strongholds, there are only three or so left; you still want to wipe them out, but that's impossible. If you keep this up, I'll get the Military District to supply them with arms. Guangxi is on the front lines, close to Vietnam's rear. I ask you to think, others are fighting American imperialism, and you are fighting a civil war. Neither of you has any conception of the threat from our enemies, you're completely clueless. By doing this do you want the American imperialists to invade, their planes flying over Nanning? We'll send you to the front lines to fight, and then you'll finally be forced to unite.[11]

As he did on several occasions, Zhou objected to arms seizures. Zhou pleaded that it was fine to have different political opinions, but this did not justify stopping rail traffic. He repeated that this was not purely a domestic issue: "If rail traffic stops, what impressions will this give the Vietnamese people?"[12] In the next meeting on September 13, Zhou continued to hammer at the same point in the face of continuing and in many ways escalating disruptions in Guangxi: "Guangxi borders Vietnam and is a coastal defense district, it's subject to infiltration by enemies. You should raise your awareness. Spies from America, Taiwan, and the Soviet revisionists can infiltrate and sabotage our railway system, even set up secret radio units to transmit intelligence about our coastal defenses and railways."[13]

By this point it was apparent that Zhou recognized the futility of this approach to Guangxi's disruptions, which continued to intensify just as the United States was rapidly escalating its troop deployments and accelerating its bombing campaign closer to Guangxi. However central his role in these negotiations, Zhou was not the ultimate arbiter of Beijing's stance toward factional conflicts in Guangxi and elsewhere in China. These decisions were ultimately made by Mao himself. He shifted his stance in September and altered the direction of the final negotiations in ways that were highly detrimental to the April faction.

### Guangxi's Distinctive Pattern

Despite the intensifying factional conflict in Guangxi, death tolls were still remarkably low, especially compared with the rest of China. This distinctive pattern, in which deadly violence was rare during 1967 but unusually severe in 1968, is evident in data extracted from more than 2,200 local histories in a separate study. Data collected for that study reveal a sharp distinction in both the pattern of factional conflict and the resulting deaths.[14] Figure 4.1 displays monthly counts of conflicts

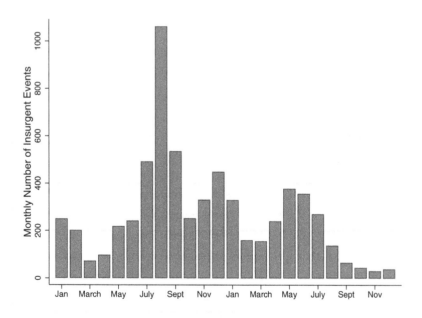

FIGURE 4.1.    Monthly Number of Insurgent Events, China excluding Guangxi, 1967–68
Source: Data set based on published annals employed in Walder (2019).

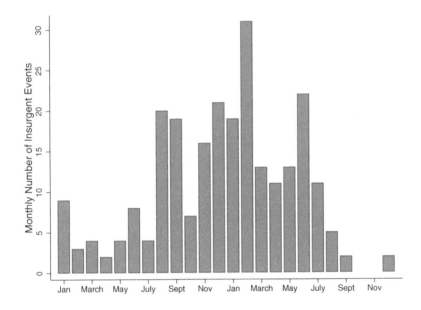

FIGURE 4.2. Monthly Number of Insurgent Events, Guangxi Only, 1967–68
Source: Data set based on published annals employed in Walder (2019).

involving rebels during 1967 and 1968 for China as a whole, excluding Guangxi. The massive upsurge in the summer of 1967 marked the high tide of violent clashes between rebel groups across China. After September the volume of rebel conflicts declined markedly. Figure 4.2 displays the trends for Guangxi from the same sources. The spike in activity in the summer of 1967 is less pronounced and is only the beginning of a sustained period of conflict that endures until July 1968.

The contrast in the number of deaths generated by these same events is even more pronounced. Figure 4.3 shows a bimodal distribution for China excluding Guangxi, with a peak in deaths that corresponds with the upsurge of rebel conflicts in 1967, and a later spike that coincided with the formation of Revolutionary Committees in mid-1968. This reflected a pattern analyzed elsewhere, in which a smaller number of much more deadly conflicts occurred near the end of the period of factional warfare.[15] Figure 4.4 shows that Guangxi's deadly violence was almost entirely concentrated in 1968, without the 1967 upsurge elsewhere in China.

Guangxi's distinctive pattern is especially evident in the more abundant descriptive material extracted from investigation reports. Figure 4.5 traces the

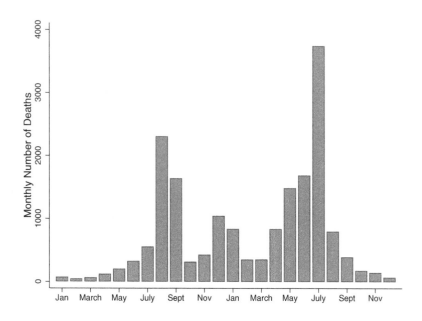

FIGURE 4.3. Deaths due to Insurgent Activity, China Excluding Guangxi (monthly count), 1967–68

Source: Data set based on published annals employed in Walder (2019).

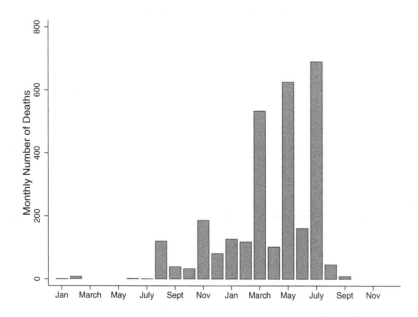

FIGURE 4.4. Deaths due to Insurgent Activity, Guangxi Only (monthly count), 1967–68

Source: Data set based on published annals employed in Walder (2019).

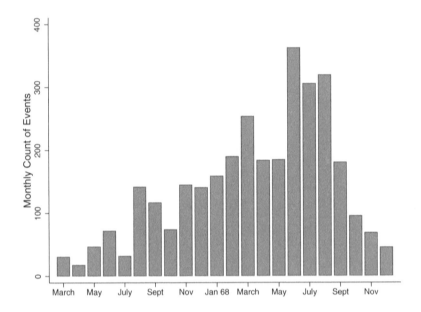

FIGURE 4.5.    Factional Activity in Guangxi (monthly count of events), March 1967–
December 1968
Source: Data set based on Guangxi Party Committee (1987).

number of factional conflicts in the period from March 1967—the month when the
splits that turned into the April and Allied factions originated—through the end of
1968. It replicates the pattern of factional activity that is evident from other sources
in figure 4.2, though with five times the number of reported events. Guangxi saw
sustained factional conflict for an entire year after July 1967. Figure 4.6 traces the
number of deaths generated by these events, but it removes from the death counts
the factional conflicts in which one side had the backing of a military unit.[16] It also
replicates the pattern already evident in figure 4.4 with less abundant evidence
from the published annals. It shows even more clearly, with accounts from four
times as many reported events, the striking lack of deadly conflict during 1967, and
the steady surge afterward during 1968.

By May 1967 local factions had taken opposed stances in two-thirds of all cities
and counties in the dispute over Wei Guoqing, and in half of them Wei's opponents
had declared an affiliation with April 22. By October, factions in 96 percent of all
cities and counties had affiliated with one of the two factions. As these affiliations
spread to encompass virtually the entire province, there still were relatively few

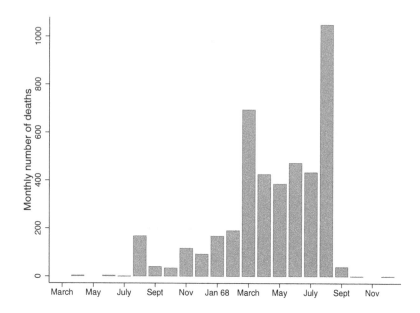

FIGURE 4.6. Deaths from Factional Activity in Guangxi (monthly count), March 1967–December 1968
Source: Data set based on Guangxi Party Committee (1987).

armed hostilities, compared to subsequent months. The investigation reports describe 379 events from May to November in which either the April or Allied faction is named as participant. These events generated a reported 402 deaths. The most common types of event, some 80 percent of the total, were an "armed battle" between the two sides (20 percent), a protest demonstration or a seizure of arms from a military depot (15 percent each), and a struggle session against a captive official, a random killing, or an attempt to seize control of a building (8 or 9 percent each).

These activities were concentrated in a few places, primarily cities. Only ten jurisdictions had ten or more reported events, including five of Guangxi's six cities (the border town of Pingxiang was the one exception). Together, the five cities and five counties alone accounted for just over half of all reported conflicts. Three places stood out with unusually high levels of factional conflict: the cities of Wuzhou and Beihai (32 and 28 events, respectively), and Yishan County (36). The death tolls were even more concentrated. Beihai alone generated 169 deaths (42 percent of the total), followed by two counties (Yishan, 36, and Quanzhou,

30). The Beihai death toll was due to three large armed battles during August.[17] Together, these three localities contributed well over half of all reported deaths during the six months of negotiations in Beijing.

### The April Faction Ascendant

In retrospect, the Beijing negotiations marked the high tide of the April faction's prospects. Through much of this period they were on the offensive. A particular target of the April faction was the provincial party newspaper, *Guangxi Daily*, which became a mouthpiece for the pro-Wei forces in Nanning after being placed under military control in late March. A mass march and demonstration at the offices of *Guangxi Daily* to present a list of demands, held on April 22, was the event that inspired the name of the nascent anti-Wei faction. The group mobilized 500 followers to invade and occupy the newspaper's offices on April 27; they remained there until May 2, when they finally withdrew after demanding a change in the leadership of the Military Control Committee and the addition of their own representatives, who would have a say in editorial content.[18]

Although the faction's leaders left for the Beijing negotiations in early May, they continued to plan strategy at their lodgings in the capital, directing political action back in Nanning to strengthen their hand in the Beijing discussions. In mid-May they held a meeting to lay out political strategy, and they planned a "power seizure" over *Guangxi Daily* as an act of resistance to the imposition of military control. After reporting their plans to Wu Jinnan, they sent messengers back to Nanning to mobilize the attack.[19]

Collective action followed shortly afterward. On May 15 more than 1,000 pro–Wu Jinnan students invaded the paper's editorial offices and confronted its Military Control Committee, after which the Military District issued a stern warning. Undeterred, the students invaded the paper's offices for three consecutive days beginning May 23 and left 100 of their members in the building. The pro-Wei forces responded by organizing a "May 25 Revolutionary Action Headquarters," the precursor to what would soon become the Allied Command. They sent their pro-Wei followers to the newspaper offices to dislodge the invaders. A battle fought with stones and clubs ensued, and reinforcements on both sides swelled the crowd to more than 5,000 people. Several ambulances rushed to the scene to treat the wounded, and the fighting finally subsided in the early morning hours of May 26.

Later that day, pro-Wei groups forced their way into the newspaper offices to drive out their opponents. The two sides occupied buildings and renewed the fighting, injuring hundreds. Finally, the April faction forces occupied the newspaper's offices and declared a formal power seizure, expelling the military control personnel. They interrupted the printing of the newspaper and took over the provincial broadcasting network by cutting power to the station. After commandeering the printing presses, they used them to issue their own news sheets.[20]

The April faction remained in possession of the *Guangxi Daily* offices at least through mid-August, despite repeated efforts by the Allied Command to eject them. One of the last major battles over the newspaper took place on August 11, and resulted in the destruction of the printing presses and the shutdown of the paper for more than two weeks.[21] April faction militants also staged several invasions of the Military District Headquarters to paste up wall posters denouncing Wei Guoqing and the military control forces. Similar confrontations between the two sides continued in Nanning, involving large numbers of people with only rudimentary weapons. Injuries were common, but deaths were rare.

While the battles over *Guangxi Daily* were under way on May 23, the CCRG liaison officer Wang Li visited the April faction delegation at their Beijing hotel and suggested that they stage a raid on the Jingxi Hotel in order to "drag out" Wei Guoqing. He pointed out that rebels from Wuhan had recently seized General Chen Zaidao at the same hotel, and that sympathetic military guards at the hotel might cooperate. The delegates agreed and resolved to hold a sit-in demonstration to chant slogans.[22] Wang Li returned to their hotel two days later and asked them why they had not yet seized Wei. He told them that Qi Benyu had said that the Guangxi rebels should not be so restrained in dealing with Wei—and Wang told the delegation that Wei was staying in a room on the fifth floor. Wang Li laid out a strategy for the raid: the April faction delegates should assemble at the reception area and stage a sit-in, make a lot of noise, and demand that Wei come out to meet them. In the meantime, Wang Li would consult with his superiors to see what their attitude was toward this mass action. If Wei refused to come out, and if the "Center" did not say anything, then they could call on a large group of Beijing Red Guards to help force their way into the building.[23]

On May 26 their "revolutionary action" to take Wei Guoqing hostage began. Wang Li went to the scene and pointed out the window of Wei's hotel room. They gathered outside at 8 p.m. and staged a loud sit-in, chanting slogans and demanding that Wei come downstairs. Shortly after midnight PLA officers arrived and ordered them to leave, saying that the Center did not agree to dragging out Wei. The April activists, confused, asked Wang Li whether their action had support at the upper levels or not. Wang Li responded that the soldiers were probably just stationed at the hotel, and that his superiors would tell them if Wei was not to be touched. The group refused to leave and continued their loud sit-in until May 31, when the CCRG sent a vehicle to take them back to the Xiyuan Hotel in anticipation of their first audience with Zhou Enlai the next day.[24]

The April delegation made a more successful attack on Wei Guoqing on August 9, during the nationwide wave of attacks on military forces instigated by an incendiary editorial published in the CCRG's mouthpiece, *Red Flag*, on August 1. Once again encouraged by Wang Li, but this time collaborating with sympathetic military officers of the Guangxi delegation, the April faction, along with 200 local Beijing Red Guards, rushed into the hotel compound and invaded Wei's suite. Wei was knocked to the ground and beaten unconscious. He was hospitalized, bleeding profusely from wounds on his leg, lower back, and face. His bodyguards were even more severely injured, and several suffered permanent disabilities. The deputy commander of the Guangxi Military District was surrounded, beaten, and stripped of his military insignia.[25] Wei was still hospitalized in late August, and missed the session with Zhou Enlai on August 24.[26]

Not until August did the two sides begin to raid arms depots to seize military weapons back in Guangxi, a development that began to generate deaths from the sporadic clashes across the province. There were no reported raids to seize arms until July, when one took place in Beihai. In August, however, forty arms seizures were reported in twenty-two localities (close to half of them in Nanning and Guilin). In September there were another eighteen, despite orders by Mao in early September authorizing PLA units to retrieve the weapons and resist further raids with force. After months of negotiations in Beijing, the two sides were finally preparing for armed warfare.

The most dramatic example was in Guilin, where the April faction affiliate staged a series of raids in August to seize weapons from the Military Subdistrict and PADs in the city and two suburban counties. The raids netted close to 5,500 rifles, 5 million rounds of ammunition, 3,100 hand grenades, 5 artillery pieces and 500 shells, and other military equipment. They then adopted a more aggressive stance toward Allied Command forces that had slowly grown up in the city, forcing them to flee to rural counties in Guilin Prefecture. In response, the Allied Command raided PAD compounds in these counties in efforts to match the April faction's firepower. The April faction consolidated control over Guilin with the cooperation of PLA Unit 6955, which had sponsored their power seizure back in January and backed them continuously. The PLA unit held a joint rally and armed parade with the April faction. The local PAD commander was compelled to apologize for his support of Wei Guoqing.[27]

A few weeks later April 22's prospects reached their highest point, and Beijing appeared ready to settle the Guangxi question in their favor. During June and July, the CCRG had set up a "Guangxi Liaison Station" to handle the negotiations, and appointed as its director Wang Li, whose back-channel efforts to undermine Wei Guoqing had earlier led to the formation of April 22, and who had continued to coordinate with the group's delegates in Beijing throughout their stay in the capital.[28] Reporters in the Liaison Station issued bulletins to the CCRG in mid-July accusing the local army units of refusing to make an acceptable self-criticism for their suppression of April 22. Qi Benyu approved the reports and sent them to the leadership, undermining the Guangxi Military District.[29] In private meetings with reporters from the Liaison Station in late August, April faction representatives were told that a final decision on the Wei Guoqing issue was imminent, and they should clearly state their preferences. They asked that Wei be transferred permanently out of Guangxi.[30]

Similar signals were relayed by Zhou Enlai. In his August 24 meeting with the two factions, he made comments indicating that the "Center" favored the April faction. Zhou went out of his way to compliment the Guilin April faction for handling matters in a positive fashion in Guilin. Even as he admonished the April faction for their disruptions of the railway system and their violent attack on Wei Guoqing at the Jingxi Hotel, he criticized the Allied Command for suppressing them in recent months and stated that the local armed forces (presumably the PLA) now supported them: "It's clear that in the past the army didn't support April 22, suppressed them. Over the past two months they've become more politically aware . . . Now this has changed, and they support you [pointing to April faction delegates]. It was wrong for the Allied Command to suppress you." In the same session, Zhou criticized the Allied Command for mobilizing "poor peasants" (apparently the village militias commanded by PADs) to march into the cities for battles with the

April faction, which, Zhou noted, did not have this capacity. And he ordered the release of Xiong Yijun, the leader of Nanning's Workers' Headquarters and a major figure in the provincial power seizure back in January, who led the breakaway organization "New Workers' Headquarters." Xiong had been incarcerated since late February, and this had been one of the key complaints of the April faction and a major reason for their antagonism toward the Military District. Zhou also ordered the Military District to formally withdraw all charges against both organizations, an order that was implemented shortly thereafter, along with an apology by the Military District for its errors.[31]

The most dramatic exchange in this meeting was one in which Zhou referred to the April faction as Guangxi's "rebel" faction: "In the past, the Military District supported one faction while suppressing the other. Now the troops should support you [pointing to the April 22 delegates]. You are rebels [*zaofan pai*] and the Military District should actively support you." He did not make a similar reference to the Allied Command, which caused them some concern. Near the end of the session one of the Allied faction delegates asked Zhou, "Then what kind of organization are *we*?" Zhou responded, "You are a mass organization [*qunzhong zuzhi*], and if you continue to make revolution, you will become a revolutionary organization."

The April faction publicized Zhou's statements with great fanfare. This spurred them to press their offensive against the Allied Command in Nanning. As the news spread, members of the Allied Command began to withdraw, and some declared that they were switching their allegiance to April 22. Some of the provincial leaders pledged to the Allied Command switched sides. Local PLA units also began to waver. The PLA's 55th Army Corps, stationed in Liuzhou, announced its support for Liuzhou's April faction. Some of the Allied delegates were so despondent over Zhou's obvious tilt toward the April faction that they abandoned the negotiations and left Beijing without informing the authorities.[32]

### The September Reversal

Just as victory for April 22 appeared imminent, the situation changed radically in ways that would not become apparent for several weeks. The day after his August 24 meeting with the Guangxi delegations, Zhou pressed Mao to make a final decision about the violent factional warfare that had broken out across China during August. The Cultural Revolution appeared to have reached a violent impasse, and as Zhou said to the acting PLA chief of staff, Yang Chengwu, who would soon meet with Mao, "Where will it all end, if this is allowed to go on?"[33] When confronted with this choice, Mao came down decisively in a way that dramatically altered the balance of forces in Guangxi. Although he had recently encouraged "left" factions like April 22 to arm themselves and fight for victory, Mao decided to blame the disorders on the April faction's longstanding sponsors in the CCRG.[34] He told Yang Chengwu that Wang Li, Guan Feng, and Qi Benyu "are wrecking the Cultural Revolution and are not good people. Tell nobody but the Premier [Zhou Enlai] about this and see to it that they are arrested. I am putting the Premier in charge of dealing with this matter." Before Zhou was informed, Mao modified his orders and said that Qi Benyu should be spared for the time being (he was taken into custody the following January).[35]

The primary charge against them was that they had encouraged rebel groups to attack PLA commanders in a *Red Flag* editorial on August 1, which urged rebels to "expose the small groups of capitalist power holders in the military, and struggle against them politically and ideologically until they are overthrown and stink."[36] Wang Li and Guan Feng were denounced in closed-door meetings at the very end of August, accused of being foreign agents. They were placed in isolation while their cases were investigated. Learning of his colleagues' fall, Qi Benyu energetically denounced them while engaging in self-criticism for making many of the same errors. The other two were taken into custody by the Beijing Garrison in mid-October and disappeared from public view.[37] Mao reassured military commanders across China that he supported them, and he ordered that factional warfare be resolved quickly and that Revolutionary Committees be formed more rapidly under the direction of the PLA.[38]

While these tectonic shifts in Cultural Revolution politics were taking place behind the scenes, there were signals in the Beijing negotiations that change was imminent. In the meeting with the delegations on September 13, Zhou adopted a more critical tone in comments on the April faction. Expressing dismay that several cease-fire agreements went unenforced, he warned the April faction, which had perhaps become overconfident and more aggressive after the previous meeting, that they "ha[d] begun to make mistakes." Zhou warned them that even though they were the earliest rebels in Guangxi, and had a good record as a rebel organization, their designation as "rebel" was conditional and depended on their current behavior. Just because they were a rebel organization in the past did not mean that this designation was permanent.[39] In a subsequent meeting on September 22, Zhou pressed the two sides to form an alliance, saying that any faction that agreed to unite would be considered revolutionary, but whoever refused would be engaging in factionalism.[40]

These hints were finally made explicit in Zhou's meeting with the delegates on November 16, during which he completely backtracked on his August 24 statement that compared the Allied Command unfavorably with the April faction. Reassuring Allied Command that they were also a "rebel organization," he stated that both sides were equally "revolutionary," and that the terms "mass organization," "rebel organization," and "revolutionary organization" were used interchangeably by the Party Center. Zhou also signaled a shift about who was to blame for the rebel divisions in Guangxi. In August he had laid the blame on the Military District for supporting one faction and suppressing the other. Now, however, he mused that the factions did not appear until Wu Jinnan made his speech of April 19, 1967, which, he said, incited the rebels to fight one another, and subsequently caused "inexperienced" military commanders to commit errors.[41] It was clear that Beijing's definition of the problem had shifted toward equal responsibility for both sides. In his final meeting with the two delegations on November 23, Zhou repeated his statement that both factions were revolutionary, and that the April faction should abandon its demand that all rebels should "unite under April 22 leadership." In this final meeting, delegates from both sides were still complaining about the behavior of their opponents back in Guangxi, and it seemed clear that troubles lay ahead.[42]

## The November Decision

The shift in Beijing's stance toward the Guangxi problem presaged a decision that denied the core demand of the April 22 faction. Wei Guoqing would remain in charge of the Military District and head a Preparatory Committee for a new government in Guangxi—a Revolutionary Committee that included veteran provincial leaders, military officers, and rebel leaders. By placing Wei in charge, Beijing signaled that Wei was likely to remain in Guangxi as the head of its Revolutionary Committee. This prospect surely filled the April faction with foreboding.

Zhou moved quickly to force the parties to agree. A series of documents issued in quick succession in mid-November sealed the arrangements. On November 8

the Guangxi Military District issued a long and detailed self-criticism for the errors that they had committed in previous months, primarily their favoring of Allied
Command at the expense of April 22.[43] Wei Guoqing made a detailed self-criticism
for the errors that he had committed during the initial months of the Cultural Revolution and for his favoring of the Allied Command faction. His self-criticism was
approved by Mao and issued as a Central Committee document four days later.
On the same day a ten-point peace accord was issued, in which the leaders of the
two factions agreed to turn in arms and cease hostilities.[44] On November 18 the
final decision on the Guangxi problem was issued as a Central Party document.
Relatively brief, it stated that Wei Guoqing and Wu Jinnan had both committed
errors and had made acceptable self-criticisms, and it emphasized yet again the
importance of resolving Guangxi's conflicts for China's support of Vietnam's fight
against American imperialism.[45]

Each of the parties in Guangxi had reason to feel disappointed with this imposed solution. After separate meetings with Allied Command delegates and rebels
from the Liuzhou Railway Bureau, Zhou held a final meeting with the delegations
on November 19.[46] He stated that he knew that the road ahead would be difficult.
He noted that the two sides had already agreed to cease hostilities on four separate
occasions, and none of the agreements had been enforced.

Zhou also issued what must have seemed a strange warning to the Allied Command delegates. Given subsequent developments, his statement indicated that he
had a firm grasp of the political dynamics in Guangxi, and of some of the dangers
ahead. Pointing to the delegates from Guilin's Allied Command, he warned them
that in view of their weak position relative to the city's dominant April faction,
they should not strive to enlarge their forces to achieve equality with their opponents, who had already agreed to equal treatment.

You should seek truth from facts, don't push for equal numbers like the local
extreme conservatives (not just ordinary conservatives) in Hunan's Lingling
Prefecture who, under the direction of evil people in charge of People's Armed
Departments, set up so called "Poor and Lower Middle Peasants Supreme People's Courts" and issue directives to kill people, mainly landlords, rich peasants, bad elements and rightists, and others, and their children. Some [of those
killed] were also rebels, a fairly large number. Now the 47th Army Corps is

handling this problem in Hunan. The evil influence of this episode is already spreading into the Guilin Military Subdistrict, in neighboring parts of Quanzhou and Guanyang counties. These two counties have both declared that they are setting up "Poor and Lower Middle Peasants Supreme People's Courts" just like in Hunan. This sounds good, like they want mass dictatorship. But in reality poor and lower middle peasants are not in charge, but instead a small number of individuals, People's Armed Departments, and city people previously removed from their posts who are now stepping forward. They are assembling local masses, declaring that this person must be shot, that person should be done in, mobilizing people this way. If you in Guilin do this to increase your numbers, and pull in this kind of people, then you have really taken a bad turn. I'm warning you, pay attention! You must draw a line between yourselves and them. Not only April 22 should draw a line with them; you in the Allied Command must draw a line even more clearly.[47]

After this final meeting, the delegations were flown back to Nanning on November 23 to try to implement this latest agreement. To greet the returning delegates, more than 1,000 people, drawn from the two factions and military units, met them at the airport.[48] Despite the ceremonial trappings, this latest agreement would prove no more workable that the previous ones. It would begin to unravel almost immediately and would slide into widespread violence on a scale not previously seen in Guangxi. The collapse was touched off by precisely the kind of activity described by Zhou Enlai in his warning to the Allied Command faction in Guilin. Considering subsequent developments, his warning was darkly prophetic, and had implications that stretched all across Guangxi.

## CHAPTER 5

# Escalation

Zhou Enlai's stern warning about killings instigated by "evil people in charge of People's Armed Departments" referred to disturbing developments in counties along Guilin Prefecture's border with Hunan Province. He referred to massacres in Hunan's Lingling Prefecture, a remote region of eight rural counties whose hills contained communities of the Yao minority.[1] During a two-month period beginning in early August 1967, 9,083 individuals were summarily executed in local killing sprees organized by branches of PADs. The epicenter of the massacres was Dao County, where there were 4,193 killings and 326 suicides during August and September 1967.[2] In his final speech to the Guangxi delegations, Zhou charged that rural PAD officers employed this as a strategy to strengthen their hand against factional opponents. Under the guise of eliminating class enemies, the PAD mobilized militia forces to massacre individuals in stigmatized political categories, along with anyone associated with opposed rebel factions. Zhou warned the delegates from Guilin not to adopt this as a strategy of achieving parity with the April faction in the region.[3]

Subsequent investigations of the massacres in Dao County and Lingling Prefecture fully substantiated Zhou's claims. Of all those killed, 84 percent were members of stigmatized "class enemy" households.[4] Subsequent investigations did not identify the other 16 percent, but Zhou implied that the killings were used as a cover to eliminate any rebel opposition in rural districts. Zhou's charges against local PAD officers also proved to be accurate: those later implicated in the killings included close to one-quarter of the county's state cadres, two-thirds of village-level cadres, and one-third of all party members.[5]

The massacres in Dao County were organized by branches of the PAD as part of an offensive against a coalition of opposed rebels. As was the case in Guangxi, the PADs in the Hunan counties were closely aligned with a favored rebel faction, which meant that they had control over village militia in the rural communities outside the county seat where most of the population lived. In Dao County the massacres began after a decisive victory in armed clashes by the anti-PAD rebels, who drove their opponents out of the county seat. The PAD mobilized their rural militia to massacre "class enemies" allegedly aligned with the anti-PAD rebels in districts under their control, and then launched counter-attacks by village militia on the county seat.[6] The rural massacres did not end until a unit from the PLA 47th Army Corps arrived to take over control from the PAD.[7] Subsequent investigations showed that the massacres were organized and directed by local security and military networks: "there were almost no genuine instances of poor and lower-middle peasants spontaneously rising up against landlords and rich peasants unless it was out of personal revenge or to take possession of women or valuables, and that apart from these personal factors, the killings showed a clear chain of command from top to bottom."[8] The investigations concluded that claims that the killings resulted from the spontaneous anger of rural residents against class enemies were a cover for something very different.

Zhou warned that the Guilin counties bordering Hunan had already begun to imitate Dao County, and the later investigations bear this out. In Guanyang, one of the two counties mentioned by Zhou, 158 people were executed during the month of September. The killings, all in rural communities, were organized by security agents under the direction of "Poor and Lower Middle Peasants' Supreme People's Courts," which in turn were under the direction of district branches of the PAD. The vast majority of those killed were reportedly members of politically stigmatized "enemy" households.[9] In Quanzhou, the other county mentioned by Zhou, a similar spate of killings in one commune claimed 76 individuals in October.[10] Both counties bordered Hunan. Zhou did not mention a third county, just south of the other two along the Hunan border—Fuchuan, located in the northern corner of Wuzhou Prefecture. During October and November a similar killing spree resulted in 89 deaths: 61 people executed, beaten to death, or thrown from cliffs; 26 suicides; and 2 who simply disappeared.[11]

The Hunan massacres were halted by the rapid intervention of the PLA's 47th Army Corps. In Guangxi, however, these massacres were the first ripples of what turned into a wave of similar killings across the province. Zhou saw these atrocities as a political strategy of beleaguered factions aligned with the rural PAD to gain momentum against stronger opponents lodged in the cities and towns. This practice turned into an instrument through which a locally dominant Allied Command faction, aligned closely with the PAD, waged final battles to eliminate their April faction opponents and establish Revolutionary Committees dominated by them. This began as soon as the members of the new Guangxi Preparatory Committee, under the direction of Wei Guoqing and the Guangxi Military District, returned from Beijing at the end of November. One of the first such instances was in Rong County, in Yulin Prefecture. There was an active April faction insurgency in the county, with 25 members of one village's Allied faction killed in a gun battle on November 6 and another 51 taken prisoner. The county PAD responded by initiating a suppression campaign, mobilizing militias in villages to carry out group executions of individuals allegedly part of an "Anti-Communist Salvation Corps" (*fangong jiuguo jun*). Close to 70 April faction activists and members of stigmatized households were beaten to death during November, and a total of 738 would die in the campaign, more than half of all people killed in the county.[12]

## The Collapse of the Preparatory Committee

The Nanning Preparatory Committee ran into difficulties almost immediately. Near the end of November, after the Guangxi Military District's self-criticism for errors committed over the previous eight months, Nanning's Allied Command invaded the Military District's headquarters to "drag out" officers who had allegedly sold them out in the Beijing negotiations. The Preparatory Committee's first meeting, chaired by Wei Guoqing, issued a set of instructions that would be largely ignored: arms held by rebels must be returned to army units; activists and members of rural militias should leave the cities and return to their home counties; and the April faction must return *Guangxi Daily* to military control.[13]

These directives amounted to wishful thinking. Factional antagonisms remained intense, and in rural counties the April faction maintained active insurgencies against their opponents, their PAD backers, and rural militias. A compromise may have been forced under Beijing's intense pressure, but there were no such negotiations at the city and county level, and each side mobilized to advance its cause in anticipation of a final settlement. There was no credibly neutral authority to enforce an equitable settlement. PAD and PLA regiments were the only possible mechanism to enforce settlements, and they were themselves parties to the conflicts. The fact that their military superiors had apologized for their "errors" meant nothing at the local level.

The situation spurred April faction units in rural counties, where they had long been disadvantaged, to mobilize their followers to protect or advance their positions. This provoked the Allied Command, and PAD networks, to counter-attack with violent repression. Several counties generated death tolls so large that they alarmed April faction leaders in Nanning. During December, intensified battles in Guiping County led to 30 deaths. In Lipu County 44 died in factional battles over a four-day period in early December, and 14 were publicly executed during a mass rally held by village cadres to "suppress counter-revolution."[14] In Bobai County, armed skirmishes between the April faction and village militias affiliated with the Allied Command resulted in close to a dozen deaths, provoking a PAD-organized campaign of suppression in which some 100 insurgents and "four-type" elements were killed over a few weeks.[15]

These events spurred protests in Nanning. In mid-December around 200 activists from ten counties staged a sit-in at the Military District Headquarters to protest local massacres by the Allied Command. The April faction formed an "Anti-massacre Committee" and submitted a demand that the Preparatory Committee prohibit "Poor Peasant Supreme People's Courts" and dispatch armed PLA troops to counties where massacres were taking place. They demanded that Wei Guoqing and the Military District resolve the problem and issue a self-criticism over their inaction. April faction leaders from more than fifty localities implored the Nanning authorities to make telephone calls to PAD commanders to demand an end to the killings.[16]

The Nanning authorities responded in late December, issuing a directive calling peasants' courts illegal, and they ordered an immediate halt to the arrests and executions. The April faction saw these directives as ineffectual, and once again demanded the dispatch of PLA soldiers to stay the hand of local PAD commanders, who had become almost indistinguishable from the Allied Command faction. Their Anti-massacre Committee staged a rally of 2,000 people at the Military District Headquarters to demand the immediate dispatch of troops.[17]

The Preparatory Committee met with the protest leaders and acknowledged the problem, but they did not send PLA troops to halt local killings. The committee was pulled in two directions at once. While the April faction was making increasingly urgent calls for direct action to halt massacres organized by the local PAD, the Preparatory Committee was also concerned that revived factional warfare in several prefectures be halted immediately. Their capacity to quell local battles, which were spread across rural districts and villages, was limited. They could not solve the problem by sending contingents of troops, which could not possibly cover the many rural communities where killings occurred. The only force capable of covering all these localities was the village militias under the PAD—the very organization implicated in the massacres.

While these developments alarmed the April faction, they were only a hint of what was to come. In February, violence exploded across four counties in Qinzhou Prefecture. The investigation reports record a total of 264 deaths in Guangxi during January. In February this number increased sharply to 4,293. Almost all these deaths (4,096) were the result of suppression campaigns or arbitrary mass killings by local forces aligned with the PAD. And out of that 4,096, almost all (3,930), were in Qinzhou Prefecture, the maritime region on the Gulf of Tonkin that was until recently part of Guangdong Province. The killings accelerated beyond all imagination in Lingshan County during February, reaching a total of 2,634 by the following month.[18] The same trends occurred in nearby Dongxing, Hepu, and Qinzhou counties.[19]

The wave of killings in Qinzhou Prefecture precipitated the irreparable breakdown of the Preparatory Committee. April faction representatives on the committee charged that the killings were coordinated by the Guangxi Military District, whose officers dominated the top posts on the committee. Their charge had surface plausibility, because county PADs were under the authority of the Qinzhou Military Subdistrict, which in turn was under the Guangxi Military District. Their suspicions were understandable, but a more reasonable charge would have been that the Military District had not acted decisively enough to enforce its recent prohibitions against mass killings.

Whatever the truth of the matter, the commanders of the Military District reacted angrily to charges that they had orchestrated the killings. They hurled back
counter-charges that the April faction was responsible for the ongoing disorders
because they were resisting the imposition of military control and the establishment of local Revolutionary Committees. They went further in their accusations
in ways that would soon accelerate the killings. The military commanders charged
that the April faction was obstructing the creation of Revolutionary Committees
because their organization was following a "black line" driven by the subversive
motivations of class enemies, revisionists, and traitors. They demanded that Wu
Jinnan and the other leaders associated with the April faction repudiate the group
and cut their ties.[20] From this point forward, the controversy between the April faction and the military commanders served only to fan the flames of violence, and
the military commanders once again became partisans in the factional conflicts.
What began as a weak restraining hand on local PAD atrocities turned into a force
that accelerated violent suppression.

As the trust between the two sides collapsed, each attributed base and conspira-
torial motives to the other. In mid-February the military commanders ordered PLA
Unit 6984, which had all along been stationed in Nanning, to a county near Liuzhou,
to help suppress an outbreak of factional fighting there. The April faction objected
to the move, suspecting that the unit would be replaced by one with more hostile
intent toward their side in the escalating controversies. The April forces in Nanning
staged several demonstrations to demand the retention of PLA Unit 6984, and they
appealed to the commanders of that unit to disobey the Military District's orders.
After the PLA unit left Nanning, the April faction held large demonstrations to demand its return. The Military District and Preparatory Committee accused the April
faction of subverting the military command structure, and they sent reports to Beijing stating that the rebel group was undermining their efforts to reestablish order.

At the end of February, the April 22 leadership in Nanning held meetings to
plan renewed armed resistance to military control. They resolved to act to curtail
mass killings on their own, by establishing "field armies," seizing arms, and preparing for a much more militant resistance movement than anything contemplated
before.[21] Arms seizures, which had declined to a reported 6 or fewer in each of the
months after the peak of 41 in August 1967, climbed to 18 in January and 31 in February, the highest level since the high tide during the previous summer.

The situation in Guangxi was about to spiral out of control, closing the window of opportunity for the Preparatory Committee to fulfill their mission quickly. They responded by issuing an urgent directive to cities and counties to establish Revolutionary Committees as rapidly as possible. Unfortunately for the April faction, the only instruments for fulfilling this directive were the county PADs.[22] There had been no negotiations or Preparatory Committees at the county level, and it is unclear how such arrangements could have been made. The April faction was arming itself and mobilizing for armed resistance against the imposition of Revolutionary Committees by the very actors against whom they had fought for more than a year. Local PAD commanders, not surprisingly, imposed Revolutionary Committees that favored themselves and the Allied Command. They now mobilized to forcibly establish Revolutionary Committees, employing their local PAD branches and militia to suppress enemies, real and imagined.

The first 46 Revolutionary Committees were established in March. Political order was reimposed by force, with little armed resistance. Of the 3,932 reported deaths in these counties during March, 88 percent were due to organized repression coordinated by the local PAD—either summary killings in villages or executions conducted as part of a political campaign. Only 11 percent of the total was the result of actual conflicts between factions, where the losing side, uniformly associated with the April alliance, suffered disproportionately.

During this period the Preparatory Committee submitted reports to Beijing that emphasized the threat of the April 22 "field armies" and their violent resistance to Revolutionary Committees.[23] There is little evidence of this in the investigation reports. There were only forty armed battles between factions during February and March in the thirty-nine counties and cities that had not established Revolutionary Committees by the end of March, and overwhelming levels of repression were applied in these places as well. Armed clashes between factions generated only 483 reported deaths during March, while repression by the PAD and militia accounted for 5,547.

The implacable pressure on the April faction led the alliance to fracture. Its headquarters split in disagreements about the decision to seize weapons and create "field armies" to resist the formation of Revolutionary Committees. The rebel leaders who disagreed with that decision immediately replaced the other April representatives on the Preparatory Committee. The expelled April faction leaders dispatched a delegation to Beijing to denounce Wei Guoqing and the Preparatory Committee for sabotaging the November agreement and imposing Revolutionary Committees that represented only one faction. They appealed to members of the CCRG for help, but there was no longer anyone in the national leadership willing to support their cause. As the Revolutionary Committees were established by force in rural counties, April faction activities were increasingly concentrated in the cities, none of which had yet established Revolutionary Committees. They remained active in the larger cities, especially Guilin and Nanning, where they could still mobilize thousands of people for rallies and marches to denounce the actions of the Preparatory Committee.[24] These numbers were swollen by defeated April faction activists fleeing repression in rural counties.

Another thirty Revolutionary Committees were established during April, including in Nanning and Guilin. After the split of the April 22 leadership, the creation of Revolutionary Committees that favored the Allied Command was a foregone conclusion. There was little reported violence during April in this group of thirty localities; there were only four factional clashes and 880 deaths from all causes. This did not mean that resistance by the April faction had ended in the cities. They still had large and active followings in Nanning, Guilin, Liuzhou, and Wuzhou. Their continued strength was dramatized by a mass rally of close to 20,000 people in Nanning's Chaoyang Stadium on April 19 to denounce the city's Revolutionary Committee that was established that day. Several days later they held an even larger rally at the same venue to celebrate the anniversary of the founding of the April 22 faction. Red Guards associated with them invaded the Military District Headquarters several days later.[25]

The Allied Command responded in early May by seizing arms from PLA units in Nanning and Liuzhou. The April faction staged their own raid to seize arms in Nanning, and a battle between the two sides followed.[26] Without the restraining hand of PLA Unit 6984, which by this point had been transferred well away from Nanning, the Allied Command forces in Nanning carried out assaults on April faction strongholds in the city, a development that portended the later battles. By the end of May, there were still seven counties and two cities (Liuzhou and Wuzhou) that had yet to establish Revolutionary Committees, and Nanning and Guilin were

far from pacified. So long as entrenched resistance continued in these four cities, the final step in the full restoration of provincial government was indefinitely
postponed.

This would not be accomplished for another three months, and only after a
spasm of violence that dwarfed even this period of rapid escalation. As noted in
chapter 4, deadly violence was remarkably rare in Guangxi during 1967. From January 1967 through the end of May 1968, there were a total of 14,640 deaths linked
to political events described in the investigation reports. More than 92 percent of
these occurred *after* the Beijing negotiations ended in November 1967. Deadly violence in Guangxi—almost all at the hands of local actors affiliated with PADs—accelerated rapidly after January 1968. Despite this alarming trend, mass killings of
the type for which Guangxi would become notorious were still rare. By the end
of May, the average death toll in Guangxi's cities and counties was 172; half of
them had recorded fewer than 27 deaths, and fifteen had experienced 5 or fewer.
Only three counties—Qinzhou, Luchuan, and Lingshan—had suffered more than
1,000 deaths, and only five other counties had recorded more than 500. Despite
high levels of factional conflict and a strong presence of the April faction, the cities
had yet to experience large death tolls. Beihai had suffered the worst violence,
with 362 recorded deaths, primarily from factional warfare during August 1967.[27]
Wuzhou, Pingxiang, and Liuzhou had recorded between 108 and 145. Nanning and
Guilin, where the April faction had its largest and most enduring followings, and
whose final battles were described in the prologue, had recorded only 45 and 38,
respectively.[28]

By the end of 1968 Guangxi would look dramatically different, due to events
from June to September. The average death toll in 86 cities and counties would
reach 986; 33 localities suffered more than 1,000 deaths; 7 counties more than 2,000,
and 3 counties (Gui, Lingshan, and Binyang) more than 3,000.[29] At the end of May
1968 Guangxi had yet to earn its reputation for unusual levels of violence. Political
developments in the province and in Beijing were crucial in pushing Guangxi over
the edge.

### Redefining the Conflicts

The essential first step in setting the conditions for mass killings was the redefini-
tion of the conflicts in Guangxi from a factional conflict between competing rebel

groups, to the suppression of an insurgency that sought to overthrow the Communist Party and restore Nationalist Party rule. As the Guangxi Military District sensed that the situation was spiraling out of control, they made increasingly extreme accusations against the April faction. In reports to Beijing, they began to characterize April faction resistance as the work of "class enemies." They followed up these charges with reports of an alleged province-wide underground network connected to Nationalist agents and former class enemies headed by the April faction. Once Beijing accepted this definition of the conflicts, the July 3 Orders would soon follow.

It was common during this period to intimidate the leaders of stubborn rebel opposition by charging that they had made common cause with class enemies. The Preparatory Committee made precisely such a charge in a dispatch to Beijing on May 14, in which they claimed that continued resistance by stubborn April faction forces was due the influence of a "small group of class enemies." They repeated this accusation several days later in a report to Beijing that falsely claimed the discovery of an active underground counter-revolutionary organization linked to the Nationalist Party on Taiwan, with branches throughout Guangxi. The report claimed that the conspirators were plotting to overthrow Communist Party rule and were linking up with local April faction affiliates. The report further claimed that the headquarters of the organization was on Nanning's Liberation Road, in a building that was the headquarters of the surviving April 22 leadership.[30] On May 20 the Preparatory Committee issued a directive to local Revolutionary Committees and PAD officers that ordered a campaign to eliminate this underground conspiracy. The orders claimed that this "Anti-Communist Salvation Corps" thrived on links to former class enemies in politically stigmatized households, such as landlords and former members of Nationalist organizations, those punished as "rightists" or "bad elements."[31] Shortly afterward they issued a report claiming the discovery in Fengshan County of an anti-Communist movement composed of "historical counter-revolutionaries and traitors."[32] On June 18 they issued additional directives ordering all local Revolutionary Committees and PADs to mobilize full-scale investigations of the group's local branches.[33]

The intentions of these military officers in making these charges are not entirely clear. Perhaps this was simply the routine rhetoric that the Chinese Communist Party always used to intimidate its opponents. Perhaps it was a deliberate cover for the anticipated application of overwhelming force against rebels that had long been prohibited by Beijing. Perhaps it was intended as cover and justification for local massacres that were already under way and that the Nanning authorities had done little to prevent. Whatever their intentions, by making these claims the Nanning authorities unleashed a wave of massacres that they may not have anticipated or intended, and that went far beyond what was needed to quell the April faction. There is some evidence for this last possibility. On June 24 the Preparatory Committee issued a directive that ordered a halt to mass killings in rural counties due to the campaign that they had initiated against the "Anti-Communist Salvation Corps."[34]

The authorities in Nanning appear to have intended a systematic suppression campaign, implemented from the top down, to neutralize continued opposition in an orderly fashion. But the rhetoric issuing from the Preparatory Committee had two other consequences that were likely unanticipated, and evidently unwelcomed. Encouraged by the authorities' animosity toward the April faction, and spurred by their denunciation as counter-revolutionaries, Allied Command factions in the cities seized weapons and planned major offensives against stubborn April faction holdouts. The Allied Command sent some 3,500 fighters to the Military District's arms depot in Nanning on June 4, seizing close to 1,900 firearms of various types, more than 1 million rounds of ammunition, and artillery pieces.[35] In Guilin, the group raided arms depots in nearby counties to prepare for a major offensive against April forces in control of the city.[36] Rebel factions armed with heavy weaponry could wreak havoc on cityscapes and thereby intensify the perception that the Nanning authorities had lost control. On June 13 Allied Command fighters fired artillery at an April faction base in one of the Nanning department stores, starting a major fire. Six days later they bombarded a building under the Hydroelectric Bureau, killing sixty-two defenders and dumping their corpses into the Yong River. And on June 23 they bombarded the wharf area controlled by the April faction from both sides of the river, sinking or damaging forty boats.[37]

A second unanticipated consequence was that rural PADs, after pacifying their localities, sent village militias into nearby cities to assist Allied faction forces in their campaign to annihilate their opponents. On June 9 the Preparatory Committee and the Military District issued a joint order for the Allied Command and rural

PADs to stop mobilizing tens of thousands of fighters to enter the cities in their campaign of extermination against April 22. They reissued their earlier prohibition against village militia forces entering the cities to fight.[38] So long as Guangxi's cities were the sites of factional violence, the formation of the provincial Revolutionary Committee would continue to be delayed.

## Toward the July 3 Orders

The reports submitted to Beijing by the Guangxi Military District emphasized armed resistance by the April faction in the cities and their continuing efforts to undermine local Revolutionary Committees. These dispatches claimed that the April faction was a front for a large underground antistate conspiracy linked to hostile foreign powers and remnants of defeated class enemies. When the Nanning authorities issued warnings that rural massacres should stop, that the Allied Command should cease arms seizures, and that rural militias should stop flooding into cities for urban warfare, their directives were issued within the province, aimed at local actors. These were not included in their dispatches to Beijing.

It is not clear to what extent Beijing had accurate information about events in Guangxi during this period, but the actual trend, as reflected in data extracted from the investigation reports, was very different from the impression that Nanning's reports must have left on China's leaders. There were 607 political events recorded across Guangxi during June 1968. Two-thirds of them (470) were campaigns orchestrated by local civilian and political authorities, and related killings. These events generated a reported 6,609 deaths. One-fifth of these events (123) were actions, like armed battles, that could plausibly be attributed to rebel factions. These events generated a reported total of 466 deaths. Whatever the impression left by the Preparatory Committee's dispatches to Beijing, the actual situation in Guangxi was one of rapidly accelerating repression against the April faction and members of politically stigmatized households. The mass killings in counties, which had begun to spread in April and May, accelerated in June. During that month deaths at the hands of local authorities continued to spread. In June alone, two counties (Mengshan and Quanzhou) recorded more than 1,000 such killings; in three counties there were more than 400; and in eight counties there were well over 100. The actual situation, completely obscured in Nanning's dispatches to Beijing, was one of intensifying massacres in rural counties, the arming and mobilization of a resurgent Allied Command, and the flow of rural militias to fight factional battles in the cities.

It is possible that the Nanning dispatches misled China's leaders about the true situation. It is also possible that figures in Beijing had a clear understanding of the situation. But it seems clear that whatever the state of their knowledge, the "Center"—namely, Mao Zedong—had lost patience with the continued disorders in Guangxi, whatever their actual cause. It had been eight months since Mao had personally approved the compromise hammered out in long negotiations supervised by Zhou Enlai. Guangxi remained one of the few provinces that had yet to reestablish a government in the form of a Revolutionary Committee. The war in Vietnam continued to rage on, the Americans continued to escalate their troop levels and bombing campaign in the North, and the Liuzhou Railway Bureau continued to suffer periodic blockages of shipments to the southern border. It was precisely during this period that China was continuing its effort to draw Vietnam to its side in the Sino-Soviet split, and to convince the Vietnamese to fight on and ignore Soviet advice to participate in peace negotiations.[39]

There was much about the two-year-old Cultural Revolution that had frustrated Mao, including the behavior of celebrated Red Guard and rebel factions in the capital's universities. During July 1968, Mao had become fed up with the continued factional battles on college campuses among his prized Beijing Red Guards. He decided to shut down the student rebels, close the universities entirely, and place them under military control. In an angry meeting with the capital's famous Red Guard leaders on July 28, he expressed his frustration and referred to harsh orders he had issued earlier that month calling for the ruthless suppression of continued factional battles:

> The Cultural Revolution has gone on for two years now! . . . I say you are divorced from the masses. The masses cannot accept civil war . . . Well, now we are issuing a nationwide directive, and whoever violates it, striking at the army, sabotaging transportation, killing people, setting fires, is committing a crime. If there is a minority who will not listen to persuasion and refuses to change, then they are bandits, Nationalists. We will surround them, and if they are stubborn, we will wipe them out.[40]

The spirit of Mao's warning to the Beijing students reflected the content of the July 3 Orders that a frustrated Mao had issued about Guangxi's ongoing disorders. The orders made clear that Beijing largely accepted the Preparatory Committee's characterization of the political situation in Guangxi, and it removed constraints on the use of overwhelming repression. The orders opened with formulaic praise about positive trends in Guangxi and stated that "both sides" in rebel disputes were revolutionary, but it essentially denied this statement when it came to continuing resistance by remnant April faction forces.

In recent months, in Liuzhou, Guilin, Nanning Prefecture, a small handful of Khrushchev-type capitalist roaders inside the Party and their representatives in Guangxi, along with traitors, secret agents, counter-revolutionary elements, and unrepentant landlords, rich peasants, bad elements, and rightists have deceived and fooled some of the masses and have repeatedly created a series of counter-revolutionary incidents:

1. Sabotaged railway transport, which has yet to be restored

2. Daring to seize supplies for support of Vietnam and refusing to return them

3. Repeatedly attacking the headquarters and troops of the People's Liberation Army, seizing the People's Liberation Army's arms and equipment, wounding and killing their officers and troops . . .

The Center considers these acts to be counter-revolutionary crimes by a small group of class enemies of sabotaging the proletarian dictatorship, sabotaging the struggle to resist America and aid Vietnam, and sabotaging the Proletarian Cultural Revolution.[41]

The July 3 Orders implicitly embraced the characterizations in the incendiary Preparatory Committee dispatches, even if they did not repeat their claims about a province-wide underground conspiracy. By characterizing the continuing resistance in Guangxi as the work of "traitors, spies, counter-revolutionaries along with landlords [and] rich peasants," the document indirectly endorsed these false claims. By characterizing ongoing resistance as counter-revolution, and by naming former class enemies as participants, the document accelerated the mass killings by county-level PADs and their associated village militias against rebel opposition and members of politically stigmatized households. The fears that Zhou Enlai expressed in his dark warning of November 1967 to the Allied Command faction in Guilin were about to be realized to an extent that he could not possibly have imagined.

## CHAPTER 6

# Suppression

Having characterized the political processes that entrenched conflict between two province-wide factions, we can now confront the central question posed at the outset of this book: why were the death tolls in Guangxi so much higher than those elsewhere in China? We have seen that deadly violence was remarkably rare in Guangxi during the six-month period of negotiations in Beijing, and that armed warfare between factions began to spread only with the breakdown of the Preparatory Committee near the end of 1967. We have also seen that the massacres in rural regions of factional opponents and members of stigmatized "four type" households began to spread across Guangxi during the first half of 1968, portending the wave of killings to come.

By the end of June 1968, the death toll from all political causes in Guangxi was still only roughly half of what it would be by the end of September. Of the close to 100,000 people killed or missing and presumed dead in Guangxi overall, almost half of the deaths (45,993) were tied to specific actions described in the investigation reports. The July 3 Orders spurred an extremely violent, two-month period of open warfare in large cities, and mass killing in rural communities, as described in the prologue. During July and August 1968, the events narrated in the investigation reports were linked to 22,242 deaths. In other words, *half* of *all* recorded deaths that can be linked to specific times and places in the investigation reports occurred during these two months.

This brief period turned Guangxi into the deadliest of China's provinces. The answer to our central question lies in understanding the actions unleashed at that time. Guangxi's death toll of 100,000 translates into a death rate of 4.0 per thousand population, roughly double the estimated national death rate (minus Guangxi) of 2.1. The investigation reports provide dates for close to half of the total documented deaths.

If the distribution of deaths over time in Guangxi approximated the distribution of the deaths for which dates are known, we can estimate Guangxi's monthly progression toward its final death rate of 4.0 per thousand. Figure 6.1 illustrates this progression during the first nine months of 1968. The graph begins in January 1968, at which point Guangxi appears to have suffered very little deadly violence.[1] This reflects the fact that Guangxi missed the wave of armed factional conflict elsewhere in China in the summer of 1967. The graph traces the steady increase in the death rate in the early months of 1968, a trend that reflects the arming of the two factions and the spread of rural killings. There was a large jump from May to June, which fits with the accounts in chapter 5. Nonetheless, by the end of June, Guangxi's estimated death rate was still just below the ultimate death rate elsewhere in China of 2.0 per thousand. This changed suddenly in July and August, when Guangxi's

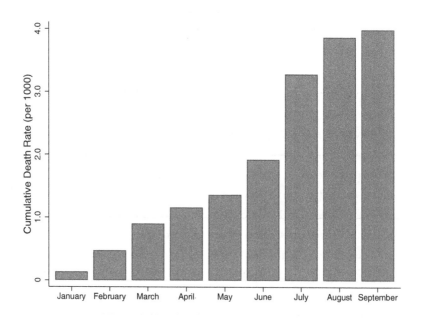

FIGURE 6.1.   Estimated Cumulative Provincial Death Rate, Guangxi, 1968

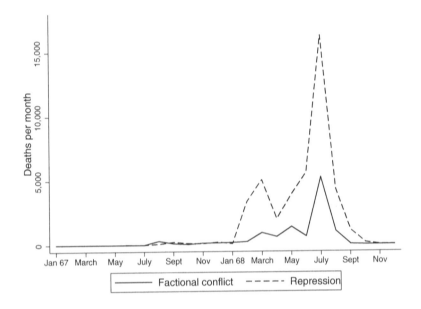

FIGURE 6.2.   Monthly Deaths from Factional Conflict versus Repression, 1967–68

cumulative death rate doubled. By September it had reached the levels for which Guangxi is notorious.

The July 3 Orders had an immediate impact, as seen in figure 6.2, which traces over a two-year period the number of deaths generated by factional conflict versus those resulting from repression by civilian or military actors. There are few deaths from any causes throughout 1967. The number of deaths due to repression begins to rise in February 1968 and escalates sharply in June. The numbers spike with the July 3 Orders. The rise in deaths from factional conflict in July is somewhat misleading: these events were classified as such only because April 22 fighters in the cities resisted and held out for several weeks against assaults in which Allied Command fighters were actively assisted by units of the PLA and rural militia commanded by county PADs.

## Rural Suppression Campaigns

I have described mass killings in rural regions as a product of organized campaigns carried out by PADs, their branches in rural districts, and their village militias. I have yet to provide systematic evidence to back up this claim. Recall that an alternative characterization of the political processes that generated Guangxi's large death tolls is that they were a form of intergroup violence, collective behavior at the village level that was not an extension of factional conflicts in cities and county seats. That characterization draws parallels between Guangxi's mass killings and genocidal violence in Rwanda, Bosnia, and other settings. The alternative is that the killings more closely resembled the massacres of suspected communists and other leftists coordinated by the Indonesian army or counter-insurgency forces in a variety of historical settings.

The portrayal of Guangxi's high death tolls as the product of collective violence against stigmatized "four type" households relied on evidence extracted from published county and city annals. These sources contained very few descriptions of factional conflict at the village level, but often provided numbing detail about killings of members of the stigmatized households in village settings. The sources also provided statistical material that made clear that only a small percentage of the overall death toll in Guangxi (as elsewhere in China) was due to factional warfare. This led to the conclusion that almost all the deaths, which occurred overwhelmingly in rural settings, must have been unrelated to the factional conflicts in towns, and that almost all of those killed therefore must have been members of stigmatized households.[2]

The more abundant detail provided in the investigation reports permits us to examine these contrasting portrayals in greater depth, and to explore local political processes in a more systematic fashion. Were villages largely isolated from the factional conflicts in Guangxi's cities and county seats, or did factional conflict also penetrate below the county level into smaller rural towns and villages? Who were those killed in rural areas: were they members of stigmatized households, or were they individuals associated with one of the two provincial factions? And who were the actors identified as the perpetrators: were they ordinary members of rural communities who were uninvolved in the factional battles of the cities and towns, or were they agents of rural authorities, in particular members of village militias or other organizations that were closely aligned with, if not identical to, the Allied Command faction? The answers to these questions will help to determine the extent to which Guangxi's high death tolls were the product of intergroup violence, or of a counter-insurgency campaign that spilled over into killings of suspected collaborators in stigmatized households.

## The Geographic Distribution of Factional Activity

Were factional conflicts between April 22 and the Allied Command largely confined to cities and county seats? Data extracted from the investigation reports permit a closer look. Table 6.1 displays the distribution of conflict events and deaths in cities and counties, and within counties, in county seats versus rural communes and villages. The top panel displays the location of 366 "armed battles" between civilian factions. Just over 70 percent of these events, and just under 30 percent of associated deaths, occurred in counties. Violent factional conflict spread far outside the cities, but it was on a smaller scale and generated fewer casualties per jurisdiction. There were an average of 17.5 armed battles in the six cities, and an average of 783 deaths per city from these battles. In the counties, by contrast, there was an average of only 3.3 armed battles, which resulted in an average of 24.4 deaths per county.[3] Armed battles between the two rebel factions were much more frequent in the cities and resulted in far more deaths per event. This fits with impressions that previous analysts have drawn from accounts in published annals: large armed confrontations between the two factions were concentrated in urban areas, as were deaths from armed factional combat.

The distribution of these events *within* counties is of greater interest. To what extent were the 261 reported armed battles between factions in counties concentrated in county seats, and to what extent did they also occur in rural districts? A slight majority of these events, and of the resulting deaths, occurred in the county seats. A large percentage of both, from 42 percent to 45 percent, occurred in rural districts. Within counties, this most violent type of factional activity was distributed fairly evenly between urban and rural districts.

Armed battles, however, are only the most dramatic and violent type of factional activity. Factions were far more active than what is indicated solely by the occurrence of armed battles. The investigation reports also contain accounts of a larger range of events that involve one or both of the factions. There were 1,570 such events in the data set. They include armed battles and also a wide range of other kinds of events: protest demonstrations or marches; raids on arms depots, storehouses or buildings; attacks on government officials or military units; the taking of prisoners; nonviolent confrontations; unarmed street brawls; isolated killings of opponents; and the violent suppression of one or another faction. The defining

TABLE 6.1.   Distribution of Factional Activity and Related Deaths, Urban versus Rural Locations

| Location | Number of Events | Percent of Events | Number of Deaths | Percent of Deaths |
|---|---|---|---|---|
| **Armed Battles** | | | | |
| Cities | 105 | 28.7 | 4,696 | 70.7 |
| Counties | 261 | 71.3 | 1,949 | 29.3 |
| *Total* | *366* | *100* | *6,645* | *100* |
| *Within Counties* | | | | |
| Urban | 150 | 57.5 | 1,072 | 55.0 |
| Rural | 110 | 42.1 | 876 | 44.9 |
| Unspecified | 1 | 0.4 | 1 | 0.1 |
| *Total* | *261* | *100* | *1,949* | *100* |
| **All Factional Activity*** | | | | |
| Cities | 308 | 19.6 | 5,165 | 33.3 |
| Counties | 1,262 | 80.4 | 10,331 | 66.7 |
| *Total* | *1,570* | *100* | *15,496* | *100* |
| *Within Counties* | | | | |
| Urban | 706 | 55.9 | 2,207 | 21.4 |
| Rural | 530 | 42.0 | 2,980 | 28.8 |
| Unspecified | 26 | 2.1 | 5,144 | 49.8 |
| *Total* | *1,262* | *100* | *10,331* | *100* |

* Defined as events in which one or both rebel factions are named as actors or harmed parties.

feature of this group of events is that the April 22 or Allied Command factions are named as either actors or harmed parties.

The lower panel of table 6.1 examines this broader range of 1,570 events. This view of factional activity yields almost the same distribution of events across cities and counties, but a somewhat higher proportion in counties. However, the proportion of deaths from this broader range of activity now swings much more heavily toward the counties, where two-thirds of resulting deaths were recorded. This reflects the many events that involve the suppression of one of the factions by their opponents or by local authorities or military units. What is significant in this category is that the event indicates the presence of factional activity, even if the faction is named only as the target of suppression. The crucial information, again, is in the lower panel that examines the distribution of the 1,262 events *within* counties. We find that the distribution of events is very close to that for armed battles, but that most resulting deaths, at least for those events whose location is known, were in rural districts.

These numbers indicate that factional conflicts reached into the rural districts of counties. The rural districts were not isolated from the province-wide factional rivalries, despite impressions derived from published local histories. This general conclusion, however, raises yet another question. The figures in table 6.1 are averages, and they surely mask wide variations across counties. How many counties had factional conflict that penetrated well into rural regions, and in how many were these conflicts largely absent?

There is, in fact, wide variation in the extent to which factional activity reached into rural districts. The twenty counties that had the largest number of conflict events had a minimum of 22 total events and a maximum of 61. In this group, there was an average of just under 15 factional events in rural districts. In these counties, factional conflict was pervasive and extended deeply into rural districts. Suppression campaigns in these counties would likely have aimed at quelling factional opponents, their sympathizers, and family members. At the opposite end of the distribution, however, the picture is completely different. In the twenty counties with the least factional activity, there was a maximum of 6 events and minimum of only 1, and an average of less than 1 event in rural districts (11 reported none). In these counties there was little factional conflict, and it was almost completely limited to urban districts. Suppression campaigns in these counties would have found few factional opponents to target, and presumably the brunt of these campaigns would fall on the "four type" households or others. Between these extremes are forty counties that reported a total of between 7 and 22 events, with an average of 5–6 in rural districts. Factional conflict occurred frequently in these rural districts, but it was not pervasive.

In short, factional conflict in rural regions was by no means limited to urban districts, but it was unevenly distributed across rural regions. It appears that somewhere between one-quarter and one-third of counties had pervasive factional conflict that extended well into rural districts. A roughly equal number had little factional conflict, and it was largely confined to county seats. Between these two extremes was a larger group where factional conflict was common in county seats and somewhat less prevalent in rural districts. This spectrum of variation defies simple characterization, but it suggests that in the rural districts of most counties there was factional opposition to target in suppression campaigns, while in a substantial minority there were few factional opponents, potentially leaving stigmatized households to bear the brunt of suppression.

### The Victims

This leads to the next question, about the identity of the victims. To what extent were they from politically stigmatized "four types," and to what extent were they April faction activists, supporters, or family members? A subset of the events recorded in the investigation reports describe the identity of the victims. These cases permit estimates that, while imprecise and incomplete, are nonetheless broadly informative.

The data set extracted from the investigation reports recorded up to three "harmed parties" that suffered death or other kinds of harm in the described events. There were 1,937 discrete events in the data set that recorded at least one death, and it was possible to identify at least one type of "harmed party" in 1,265 of these cases. In 137 cases two harmed parties were identified, and in 7 of them three were recorded. Among the 1,409 harmed parties that were named, the April faction was mentioned in more than half, far more than any other group. In the 144 cases where more than one harmed party was recorded, however, it is impossible to apportion the deaths among the groups named. To eliminate this ambiguity, we examine only those events where just one harmed party was named. These cases include all events that resulted in a death, regardless of the type of event or who were the actors involved.

Table 6.2 summarizes information about harmed parties drawn from these cases. Members of the April faction were the victims in most events, 57 percent of the total. However, this percentage was much higher in the cities than the counties. The April faction made up almost 90 percent of those killed in the cities, but just over one-third in the counties. This was still the largest single category in the counties, larger still than the 23.4 percent who were identified as members of "four type" households. There is one large, ill-defined category, that of "masses"— individuals not identified as civilian or military authorities, affiliates of factions, or members of stigmatized households. It is possible that some members of stigmatized households were counted in this category, but it is also possible that relatives and associates of the April faction were included. We therefore cannot conclude with

TABLE 6.2.   Identities of Those Killed, Cities versus Counties (numbers killed, by group)

| Identity | Cities (percent) | Counties (percent) | Guangxi (percent) |
|---|---|---|---|
| April faction | 4,637 (89.6) | 2,636 (34.9) | 7,273 (57.1) |
| "Masses" | 64 (1.2) | 2,050 (27.2) | 2,114 (16.6) |
| Politically stigmatized households | 33 (0.6) | 1,769 (23.4) | 1,802 (14.2) |
| Cadres | 15 (0.3) | 318 (4.2) | 333 (2.6) |
| Allied faction | 171 (3.3) | 62 (0.8) | 233 (1.8) |
| Counter-revolutionary groups | 18 (0.3) | 173 (2.3) | 191 (1.5) |
| Others/unclear | 239 (4.6) | 542 (7.2) | 781 (6.1) |
| Total deaths | 5,177 | 7,550 | 12,727 |

Note: Numbers of dead recorded in 1,265 events that name only one harmed party; excludes 144 cases that name more than one.

confidence the relative balance of April faction members and stigmatized households. But we can conclude that both groups were prominent among the victimized. We can also conclude that members of stigmatized households were far more likely to be targeted in counties than cities, and the April faction less likely.

Our primary interest is in killings that were concentrated in the rural districts of counties. Table 6.3 examines a subset of 911 events in counties in which the location in an urban versus rural district was known. We see the same contrast between urban and rural districts in counties as between the cities and counties. The April faction represents a large majority of the deaths in urban districts—close to two-thirds—but only one-fourth of the deaths recorded in the rural districts. The numbers associated with the April faction are less than those recorded for both the "masses" and the stigmatized households. The more rural the setting, the smaller the percentage of the victims in the April faction, and the larger the percentage in stigmatized households. There is still uncertainty about these proportions due to the ambiguous nature of the "masses" category.

TABLE 6.3.  Identities of Those Killed in Counties (numbers killed, by group)

| Group | Urban Districts (percent of total) | Rural Districts (percent of total) | Counties Overall (percent of total) |
|---|---|---|---|
| April faction | 1,045 (64.4) | 1,309 (25.2) | 2,354 (37.2) |
| "Masses" | 157 (9.7) | 1,778 (34.3) | 1,935 (28.4) |
| Politically stigmatized households | 59 (3.6) | 1,411 (27.2) | 1,470 (21.6) |
| Counter-revolutionary groups | 11 (0.7) | 161 (3.1) | 172 (2.5) |
| Cadres | 120 (7.4) | 167 (3.2) | 287 (4.2) |
| Allied faction | 38 (2.4) | 24 (0.5) | 62 (0.9) |
| Others | 194 (11.9) | 339 (6.5) | 533 (7.8) |
| Total deaths | 1,624 (100) | 5,189 (100) | 6,813 (100) |

Note: Numbers of dead recorded in 911 events that name only one harmed party; excludes 18 events with unspecified locations.

We showed earlier that factional activity varied widely across the eighty counties. The ratio of April faction members to individuals from stigmatized households as victims in rural killings also varies widely. If we calculate the percentage of deaths in a county identified with the April faction, we find that in 25 percent of the counties this group constitutes from 50 percent to 100 percent of the total, and in another 25 percent no members at all of the April faction are identified among the killed. Similarly, if we calculate the same percentages for the stigmatized households, we find that in 20 percent of the counties they make up from 50 percent to 100 percent of the total, and in another one-third of the counties no members of this category are mentioned.

The most precise accounting of the prevalence of members of stigmatized households among those killed is to be found in summary statistics provided in twenty-five of the investigation reports. In this subset of counties, whose representativeness is unknown, the reported percentage of those killed who were identified as members of stigmatized households ranged from 13.2 percent to 76.9 percent, an average of 46.7 percent. It is possible that this estimate is biased upward because the compilers of the reports viewed this percentage as lamentably high and found it worthy of emphasis, but the figure is consistent with the evidence presented in table 6.3.

Based on this evidence, we can confidently conclude that the portrayal of mass killings in rural Guangxi as pogroms against stigmatized "four type" households greatly underestimated the extent of factional activity in rural regions and the victimization of individuals associated with the April faction. However, this portrayal does accurately characterize events in a large minority of rural counties in Guangxi. These counties had little factional activity, and such activity was restricted almost exclusively to urban districts. In these counties, rural suppression campaigns, lacking factional targets, focused heavily on stigmatized households as alleged supporters of a province-wide counter-revolutionary conspiracy. In most counties where factional activity was more widespread, especially in the one-quarter of them where it was pervasive in rural districts, suppression campaigns focused more heavily on members of the April faction—a pattern that was even more pronounced in the cities.

This also indicates that only in a minority of counties did the victims of mass killings in Guangxi resemble those in Dao County, Hunan. The detailed investigations into the Dao County case demonstrated that the vast majority killed in Lingling Prefecture—more than 83 percent—were members of stigmatized "four type" households.[4] Mass killings in Guangxi spread far and wide across the province, unlike Hunan, where they were limited to one prefecture and within that prefecture were concentrated in one county. The killings were stopped through intervention by outside PLA units. Rural killings in Guangxi claimed far more victims among insurgent rebels who resisted the imposition of Revolutionary Committees. Guangxi's authorities named stigmatized households as complicit with the April faction in a province-wide anti-Communist conspiracy. If there were few people associated with the April faction in a village, the default option was the stigmatized households, who were present almost everywhere.

## The Perpetrators

The crucial question, then, is this: who were the actors identified in events that led to deaths? There are 1,957 discrete events in the data set that report at least

TABLE 6.4.  Actors Identified in Events That Generate Deaths

| Actors | Number of Mentions (percent) | Deaths (percent) |
|---|---|---|
| Authorities | 1,949 (73.2) | 27,145 (85.4) |
| *Commune/Brigade Leaders* | *765* | *8,531* |
| *Rural Militia/Peasants Assns./Pickets* | *566* | *1,630* |
| *Revolutionary Committees* | *336* | *11,950* |
| *Security/Military* | *282* | *5,034* |
| Allied Faction | 380 (14.2) | 4,073 (12.8) |
| April Faction | 90 (3.4) | 375 (1.2) |
| Red Guards/Rebels | 54 (2.0) | 134 (0.4) |
| "Masses" | 19 (0.7) | 59 (0.2) |
| Total | 2,492 (100) | 31,786 (100) |

Note: The table excludes 32 events that named miscellaneous actors not included in the above categories.

one death.[5] Actors are identified more commonly than victims: at least one actor is named in 1,821 cases; two actors are named in 631 of these cases, and three are named in 73. In total, there are 2,525 actors named as perpetrators in events that result in deaths. The first column in table 6.4 tabulates the number of times that each type of actor is mentioned, whether they are the first, second, or third named. The overwhelming majority of actors named, close to three-quarters, are civilian or military authorities. The most common among these are rural leaders in districts (communes) and villages (production brigades). The second most common are village militias, poor peasants' associations, or picket corps formed by village leaders. All these actors are residents of rural communities—but they are at the same time political authorities or their agents. Somewhat less commonly named are Revolutionary Committees—the new governments created in counties and districts during 1968—and security or military actors (the PAD, PLA, or branches of the Public Security Bureau). The only other actor named with any frequency is the Allied Command faction, which is closely associated with local authorities. In other words, almost all the actors named in events that generated deaths were either individuals in positions of power or their village-level agents in military or security networks.

The second column of table 6.4 displays the deaths associated with each of these groups of actors. Because more than one-third of the cases name more than one actor, the tabulations include only the first-named actor in 1,817 events.[6] The results echo the tabulations in the first column, but an even greater percentage of the deaths are associated with actors who are civilian authorities or agents of military or security forces. When combined with the deaths associated with the Allied faction, almost all the deaths recorded in these materials were due to actions taken by local authorities or their allies, primarily in rural settings.

These results are at odds with a portrayal of rural killings as intergroup violence in which residents of rural communities mobilize to massacre their neighbors. We have already found that there was a sizeable minority of counties where there was little factional conflict and almost none in rural communities, and where a large minority of the victims were members of stigmatized "four type" households. Now, however, we find that virtually all the actors named as perpetrators of these killings are either rural leaders, PADs, or villagers mobilized by them as members of militias or poor peasants' associations. The aggregate portrayal of rural killings in these materials contradicts the idea that villagers who were uninvolved in factional conflicts unleashed deadly violence against neighbors in stigmatized political categories in ways that resembled communal violence in other settings. The evidence points overwhelmingly to an organized campaign orchestrated by agents who were associated with networks of state power.

To be sure, the individuals who engaged in the actual killings in villages were very often also members of the same local communities. In some cases, they were complicit in the murder of individuals known to them personally. When described in less detailed accounts published in local annals, these killings could appear to be inexplicably cruel forms of community behavior that spun out of the control of local authorities. The more fine-grained focus afforded by the investigation reports, however, suggests instead that the villagers who carried out the slaughter were in fact members of rural militias commanded by PADs, or members of poor peasants' associations or other groups that acted under the direction of village leaders or recently established Revolutionary Committees at the county and district level. The fact that so many of the killings were carried out by co-villagers obscures the crucial fact that the actions were coordinated through networks mobilized by local authorities. It is hard to account for the massive upsurge of rural killings in the wake of the July 3 Orders without such coordination.

The scale of the killings may well have escalated in ways unanticipated by the authorities in Nanning. But the central question is: whose actions spun out of control? Did local authorities lose control over villagers who harbored latent animosities toward stigmatized "four type" households? The evidence suggests overwhelmingly that village leaders and their militias were very much in control of the entire process. If in fact there was something that escalated out of control, it was the actions of local authorities and villagers in organizations under their direction.

### The Spread of Mass Killings

How widespread were the mass killings that elevated Guangxi's overall death toll, and where and when did they occur? The data extracted from the investigation reports permit confident answers. There were 44,107 deaths linked to events collected in the data set.[7] Of these, 35,894, or 81 percent, were classified as actions of authorities—campaigns organized by local authorities or killings that occurred during their course. Another 6,247, or 14.6 percent of the total, were the product of armed battles between factions. We have already seen that mass killings were a rural phenomenon. A total of 38,800 reported deaths were in counties. Of these, 35,382 were classified as campaigns or local killings—91 percent of the total. In counties, only 1,793 deaths, or 4.6 percent, were the product of factional battles.

The total death toll in counties ranged widely, from 95 to 3,951, with a median of 749 and an average of 965. Thirty counties had more than 1,000 deaths. If we assume that 91 percent of the deaths in each county were the product of actions by authorities and related killings, this results in an estimate of an average of 878 deaths per county, and a median of 681. By this measure, twenty-eight counties had more than 1,000 deaths overall that could be attributed to local mass killings during the entire period.

To track the occurrence of mass killings across counties and over time, we need to establish the number of deaths from these causes in a single county in a single month that constitutes evidence that killings are under way. There is no obvious cutoff point for determining when such killings can be defined as "mass." In his warning to the Allied faction delegation in his final meeting with them in November 1967, Zhou Enlai expressed alarm about the first cases in counties bordering Hunan, where 76 people had been killed recently in one of them. For purposes of illustration, I define 50 or more deaths in a single month that are not the result of factional activity as the cutoff point for designating a county as experiencing mass killings. Because the reported deaths are undercounts, and because it is difficult in many cases to link reported deaths to a single month, a report of 50 deaths is likely to signify substantial killings in a locality.[8] By this definition, mass killings were detected during 98 months in 52 counties. This suggests that 28 counties did not have mass killings. Of the 52 counties that had them, 22 had them only in one month. The remaining 30 counties had them during two to seven months. Evidently, mass killings were distributed across counties as unevenly as factional conflict.

Table 6.5 tracks these incidents over time. The first instances of mass killings in Guangxi were in October 1967, in two counties that bordered Hunan's Dao County. There were another two in November—one of which was in the same border region. Perhaps because of Zhou Enlai's harsh November warning, there were only two additional instances over the next three months. The killings began to spread rapidly in March 1968, the month that coincided with the drive to establish Revolutionary Committees. From this point onward the number of counties experiencing such killings, and the average numbers killed, rise rapidly.

Perhaps the most significant information conveyed by this table is that killings were already well under way by June 1968—in 22 counties that month, taking an average of 198 victims per county. Such killings had already occurred in 23 counties over the previous three months. This reveals that they were already widespread and accelerating before the July 3 Orders, which essentially encouraged the intensification of this trend. The July 3 Orders were a response to wildly inaccurate reports by the Guangxi Military District and Preparatory Committee that emphasized the continuing armed resistance of the April faction and the dangers posed by a fictional province-wide conspiracy by historical class enemies and foreign agents. The actual situation in Guangxi was that rural massacres committed by the lowest rungs of the provincial military networks were spreading rapidly, eliminating any

TABLE 6.5.  Reported Mass Killings, by Month*

| Month | Number of Counties | Average Deaths | Maximum | Minimum |
|---|---|---|---|---|
| October 1967 | 2 | 168 | 260 | 76 |
| November 1967 | 2 | 82 | 95 | 69 |
| December 1967 | 1 | 89 | 89 | 89 |
| January 1968 | 0 | 0 | 0 | 0 |
| February 1968 | 1 | 390 | 390 | 390 |
| March 1968 | 9 | 702 | 2832 | 119 |
| April 1968 | 7 | 229 | 814 | 93 |
| May 1968 | 7 | 136 | 348 | 59 |
| June 1968 | 22 | 198 | 457 | 51 |
| July 1968 | 20 | 273 | 1162 | 55 |
| August 1968 | 19 | 503 | 3689 | 51 |
| September 1968 | 8 | 212 | 703 | 63 |
| October 1968 | 0 | 0 | 0 | 0 |

* Defined as 50 or more reported deaths from other than factional activity in a county in a single month. The table necessarily excludes reports of mass killings that span longer periods.

remnants of the April faction in counties and liquidating other rural residents who were otherwise uninvolved.

## The Timing of Local Killings

We have seen that rural killings were intensified by the July 3 Orders, but they were well under way prior to July. The timing of the killings was related to local political developments, in particular the establishment of Revolutionary Committees that signified an imposed political settlement by PADs, which heavily favored the Allied Command. All but a few of these new county governments (73 out of 80) were established by early May 1968, well before the intensified killings spurred by the July 3 Orders. The last seven were established in August, during that final spasm of violence.

The rural violence was closely associated with the drive to defeat rebel insurgents just before or after a county-level Revolutionary Committee was established, and in subsequent months during efforts to rebuild rural governments. Guangxi's counties were divided into rural "districts" (*qu*) or "towns" (*zhen*). The districts, in turn, were divided into "villages" (*xiang*).[9] The districts and towns were the lowest level in the state's bureaucracy, and each had a local branch of the PAD.[10] District officials were part of the national state's administrative bureaucracy, and they were on the state payroll. During this period, Revolutionary Committees were established at the district and town level after the county's Revolutionary Committee was established.

Below the districts were villages, the lowest level of government administration, but unlike the case in districts, village leaders and militia heads were not considered state cadres, even though they were usually members of the Communist Party and linked to the state through their party branch. They were registered as rural residents, lived in villages, and received grain rations and salaries from village funds. A typical example of the scale of these rural hierarchies is Pingle County, in Guilin Prefecture. At the time it had 1 town (the county seat) and 12 districts, and under the districts were 111 villages, an average of close to 9 villages per district.[11] These villages are administrative constructions, not actual settlements. Administrative villages encompass a range of separate "natural villages" (*ziran cun,* or *ziran tun*), the clusters of settlements where people live. Depending on local topography and population density, the number of natural villages covered by an administrative village can range widely.[12]

The suppression campaigns out of which Revolutionary Committees were established and consolidated were carried out in rural regions by the PADs of districts, which mobilized village militias for the task. After Revolutionary Committees were established in a district, the campaigns were carried out under the direction of newly appointed district heads. With 73 out of 80 county Revolutionary Committees established by early May, the killings in rural regions after that point were almost always carried out by recently formed Revolutionary Committees at the district level, the district PADs, and the village militias.

Figure 6.3 shows the distribution of deaths due to campaigns to consolidate political order in the eighty counties, relative to the month that a county-level Revolutionary Committee was established. Negative numbers indicate calendar months before that month, which is indicated as month zero. Positive numbers indicate calendar months afterward. The figure makes clear that killings did not generally commence on a large scale until the month prior to the establishment of the new county government. There is a large spike in deaths immediately prior to that month, after which the monthly totals abate, to a steady rate at roughly half that level over the next four to five months, as order is imposed in districts and villages. In the fifth month after the establishment of a Revolutionary Committee,

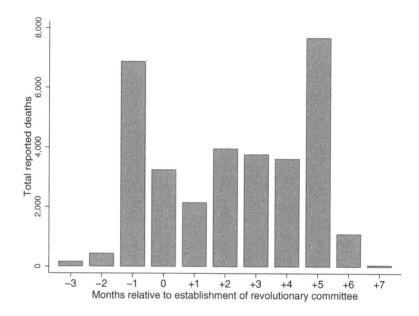

FIGURE 6.3.    Killings in Counties, Months Relative to Local Revolutionary Committee

there is a final large spike, with the highest monthly death tolls overall. This reflects the impact of the July 3 Orders, which intensified ongoing killings in the large number of counties that established Revolutionary Committees in March and April.

The political settlements imposed on the counties left PADs in command of rural governments. The distribution of power at the end of this process reflects the prior militarization of county administration after the collapse of county governments in early 1967.[13] According to a survey of published county-level organizational histories of the Communist Party, only 16 (20 percent) of county first party secretaries in May 1966 survived to head the new Revolutionary Committee; 6 of them had also been the political commissars of the PAD. Only 24 percent of the members of the 1966 Party Committees survived to hold ranking positions on Revolutionary Committees. The Cultural Revolution in Guangxi's counties had a devastating impact on the civilian party leadership.

The new Revolutionary Committees in the counties were dominated by PADs. Almost all of them (88 percent, or 70 out of 80), were headed by the person who was head of the PAD or its political commissar in May 1966. Thirty-seven percent of all the seats on the new Revolutionary Committees were held by officers of the PAD, and these individuals were concentrated in the higher ranking and more powerful posts. The violence waged to consolidate this new order was essentially carried out by the county PAD and its rural militia networks to make permanent the temporary arrangements imposed in early 1967, and which were resisted in so many regions by dissident rebels in the April faction for many months afterward.

## CHAPTER 7

# Narratives

Statistical patterns shed light on important questions, but they abstract from the events that generate the numbers. Narrative accounts contain additional information that cannot be conveyed numerically. There was wide variation in the processes that unfolded among cities and counties that generated the statistical patterns highlighted in previous chapters. We have seen that there were many counties where the April faction was active, while in many others factional conflict was largely absent. We have also seen that there were many counties where most victims of suppression were tied to the April faction, while in others most were from politically stigmatized households.

The counties were where almost all the deaths occurred. Guangxi's eighty counties generated 94 percent of all recorded deaths, but the deaths were concentrated in a relatively small number of counties. More than half of all deaths occurred in only twenty of them. Table 7.1 divides the counties into four groups of twenty ranked by the number of reported deaths. Those with the lowest death counts generated only 6.4 percent of all deaths, and the next highest group only 14.9 percent. These groups together had average death rates of 2.1 per thousand, the average for the rest of China. The forty other counties were very different. They generated almost 80 percent of all deaths and had average death rates more than twice as high.

Large death counts depend heavily on the total population of a county; death *rates* are a more direct measure of the intensity of violence. Table 7.2

TABLE 7.1. Death Tolls and Death Rates in Counties, by Quartile

| Quartile | Total Deaths | Percentage of Total Deaths | Deaths per County | Average Death Rate (per 1,000) | N |
|---|---|---|---|---|---|
| 1 | 4,963 | 6.4 | 248 | 2.0 | 20 |
| 2 | 11,514 | 14.9 | 576 | 2.2 | 20 |
| 3 | 20,882 | 27.1 | 1,044 | 4.9 | 20 |
| 4 | 39,823 | 51.6 | 1,991 | 5.6 | 20 |
| Total | 77,182 | 100 | 965 | 3.6 | 80 |

TABLE 7.2. Guangxi's Deadliest 25 Counties (by death rate)

| County Name | Prefecture | Total Deaths | Death Rate (per 1,000) |
|---|---|---|---|
| Shangsi | Qinzhou | 1,701 | 14.4 |
| Fengshan | Hechi | 1,331 | 13.6 |
| Lingui | Guilin City | 2,051 | 8.0 |
| Binyang | Nanning | 3,951 | 7.8 |
| Bama Yaozu | Hechi | 1,287 | 7.7 |
| Pingle | Guilin | 1,926 | 7.6 |
| Rongan | Liuzhou | 1,416 | 7.4 |
| Shanglin | Nanning | 1,923 | 7.1 |
| Ziyuan | Guilin | 757 | 7.0 |
| Mengshan | Wuzhou | 859 | 6.9 |
| Luocheng | Hechi | 1,389 | 6.9 |
| Tiandeng | Nanning | 1,651 | 6.6 |
| Lingchuan | Guilin | 1,415 | 6.4 |
| Longan | Nanning | 1,363 | 6.1 |
| Wuming | Nanning City | 2,403 | 6.1 |
| Chongzuo | Nanning | 1,029 | 5.6 |
| Yongfu | Guilin | 905 | 5.5 |
| Lingshan | Qinzhou | 3,220 | 5.1 |
| Sanjiang Dongzu | Liuzhou | 954 | 5.0 |
| Lingyun | Bose | 460 | 4.6 |
| Mashan | Nanning | 1,392 | 4.5 |
| Quanzhou | Guilin | 2,156 | 4.4 |
| Liujiang | Liuzhou City | 1,232 | 4.2 |
| Luchuan | Yulin | 1,557 | 4.1 |
| Gui | Yulin | 3,171 | 4.1 |

lists the twenty-five most violent counties in Guangxi, ranked by death rates. As a group, these twenty-five counties generated a total of 39,683 deaths, just over half of the total. Their average death rate of 6.7 per thousand was triple that of the remaining fifty-five counties at 2.2 per thousand. In this chapter I will select narrative accounts from this list, drawing on the investigation reports to describe the varied local processes that made Guangxi the most violent of China's regions.

## Contrasting Extremes: Fengshan and Binyang

Variation in county-level events can be highlighted with a contrast between two counties that were among the most violent, but whose politics were as different as can be imagined. Events in Fengshan County closely resembled the final military suppression of the April faction in Nanning, described in the prologue, much more than the killings of noncombatants that were so widespread in many rural counties. The rebel faction affiliated with the April alliance in Fengshan mobilized a powerful insurgency that defeated militia forces under the PAD, and by early 1968 they dominated the county seat and nearby districts. A coordinated offensive by regular PLA units and militia forces from nearby counties in August 1968 crushed them, with massive casualties. The massacres in Binyang County, briefly described in the prologue, were a total contrast. There was little factional conflict there after the imposition of a Revolutionary Committee in March. Binyang's leaders nonetheless coordinated the most extreme suppression campaign of any jurisdiction in Guangxi, and its overall death count was by far the highest in the province.

### Fengshan County

This county on the western border of Hechi Prefecture had a population that was overwhelmingly Zhuang.[1] Its overall death toll of 1,331 was well above average, but with a population close to 98,000 its death rate of 13.6 per thousand was the second highest in Guangxi, more than triple the provincial average.

Two features of Fengshan's history influenced events in 1968. First, the county had briefly been at the center of Guangxi's only Communist base area.[2] In late 1927 Communist forces in the region established a base on the border between Donglan and Fengshan counties in the name of the Zhuang Peasant Movement. The base later expanded into neighboring Lingyun and Bose counties and dropped its identification with poor Zhuang peasants. The Red 7th Army was established there and grew to 10,000 soldiers before marching east to join Mao Zedong's Jiangxi base area in 1930, leading quickly to the collapse of the Communist movement in the region.[3] This gave Fengshan a large cohort of Red Army veterans, many of whom returned to the county to be incorporated into leadership positions at all levels during the 1950s.[4]

The second relevant feature of Fengshan's history is that it was the site of a stubborn guerrilla insurgency of remnant Nationalist forces that resisted the imposition of the new Communist government established in 1950. At its height, this "Fengshan Anti-Communist Salvation Corps" (*Fengshan fangong jiuguo jun*) had more than 2,000 armed fighters. This local security threat was not eliminated until the end of 1952.[5]

These two features of local history became entangled in May 1968, when the PAD falsely charged that the large rebel insurgency threatening them, led by Red Army veterans, was in fact the reincarnation of the old "Anti-Communist Salvation Corps." This reverberated across Guangxi after the provincial Military District eagerly embraced this characterization and charged that the April 22 faction was fronting for anti-Communist insurgencies throughout Guangxi. This was the core element of the charges that unleashed massacres of April faction activists together with stigmatized "four type" households.[6]

Fengshan's rebel factions formed (as described near the end of chapter 3) over the question of whether two former county leaders should be punished for actions during the Great Leap Forward that created and then exacerbated a local famine. Rebel groups founded by Red Army veterans led the attacks on the two, whose actions had devastated the county, killing close to 10 percent of its population.[7] The county's published annals contain a description of horrific events that occurred only six or seven years before: people eating bark and leaves, fleeing the county to beg, entire families starving to death, rats eating corpses, families selling children for food, and even instances of cannibalism.[8] The charges brought against these former county leaders—who had been promoted to higher office despite their actions—resonated with many rural residents. They also appealed to leaders at all levels who had been punished as "right-wing elements" for resisting the disastrous policies.

Factions formed after the PAD declared that criticism of Mao's disastrous Great Leap Forward was politically reactionary. They banned the groups led by the Red Army veterans, splitting Fengshan's rebel movement, part of which agreed that the recent disasters of radical Maoism were an illegitimate political issue. The Red Army veterans, however, had broad support among rural residents who had suffered and officials who had been punished for resisting policies that had led to so many deaths. The rebels who sided with the PAD affiliated with the Allied Command, and those who opposed the PAD's ban formed a faction that affiliated with April 22.[9]

The dissident rebel campaign gained momentum in January 1968 when rebels seized arms from the PAD in the county seat, took the PAD commander hostage, and raided the Allied Command headquarters. From that point on they controlled the county seat and sent delegations into rural districts to persuade the commanders of village militias to join their side. The command structure of the PAD, which remained intact in other counties, began to disintegrate, and by March the insurgents clearly had the upper hand. Expelled from the county seat and losing the support of village militias, Allied Command activists sent delegations to Nanning to appeal for help from the provincial Military District. Allied Command fighters fled the county and sought help from PAD-backed allies in neighboring counties. In mid-April the Military District sent a detachment of PLA troops to the county in an unsuccessful attempt to broker a cease-fire. April faction forces elsewhere in Guangxi sent arms and supplies to reinforce their Fengshan allies.[10]

In early June the insurgents seized food stocks and other supplies in preparation for the coming battles. In mid-June their campaign reached its high point: they attacked the PAD headquarters, carting off arms, ammunition, military uniforms, and government documents, while killing one PAD officer. Shortly afterward they invaded a PLA arms depot, and on June 23 they attacked a local base where troops from PLA Regiment 6911 were stationed, seizing arms and supplies. A PLA convoy bringing military supplies into the county was ambushed and looted. Several soldiers were killed and many more were beaten. When a PLA officer attempted to negotiate the return of the seized arms in the county seat on July 3, shooting broke out, with dead and wounded on both sides. The troops counter-attacked, driving the insurgents out of the county seat. They retreated to two mountain districts, setting up new bases of operation. These happened to be the same locations where the remnant Nationalist forces had launched their "Anti-Communist Salvation Corps" in 1950.[11]

After the issuance of Beijing's July 3 Orders, preparations began for a final military assault on the insurgents' mountain strongholds. On July 30 a combined force of PLA troops and militias from three neighboring counties launched the first major assault on one of the insurgent bases. By August 10 they were able to capture or kill all the insurgents. Hechi Prefecture's Military Subdistrict then assembled an even larger force of troops from PLA Unit 6911 and more than 3,000 militia fighters from nine different counties for the final campaign against the remaining mountain base. After eight days of combat, they killed or captured almost all the insurgents.[12]

During the offensive, 438 insurgents were killed, but a major suppression campaign against April faction sympathizers followed. Mass killings spread across the villages, targeting those associated with the insurgency. The killings continued for more than a month: 543 people were killed after the Revolutionary Committee was established on August 25, according to an "incomplete" count. Of the 1,331 confirmed deaths related to Fengshan's factional conflicts, 76 percent occurred from July to October, all of them associated with the final suppression of insurgents. Many of the dead had been closely associated with the local party establishment, a fact that indicates the way the factional divisions had split the county's power structure. The dead, almost all on the side of the April-affiliated faction, included 246 cadres, 20 Red Army veterans, and 129 former guerrilla partisans.[13]

## Binyang County

There was no such insurgency in Binyang, which was firmly under the control of military authorities throughout 1968. Located in Nanning Prefecture, near the geographic center of Guangxi, Binyang's county seat was fifty miles from downtown Nanning. Binyang's population was predominantly Han, with an ethnic minority population of 18 percent, almost all Zhuang.[14] It had a significant Hakka population, which numbered just under 20 percent of the county's total. Binyang's death toll of 3,951 was easily the largest of any county or city, almost all of it generated in an astonishingly intense two-week period. The county's death rate of 7.8 per thousand was the fourth highest in Guangxi, more than double the provincial average. Despite the lack of serious factional violence in the preceding months, the July 3 Orders were carried out with an intensity that was rarely matched elsewhere.

Binyang had unusual strategic significance: the province's sole north-south railway line split into two branches at the town of Litang, with one of the branches heading southwest toward the Vietnam border. This was the key railway junction whose blockage so frustrated Zhou Enlai during his meetings with faction leaders in Beijing during 1967. Despite the occasional stoppages at the railway junction and activity by both the Allied Command and April factions, there was little violent conflict in the county during 1967 and into early 1968.

Perhaps because of Litang's strategic importance, Binyang's Revolutionary Committee was established early, under the firm hand of regular PLA troops rather than the local PAD. The head of the Revolutionary Committee established in March 1968 was the deputy commander of PLA Unit 6949, and the Standing Committee was dominated by military figures: the PAD head, its political commissar, and another PAD deputy head, along with the PLA unit's political director.[15] With little apparent difficulty, the military officers forged an agreement between the county's two rebel factions. The investigation reports give the impression that the authorities were firmly in command. In May the military authorities set up investigation teams to conduct a purge of more than 300 county cadres and others, a campaign marred by abusive struggle sessions, beatings, coercive interrogations, and suicides.[16] Three months after the Revolutionary Committee was created, there was a small upsurge of conflict between local factions, likely under the influence of the battles in nearby Nanning. The first rash of violent deaths in the county occurred only in June 1968, when 39 factional activists died in a series of isolated incidents.[17]

None of this was enough to account for the draconian suppression campaign unleashed in the county. The impetus appears to have been a reaction to events in Nanning rather than to events in Binyang. The final battle to crush the April faction holdouts in the nearby capital began on July 16, and the battle was still escalating five days later when Binyang's Revolutionary Committee convened an urgent telephone conference of leaders at all levels of government to implement the July 3 Orders. During that call, the PAD's political commissar, now deputy head of the Revolutionary Committee, harangued his subordinates to push the campaign, saying: "We must bravely stand at the forefront of the movement and fiercely attack the class enemies! Resolutely struggle against the unrepentant and incorrigible ones, resolutely dispose of them, dictatorship is mass dictatorship, if the masses see someone as bad, they must be firmly struck down!" The county's leaders formed a committee to run the campaign. At one meeting with district security workers and heads of police stations, PLA officers on the county Revolutionary Committee gave speeches, during which they emphasized that there should be no effort to hold back on deadly violence: "Dictatorship is mass dictatorship, don't pour cold water on it"; "Bad people must be dealt with, it doesn't matter if a bunch of them are killed, trust the masses."[18]

The day after this meeting, the head of the Revolutionary Committee in Xinbin town ordered all "four type elements" to assemble, and they were paraded through the streets with placards identifying them as such. During the procession, organized by the town's PAD head, 14 of the individuals were beaten to death—the county's first such incident. PAD officers in town that day for political instruction were sent to observe. The next day one of them, a militia battalion commander in a nearby commune, ordered the company commanders of the village militia to assemble all the commune's "four types" at the county seat the next day. He led a militia company to escort them to a mountain ridge late that night and had the 24 prisoners line up in rows, where they were executed by firing squad, some having to be shot a second time.[19]

The wave of killings soon expanded beyond "four types" to include a much larger set of people with political problems, known as "23 types."[20] On July 28 the county's PAD head called on all individuals in this category to be sent as prisoners to the county seat. He then had "the masses" beat them to death with wooden clubs, 90 victims in all. Several of the victims were doctors and administrators in the county hospital.[21] The next day, the PLA officer who headed the county Revolutionary Committee called a meeting of all militia and security personnel and gave a detailed report on the late-night executions of "four types" in Xinbin town. He praised the killings but argued that they lacked "educational value." He is quoted as having said:

> In the first phase of the campaign, it's no problem that activists shoot a few in the beginning, but we should guide people to use their fists, stones, and wooden clubs. Only this will educate the masses, its educational value is greater. Binyang has more than 4,000 four type elements. You've tried to remold them for more than a decade now; I don't think even one of them has really remolded their thinking. The masses have spent all kinds of effort supervising them. Wouldn't it be better to expend all this effort increasing production? Turning these people over to mass dictatorship, we can handle this problem in only 3 days, without wasting a single bullet . . . this campaign must crush to death around one third or one fourth of these enemies.[22]

The Revolutionary Committee reprimanded district PAD commanders who were slow in carrying out similar killings. At a meeting convened by the county on July 29, districts that were slow in completing this task were ordered to "unleash the masses, expose the enemies, then unfold the struggle, and those who deserve to die should be turned over to the masses to deal with them. Militia battalion commanders should take the lead." After attending that morning's meeting, the party branch secretary of one of the communes convened a group of village leaders to draw up lists of "four type elements," and the next day convened another meeting to call for an expanded roundup of "23 types." The enlarged list of 30 was assembled at the commune seat, tied up in pairs, and escorted to a coal mine shaft at the edge of the village. All 30 were thrown into the pit, which was then filled with water, drowning them.[23]

A common theme emerges from the many atrocities described in the accounts for Binyang: rural leaders return from mobilization meetings at higher levels, they draw up lists of suspects, and have the victims killed by members of village militias. In two separate communes in two different districts on July 31 and August 1, commune militia battalions, returning from the same county-level mobilization meeting, quickly draw up lists of enemies, organize mass rallies to denounce them, and send them off with village militias to be killed. In one commune, 24 are killed, in the other 33, all in large batches. The reports name the militia members who did the killings, and they describe how they did the work with knives, stones, and wooden clubs.

In a third district, the Revolutionary Committee head visited a commune and criticized its leaders for lagging in the campaign. The next afternoon, the commune head ordered each section to assemble all "four type elements" at the commune headquarters. One section sent 20, all of whom were beaten to death; another sent 32, and after some discussion it was decided to kill only 24 of them (some women were spared). They were turned over to the village militia, who clubbed or shot them to death. Some village leaders were reluctant, and they were pressured to comply. The head of the county Revolutionary Committee telephoned one district head to criticize him for falling behind. In response, the district head relayed the criticism to all villages, and ordered their leaders, if they were "too timid," to turn over all "four type elements" to the district for execution. He sent armed "picket corps" to take 34 "four types" out of four reluctant villages, and had all of them shot to death at a single location.[24]

The wave of killings in Binyang was highly organized and implemented in a crash campaign by county authorities. Over an eleven-day period (July 26 to August 6), 3,681 were killed or committed suicide to avoid a more painful death. The vast majority were rural residents who were ordinary farmers. The described methods of execution included shooting, stabbing, hanging, strangulation, stoning, beating with clubs, drowning, and even burying victims alive. A summary statement in the investigation report stated that the killing of male household heads destroyed 170 households, their members scattered elsewhere; 14 households were exterminated entirely, and targeted families usually had their homes looted.[25]

Binyang's Revolutionary Committee mobilized its security apparatus to exterminate individuals in stigmatized categories with near-industrial efficiency. The bloodbath far surpassed the campaigns against class enemies and political opponents when the new regime was consolidated in the early 1950s. From 1950 to 1953, just over 3,100 individuals were designated as enemies, 254 of whom were executed after public trials. The rest were subjected to various forms of detention and reeducation, and then released to their native villages with stigmatizing labels that subjected them to continual scrutiny by security forces and various forms of discrimination.[26] The eleven-day reign of terror in 1968 reached a level of intensity never attained in the county when the new regime was being consolidated. The death toll was more than double that of the provincial capital of Nanning, and almost four times larger than the provincial average. Just over 55 percent were members of "four type" households, which means that even in a locality without a thriving April faction, many of their former members and sympathizers were included in the expanded "23 types."[27]

## The Guilin Region

The Guilin region included the relatively compact city of Guilin, two large suburban counties under city jurisdiction, and ten counties in the surrounding Guilin Prefecture, which wraps around the city boundaries on three sides (see map 7.1). Average death rates in the Guilin region (4.6 per thousand) were the second highest in Guangxi, slightly lower than those in Qinzhou Prefecture. Six counties in the region are among the twenty-five most violent, listed in table 7.2. Table 7.3 indicates that violence there was concentrated in six counties whose death rates were well above the provincial average of 3.6 per thousand. Three of them had extremely

MAP 7.1. The Guilin Region

TABLE 7.3. Death Rates in the Guilin Region

| Jurisdiction | Death Rate (per thousand) | Total Deaths | Percent Han Chinese | Hakka Population (percent)* |
|---|---|---|---|---|
| Lingui County | 8.0 | 2,051 | 93.0 | 2.7 |
| Pingle County | 7.6 | 1,926 | 95.0 | 3.9 |
| Ziyuan County | 7.0 | 757 | 80.0 | 0 |
| Lingchuan County | 6.4 | 1,415 | 95.2 | 0 |
| Yongfu County | 5.5 | 905 | 91.9 | 1.2 |
| Quanzhou County | 4.4 | 2,156 | 95.6 | 0 |
| Guilin | 4.2 | 1,038 | 87.4 | .3 |
| Xing'an County | 3.8 | 869 | 89.8 | 0 |
| Yangshuo County | 3.5 | 639 | 88.8 | 3.7 |
| Lipu County | 3.1 | 755 | 86.0 | 8.7 |
| Longsheng Autonomous County | 2.5 | 281 | 24.9 | 0 |
| Gongcheng Autonomous County | 2.3 | 404 | 68.7 | 2.4 |
| Guanyang County | 1.7 | 304 | 93.9 | 1.2 |

* Source: http://www.360doc.com/content/11/0109/17/164198_85241080.shtml; accessed January 11, 2021.

high death rates that ranged from 7 to 8 per thousand. At the opposite end were four counties that were well below average. Two of them were the only counties with large ethnic minority populations, and one other was the only one with a significant Hakka population (Lipu).[28] The county with by far the lowest death rate, Guanyang, was one of the two harshly criticized by Zhou Enlai for orchestrating the first mass killings in the province in November 1967 meetings with faction leaders in Beijing (described near the end of chapter 4).[29]

Guilin was the stronghold of the April 22 faction, which had the support of main force PLA Unit 6955 stationed in the city. The April faction was present in all the counties. Table 7.4, which also ranks jurisdictions by death rates, displays two indicators of April faction activity: the number of reported armed battles between factions, and the number of mentions of the April faction in connection with events described in the investigation reports. The city of Guilin, as the longtime stronghold of the April faction and the site of the epic final battles, was the location of the vast majority of recorded April faction activity. Even though there were no April faction insurgencies in these counties approaching the scale of the one in Fengshan, all of them reported activity by the faction. There were armed battles in all the counties, regardless of their distance from the city. The counties with the highest death rates reported much higher levels of April faction activity than those in the bottom half of the table. The April faction was very active in counties like Lingui and Lingchuan, which were Guilin suburbs, but it was also active in counties like Pingle and Ziyuan, which were distant.

One way in which counties were drawn into Guilin's factional battles was the involvement of their rural militias in the urban warfare that began in June 1968. All twelve counties in the region sent militia forces to Guilin, a total of more than 8,000 fighters. Some sent well over 1,000, but no county sent fewer than 300 (table 7.4). The severity of the fighting in the region delayed the formation of five local revolutionary Committees until late August. The only other county in Guangxi where a Revolutionary Committee was established this late was Fengshan (August 26), where a major military offensive was needed to quell the April faction insurgency.

The involvement of rural militias in the prolonged urban battles intensified campaigns back in the counties against members and sympathizers of the April faction and their alleged co-conspirators among the "four type elements." Militia battalions that returned from these battles with their dead and wounded were prone to vengeful killing sprees. The identities of those killed reflect the prevalence

TABLE 7.4.  Political Activity in the Guilin Region

| Jurisdiction | Death Rate (per thousand) | Armed Battles# | April Faction Activity† | Militia Forces Sent to Guilin* | Miles to Guilin (by road) | Revolutionary Committee Date |
|---|---|---|---|---|---|---|
| Lingui County | 8.0 | 7 | 23 | 380 | 8 | August 26 |
| Pingle County | 7.6 | 5 | 22 | 450 | 61 | April 23 |
| Ziyuan County | 7.0 | 4 | 6 | 340 | 67 | August 26 |
| Lingchuan County | 6.4 | 3 | 14 | 1,000 | 13 | August 24 |
| Yongfu County | 5.5 | 7 | 17 | 430 | 33 | August 20 |
| Quanzhou County | 4.4 | 3 | 17 | 1,000 | 77 | May 8 |
| Guilin | 4.2 | 38 | 76 | n.a. | 0 | April 14 |
| Xing'an County | 3.8 | 2 | 2 | 1,470 | 43 | April 15 |
| Yangshuo County | 3.5 | 2 | 4 | 820 | 45 | March 27 |
| Lipu County | 3.1 | 4 | 11 | 660 | 70 | August 27 |
| Longsheng Autonomous County | 2.5 | 2 | 4 | 350 | 56 | March 27 |
| Gongcheng Autonomous County | 2.3 | 1 | 5 | 400 | 71 | April 9 |
| Guanyang County | 1.7 | 1 | 2 | 310 | 92 | April 18 |

# Defined as an armed battle in which the April faction is a participant.
† Defined as event in which the April faction is named as an actor or harmed party.
* Source: Guangxi Party Committee (1987, 3:649–50).

of the April faction across the region and the mixed character of the suppression campaigns. The profiles of the dead recall both the targeting of active supporters of the April faction so prevalent in Fengshan County and the coordinated liquidation of "four type elements" in Binyang. Six of the counties in the region provided statistical breakdowns of the identity of those killed. "Four type elements" were prominent among the dead, but no more than a large minority in three counties with high death rates: Yongfu (36 percent), Lingchuan (39 percent), and Lingui (46 percent). In three counties with lower death rates, and where the April faction had a more limited presence, the "four types" were a slim majority: Xing'an (60 percent), Gongcheng (55 percent), and Guanyang (53 percent).[30]

Guilin's battles were spurred by the early formation of Revolutionary Committees in Guilin City and Guilin Prefecture in April 1968—events intended to mark the cessation of factional conflicts. PLA Unit 6955 had long supported the April faction rebels that seized power back in January 1967, and Allied Command rebels had been driven out of the city in the summer of 1967, returning to the city in significant numbers only after the November 1967 agreement orchestrated in Beijing. The Allied Command had the support of air force and several other PLA units in the region, along with the local units under the Guilin Military Subdistrict and the PAD.

These military units greatly aided the revival of the Allied Command forces in Guilin in early 1968. They, and not PLA Unit 6955, were put in charge of forming the Guilin Revolutionary Committee. This support was reflected in a committee whose membership heavily favored the Allied Command. Top officers from PLA Unit 6955, which had long protected the April faction, were denied seats, along with prominent leaders of the April faction and former city officials who supported them. The faction's leaders angrily protested the arrangements, and some of the largest rebel groups in its coalition boycotted the mass rally held to celebrate the Revolutionary Committee. Others attended the rally and disrupted it, and they were arrested and imprisoned after arguing heatedly with the head of the Military Subdistrict. Their supporters protested at the Military District Headquarters, fought with guards there, and were arrested in turn. Their supporters staged a large sit-in, which was harassed by supporters of the Allied faction.

The Allied Command, for obvious reasons, wholeheartedly supported the new Revolutionary Committee, denounced their opponents for sabotaging it, and initiated street clashes. Instead of quelling local disorders, the laboriously arranged truce between the two sides immediately fell apart, and large-scale hostilities, long suppressed by the earlier dominance of the April faction, broke out for the first time.[31]

During May, both sides staged large raids on arms depots, with the April faction seizing the lion's share of weaponry and ammunition. The Allied Command, drawing on its support from the PADs of the city and the surrounding twelve counties, mobilized a military operation to retake the city and wipe out the April faction. More than 120 PAD officers oversaw the preparations. Their offensive began in late June, after the militia raided a large arms depot in Xing'an County in order to match the April faction's superior weaponry. Their forces then surrounded the city and began their final offensive.[32] The high death rates in the surrounding counties were generated during this final period, during which the region's once-strong April faction was decisively defeated. The two counties with the highest death rates, Lingui and Pingle, reflect the mixed character of the rural suppression campaigns.

*Lingui County*

Only a short distance from the city center, this suburban county had an active April faction. The group's high point in the county was reached in August 1967. A series of arms seizures yielded a cache of military weaponry that led to the retreat of the Allied faction from the county seat, from which they mobilized militias from rural communes to fight their way back. Shortly afterward Zhou Enlai, in the Beijing negotiations, referred to the April 22 faction as "revolutionary" and the Allied faction as a mere "mass organization." This caused several PLA units to back away from their support of the Allied Command. The head of Lingui's PAD issued a public self-criticism for favoring the wrong side and for mobilizing rural militia against April faction strongholds in the county seat. Emboldened, the April faction declared a power seizure over Lingui, ostensibly pushing the PAD aside and organizing a series of public denunciation meetings against PAD officers.[33]

This victory was short-lived, because the mid-November agreement concluded in Beijing permitted the Allied faction to participate in the formation of a county Revolutionary Committee on an equal footing. At the same time, it put a presumably repentant PAD in charge of forming a new local government. Communes in the county sent delegations of "poor and lower middle peasants" to the county seat to reinforce the Allied faction and establish bases of operation. Sporadic minor clashes between the April faction and rural militias continued into early 1968.[34]

The turning point came in March 1968, when the PAD negotiated an agreement between the two sides to unite and form a Revolutionary Committee. These committees were formed in quick succession in each of the communes during the month of April. Not surprisingly, all of them were dominated by district PAD officers and leaders of the Allied Command. The April faction loudly protested and sent a delegation to Nanning to report that they were being suppressed under cover of a "great alliance." Their adamant opposition prevented the final step, the formation of a county Revolutionary Committee, which was delayed until August.[35]

The Allied Command, for their part, became enthusiastic supporters of the drive to create a Revolutionary Committee, pushing them into an even closer alliance with the PAD. They and the PAD charged that the April faction was sabotaging a process sanctioned by Beijing and approved by Mao Zedong. They echoed the false charges that were being made by the provincial Military District that the resistance was part of a plot by class enemies to overthrow Communist Party power.

At a mobilization meeting near the end of May, the county PAD unleashed a suppression campaign described as "a force 12 typhoon" that would blow away any remaining resistance, focusing on the April faction along with "four type elements" and their offspring, who allegedly were the April group's allies. According to the investigation report, "after the meeting, all of the communes established 'headquarters to defend the Revolutionary Committee' and organized 'militia' to enter communes and production brigades and unleash a force 12 typhoon and unceasingly force such accusations as 'Anti-Communist Salvation Corps,' 'assassination teams,' and so forth on innocent masses, cadres, and students, turning them into class enemies."[36]

The killings were concentrated in a brief period and were spread widely. There were killings in all but 2 of the 161 administrative villages. Prior to this campaign, factional conflicts had generated very few deaths—only 5 people were killed prior to June 1968. Over the next four months, 1,783 were killed, and close to 250 more committed suicide to avoid being subjected to torture, beating to death with clubs, stabbing, stoning, being buried alive, or being tied up in a burlap bag and thrown into the Li River.[37] The campaign swept up large numbers from "four type" households along with the many April faction activists in the county. Close to half of the 2,051 who died were associated with the "four types" (558 "four type elements" and 387 of their sons and daughters).[38]

As in Binyang, the killings in rural districts were carried out by the militias. In one typical example, of a kind repeated constantly in the detailed reports, on July 23 the head of Dutou Commune's Revolutionary Committee convened a meeting of commune and brigade leaders and reported that three days earlier in nearby Liangjiang Commune, 41 people were executed by militia immediately after their crimes were exposed at a mass rally. He ordered each of the production brigades to report on April faction activists and "four type elements" and their sons and daughters. Based on these reports a list of those to be liquidated was drawn up, and the next day 20 people were executed: 5 were beaten to death at a mass rally, and the other 15 were taken by truck to another location and shot by militia.[39] The campaign also liquidated 267 people who worked in county administrative offices and the agencies and workplaces under them in the county seat. The killings were carried out by a "picket corps" (*jiucha dui*) formed under the direction of the PAD, a death squad that was responsible for carrying out executions of the campaign's targets.[40] The report on the campaign observed that "it is not hard to see that the killings of 1968 were massacres carried out in a planned, organized, and top-down manner."[41]

*Pingle County*

Like Lingui, Pingle had a very active April faction, despite its location on the southern border of the prefecture, more than sixty miles distant from Guilin (see table 7.4). Arms seizures and small-scale battles between the PAD-backed Allied Command and their April faction opponents persisted during the last half of 1967, generating 16 deaths. In October one district in the county mobilized its security forces to summarily execute 12 individuals in "four type" households, a foretaste of things to come. Near the end of December, after the conclusion of the negotiated agreements in Beijing, the PAD orchestrated a meeting in which the leaders of the two rebel factions agreed to a "great alliance," preliminary to the formation of a Revolutionary Committee. After the mass rally to celebrate the presumed conclusion of hostilities, each faction staged a parade in the county seat to signal their approval. When the two processions converged at the town's department store, a fistfight broke out, signaling trouble to come. Several days later the PAD nonetheless held a mass rally attended by 4,000 members of the two factions to celebrate the fragile agreement.[42]

Negotiations continued between the two sides, presided over by the PAD, resulting in March in a formal agreement to finally end the hostilities. After the Revolutionary Committee was formed the next month, however, the April faction vehemently protested that it was tilted strongly against their side and was dominated by the Allied Command and its PAD supporters. Claiming that the new government was a thinly disguised suppression of their faction, the April faction refused to recognize it and vowed to resist.[43]

Brushing these objections aside, the PAD forged ahead to consolidate their power. They launched a suppression campaign reputedly aimed at uncovering the spies and counter-revolutionaries that were opposed to the new order. For its part, the Allied Command supported the campaign and organized combat teams to "defend Red power." With the approval of the PAD, they mobilized fighters to attack April faction strongholds in the county seat and sent small squads to Guilin to support the retaking of the city from the April faction. In June their forces in Guilin sent urgent requests for reinforcements, reporting that the battle was not going well and was at a crisis point. The PAD and Allied Command held large rallies to whip up support for the battle in Guilin, and they began to send truckloads of fighters to join in the battle.

As this urgent mobilization proceeded, the Allied Command set up a detention center and ordered its armed followers in rural districts to round up the "21 types," defined as various kinds of historical enemies of the regime along with their alleged sympathizers in the April faction.[44] More than 300 suspects were incarcerated in the detention center and subjected to vicious beatings and various forms of torture. No fewer than 40 people were killed in short order. Near the end of June, the Revolutionary Committee ordered a broader campaign that targeted the same alleged conspirators.[45] From this point forward the April faction was essentially defeated in Pingle, appearing in descriptions of events only as victims of suppression.

Although violent suppression of the April faction and their alleged co-conspirators was already under way, the July 3 Orders removed any remaining constraints on official violence. In early July, as the fighting in Guilin intensified, the local authorities mobilized larger groups of fighters to help in the battle, and soon sent more than 400 members of village militias, along with uncounted numbers of fighters from the Allied Command. In a July 12 battle in Guilin, Pingle County's Allied Command and militia fighters suffered 12 deaths, with another 18 severely wounded. Hearing of the casualties, militia members in Pingle vented their rage by invading the Allied Command's detention center, beating to death several April faction leaders and "four type elements" incarcerated there. Later that same day, another group dragged 12 individuals out of the detention center and shot them to death at the county high school. When the corpses of the fighters killed in Guilin were returned to Pingle, several memorial meetings were held. The commemorations included public executions of individuals in the enemy camp. On July 15, 4 people were shot to death as part of a memorial meeting; on July 23, 3 more were executed, and at the largest one on August 14, 16 were shot as part of the commemoration.[46]

As the Revolutionary Committee mobilized to implement the July 3 Orders, it began a campaign ostensibly aimed at stamping out "counter-revolution." The campaign discovered 98 alleged underground counter-revolutionary organizations over the next two months, resulting in the deaths of 1,298 individuals in rural districts who were identified by local authorities and executed by local militias.[47] During this campaign the Allied Command apparently was given free rein by the authorities. On August 5 one of their combat teams targeted a village where April faction supporters were concentrated. They surrounded the village, summarily executing a handful of people while taking 75 others into custody, all the known April faction supporters. Over the next three days, 16 of them were executed.[48] After the final defeat of the April faction in Guilin, the roundup of their allies in Pingle intensified. The Allied faction increased the number of prisoners in their detention center and during a ten-day period after August 24 executed 65 of the prisoners in small batches.[49]

As the victorious militia returned from Guilin, the authorities turned to remnants of the April faction, who were fleeing to mountainous districts. The county's leaders noted that villagers were often sympathetic to those who fled, so they could not rely on the Allied Command to finish the job. The PAD launched a campaign to "suppress bandits" (*jiao fei*), employing a term used in the suppression of counter-revolutionaries in the early 1950s. More than 700 militia fighters were sent to mountain districts where remnants of the April faction had fled. During one mid-September operation 21 were killed, and another 76 "bandits" were later executed. At the end of September new members were appointed to replace the six April faction leaders who were initially named to the Revolutionary Committee when it was formed five months before. This was necessary because all six had been killed.[50] What was intended as a "great alliance" between the two rebel factions became a new power structure composed exclusively of the PAD and the Allied Command.

## Shangsi County

Shangsi County, located on the western edge of Qinzhou Prefecture, had the highest death rate of any county in Guangxi (14.4 per thousand), one of only two (along with Fengshan) where more than 1 percent of the population was killed. Qinzhou Prefecture was a collection of six counties and one city (Beihai) with a shoreline on the Gulf of Tonkin. The region was historically part of Guangdong Province, except for Shangsi, which was carved off to join the new prefecture when it was

transferred to Guangxi in 1965. Qinzhou had the highest death rate of any prefecture, 4.9 per thousand. One other county in the prefecture, Lingshan, had the
second-highest overall death total (3,220), after Binyang (see table 7.2). Shangsi was
overwhelmingly Zhuang, with only 8.6 percent of its population classified as Han.

The issue that initially split Shangsi's rebels in early 1967 was the recently
concluded Socialist Education Campaign, which had removed many county and
commune leaders from their positions for various alleged infractions in 1965 and
early 1966. Near the end of December 1966, more than 1,000 cadres, Red Guards,
and other individuals held a rally to declare the formation of an alliance known
as the "Rebel Brigade." The group was united by their objection to the outcome of
the recent campaign, which they said reflected the "bourgeois reactionary line" of
the county's leaders. It included victims of that campaign along with rank-and-file
cadres compelled to carry it out, and who now repudiated it.[51]

A wave of power seizures over party and government offices swept across the
county from late January 1967 and into February. Seeing that the county administration was paralyzed, with no rebel alliance stepping forward to seize overall
power, on February 7 the PAD stepped in to take over the county administration.
Two days later they formed a coalition of rebels known as the "Great Alliance Committee," designating them as the genuine rebel faction. At the founding rally one
of the PAD officers gave a speech and condemned the Rebel Brigade as a "typical
counter-revolutionary organization" because it was trying to overturn the results of
the Socialist Education Campaign. Because that campaign targeted allegedly anti-
socialist and reactionary elements inside the leadership and among the masses,
he reasoned that any effort to overturn the results was anti-party and by definition
counter-revolutionary. Not coincidentally, the PAD had been heavily involved in
directing that campaign. This became the wedge that split Shangsi's rebels, an extreme charge against a large rebel group that made it impossible for them to back
down. Several months later the Rebel Brigade changed its name and aligned with
April 22, while the Great Alliance Committee, supported by the PAD, aligned with
the Allied Command.[52]

The PAD adopted a harsh stance toward the Rebel Brigade and vowed to suppress it. The rebels in the Alliance Committee waged a propaganda campaign that
denounced their rivals as counter-revolutionary. The Rebel Brigade repudiated the
charge as false and slanderous, and demanded that it be withdrawn. Instead, the

PAD attacked, and in late March they vowed to "protect the Cultural Revolution" and launched a series of public denunciation rallies, or "struggle sessions," against 90 "four type elements" and cadres who had lost their positions in the Socialist Education Campaign. The PAD never backed away from its stance, but Beijing's April 1967 prohibition against arrests of rebels and the use of force against them permitted the dissident rebel movement to survive. Wall poster debates continued, and more than 100 April faction activists staged a sit-in protest at the county PAD headquarters in mid-October, demanding that the charges be reversed. There were no violent clashes reported in the county during 1967, and no deaths. Instead, the split in the rebel movement and the antagonism between the April faction and the PAD simply festered as the negotiations in Beijing dragged on.[53]

The county was relatively quiet after the end of the Beijing negotiations, but after the breakdown of the Preparatory Committee in Nanning, the Shangsi PAD encouraged preemptive killings of "four type elements" and others. At a February conference of county leaders down to the village level, the PAD head gave a speech in which he stated that in the past the "dictatorship over enemies" was carried out by the security agencies and court system, but "now we will carry out mass dictatorship." He continued, "All four type elements are criminals, the masses hate them; if they want to kill them, so be it." One of the commune PAD heads agreed, saying that "four type elements, dregs and leftover evils of the Nationalist regime, are all criminals, kill them."[54]

To launch the effort, in early March the PAD appointed one of their officers to set up a unit to carry out killings. Headed by a production brigade head and the commander of a militia battalion, it was directed by the PAD. Its mission was to kill individuals on death lists. The county ordered all communes to set up a leading group for the campaign, an office for directing targeted killings, and to assign a special company of village militia to carry out the task. Later that month the PAD held a meeting of 143 militia company commanders along with security chiefs from each of the villages, pushing them to liquidate class enemies.[55]

The first wave of killings spread across the county in April 1968. One commune executed 29 "four type elements." In another, 19 people were assembled in one place and mowed down with a machine gun. In a third, 76 were shot, clubbed, or stoned to death; their corpses were mutilated, with genitals and livers carved out. The killings continued through the end of May, by which point a total of 697 had been killed. As the carnage was under way, the county's Revolutionary Committee was established on April 13.[56]

Near the end of May an attempt to disarm an individual in the April faction in one village led to the shooting death of a militia commander. The Revolutionary Committee responded by directing village militias to be on guard against "bandits," and they reported the isolated shooting incident to their superiors at the prefecture as "bandit activity." Shortly after Beijing's July 3 Orders, Qinzhou Prefecture, relying on this report, informed provincial authorities that Shangsi harbored "local bandits." The province responded by issuing a document stating that Shangsi was plagued by bandit activity, in which deceived masses were incited by evil people to go up into the hills, and among them were "four type elements." This report meant that the county authorities were now trapped by their false rhetoric about the isolated shooting. The investigation report noted somewhat sardonically: "the county PAD not only couldn't take back its earlier report, but now they were obligated to submit even more reports about so-called 'bandit activities.'"[57]

The prefecture authorities, alarmed by reports of bandits, mandated a large sweep of the county's hills and valleys by more than 1,000 militia members. Not surprisingly, the manhunt failed to find even a single "bandit." Instead of admitting that there were none, thus revealing that their initial report was false or that their security sweep had failed, the county authorities charged that there was a widespread conspiracy in the county to *hide* the bandits. They launched a new campaign against those who allegedly were providing nonexistent bandits with support and safe passage, or who secretly sympathized with them. This turned renewed suspicion onto members and sympathizers of the April faction, along with the unfortunate "four types," and led to yet another wave of mass killings. By the time the campaign ended in September, another 973 innocent people had been killed in the search for supporters of nonexistent bandits. In one village, 68 people were killed, almost 5 percent of the entire population.[58]

The local authorities' deadly efforts to justify their earlier false reports are reminiscent of the bureaucratic origins of the Great Leap famine several years before. We have already seen that false reports about grain output submitted in Fengshan County compelled local authorities, unable to sell corresponding grain shipments to the state, to claim that peasants were "hiding grain." Their coercive campaign against nonexistent grain hoarding exacerbated the death toll of the resulting famine. A hauntingly similar process was at work in Shangsi. Had the authorities reported the late May shooting simply as an isolated incident involving one April faction activist, Shangsi's death toll likely would have been unexceptional.

### Lingyun County: An Outlier in Bose Prefecture

Bose was at the opposite end of the spectrum from Guilin and Qinzhou Prefectures. Its twelve counties had the lowest average death rate (2.0 per thousand) of any prefecture, slightly below the average for the rest of China. Eleven of its counties had death rates that ranged from 1.2 to 2.9 per thousand. Lingyun, with a death rate of 4.6 per thousand, was a striking exception. Bose Prefecture's population was overwhelmingly Zhuang, with an average of only 16 percent Han Chinese. Lingyun County had by far the largest Han population, at 46 percent.[59]

The investigation reports for Lingyun focus on the actions of Wang Detang, the political commissar of the county's PAD, who played a key role in the county's power seizure, placing himself in charge and emerging as head of its Revolutionary Committee in March 1968. As we have seen in the cases of Shangsi and Binyang counties, the proclivities of the head of a Revolutionary Committee could set the tone for local suppression campaigns. Wang was one such figure, and his actions were condemned as criminal in the post-Mao era.

There are hints in Wang's personal history and in the county's leadership structure that ethnic tensions or frictions between locals and northerners may have influenced his behavior. Wang was an outsider, a PLA veteran with an elementary school education from Liaoning Province in the far north, who joined the CCP at age twenty in 1945. He arrived with his PLA unit during its conquest of the region in 1950 and stayed behind to help set up local militia forces and consolidate the new government, eventually rising through the PAD ranks to become its political commissar and one of the county's top party officials.[60] Northerners who arrived in the far south along with the conquering PLA, and who stayed to serve as local cadres, frequently were sources of local tension in the early years of the People's Republic.[61] Language alone presented a difficult barrier. Wang was highly unlikely to have learned the Zhuang language, and he would have found the local Chinese dialect to be very difficult.[62]

We can only speculate that Wang's aggressive actions during the Cultural Revolution may have been driven by his perception that as an outsider he had a tenuous position in the county. Wang was the lowest ranking of seven members of the standing committee of Lingyun's Party Committee in May 1966, having been in that post for less than two years. He was one of only two Han Chinese on that committee. Wang obtained his first county-level leadership post in 1954 as the second-ranking deputy political commissar of the PAD. He was elevated to the county's Party Committee in 1956 but was dropped from June 1960 until his elevation into the party's Standing Committee in September 1964.[63] The interruption in Wang's career path from 1961 to 1964 suggests that he was sidelined for his actions during the Great Leap Forward, sanctions that were reversed shortly before the onset of the Cultural Revolution.[64]

Whatever Wang's motivations, he acted decisively to direct the county's power seizure, assume interim control, and guide rebel persecutions toward the county's current party secretary, Zhao Yongxi, an ethnic Zhuang. Zhao became the county's party secretary in May 1966, after having served as acting party secretary since July of the previous year.[65] Near the end of January 1967, cadre rebels in the county seat were poised to seize power, but the act was delayed by disagreements about the severity of Zhao's political errors. Some argued that he had resisted the local student movement, but others pointed out that he was the son of a revolutionary martyr and had been in the county for only a year. The disagreements delayed the power seizure.[66]

Wang Detang, the one member of the party's Standing Committee connected to the PAD, intervened to complete the power seizure, claiming that the cadre rebels were too passive. He pulled together a Power Seizure Committee of less hesitant cadre rebels and overthrew the entire county leadership, including most of the department heads. PAD officers assumed control of the county administration. A parade by armed militia forces marched through the streets of the county seat to demonstrate support, but opponents referred to this as a military coup.

Factions formed over the treatment of the deposed party secretary. During April and May, the PAD intensified its campaign against Zhao, making extreme accusations. Cadre rebels in the party organs felt that these charges were overblown, and near the end of May they invaded a meeting that Wang convened to detail the charges against Zhao, demanding that Wang justify his extreme charges. Wang counter-attacked, mobilizing a group of cadre rebels from the government offices to support his position. He charged that the dissident rebels were engaged in a counter-revolutionary campaign to oppose the army, further charging that Zhao Yongxi was manipulating them behind the scenes to overturn the power seizure. Clear factional divisions formed during the summer, with the supporters of Wang aligning with the Allied Command, and their opponents joining the April alliance.

During the last half of 1967 there was little deadly violence in Lingyun. The two sides hurled accusations against each other in wall posters and loudspeaker broadcasts. Things changed after the Beijing negotiations concluded in November, and it became clear that a final political settlement was coming. Violent conflict between the two sides intensified.[67] The local April faction staged attacks on the Allied Command in January and February 1968, serving only to provoke a wave of repression by the PAD and rural militias.

In mid-February Wang reinforced the Allied Command by calling in more than 300 militia fighters from surrounding villages into the county seat. Armed with rifles, they wiped out the remaining April faction fighters in the town, summarily executing leaders and imprisoning the others. Wang then formed a Revolutionary Committee on March 18, placing himself in charge. From that point forward a suppression campaign carried out over several months the same kind of actions that were concentrated in a very short period in Binyang County. The chroniclers of the events summarized them in this way:

> A wave of indiscriminate beatings and killings swept across the county seat and into villages. In every district and commune there were cases of people indiscriminately beaten to death and group killings. On June 19, 1968, the county's former party secretary, Zhao Yongxi, was beaten to death in broad daylight. Some cadres and masses were shot to death in groups, some were cruelly beaten to death, some were hounded to suicide, some were buried alive, some were beaten to death and their corpses flung into deep pits, and some families were completely exterminated.[68]

There are no reported actions by the April faction after February 1968. All of the events described after that month are actions by county, district, or commune Revolutionary Committees and village militias. From February to October 1968, the victims are all described as members of the April faction or "four types." The suppression campaign unfolded gradually but accelerated in June and into August. By the time it concluded, its cumulative effect was considerable. Close to 2,500 individuals were subjected to violent "struggle sessions," 300 were shot or beaten to death, and 748 suffered permanent disabilities. Another 158 committed suicide to avoid such treatment. One-third of the dead were from "four type" households, and most of the others were affiliated with the large April faction. Killings occurred in close to 87 percent of the county's villages, the vast majority after their village Revolutionary Committees were formed. The investigations concluded that the killings were organized and carried out by the authorities.[69]

## Atrocities

The killings of noncombatants and the massacre of surrendered or defeated April faction activists described in this chapter would be considered war crimes in any other setting, and the targeting of "four type" households resembles genocidal violence against outgroups defined by ethnicity or religion. Local narratives also contain descriptions of other kinds of atrocities: massacres of entire households, sexual violence, mutilation and display of corpses, and even the public eating of body parts of the killed. The emotional power of these descriptions helped to persuade past analysts that Guangxi's high death tolls were the product of community hatreds unleashed during a brief and deadly period in the summer of 1968. It is worth taking a closer look at the circumstances under which these acts occurred, and whether it was members of village militias, or neighbors and other ordinary villagers, who were responsible for these acts.

As we consider whether some of these acts were the product of community-level collective behavior, we need to recall the physical locations that define communities in the Chinese countryside. Counties in Guangxi at the time were divided into districts (*qu*). Below districts were "villages" that were administrative units that governed a collection of smaller settlements, referred to as "natural villages" or "hamlets" (*ziran cun, ziran tun, cunluo*). These smaller residential clusters, which could be widely separated, defined the rural communities within which neighbors were likely to know one another. In Binyang County, for example, there were 148 administrative villages and 1,705 natural villages. Administrative villages, which had an average population of 3,214, contained an average of 11 natural villages, and each had an average population of close to 300. At times, several natural villages might be grouped as collective production units, but this did not change the residential settlement pattern.[70]

Binyang was in a lowland region, and its natural villages were fewer in number and had larger populations than hilly and mountainous regions with lower population density, where the settlements were much smaller and more widely dispersed. Fengshan County had 2,143 natural villages under its 86 administrative villages, an average of 25 apiece. The natural villages were often tiny settlements that clustered an average of close to 10 households. The administrative villages had an average population of 1,087, and the natural villages averaged only 44 people each. In addition, in an ethnically diverse county such as Fengshan, natural villages were generally segregated by ethnicity.[71]

The killings described earlier in this chapter were almost always done by rural militia forces or by specially formed "picket corps," essentially death squads, that carried out killings under the direction of the PAD or Revolutionary Committees. Individuals who served in militia forces acted under the direction of leaders at higher levels, but they also lived in villages. The militias that carried out killings were organized by administrative villages. Although every able-bodied and "politically reliable" resident of a county between ages eighteen and thirty-five was enrolled in a militia unit, actual militia work was carried out by regular units known as "armed militia" (*wuzhuang minbing*). These were the units that left to fight in cities in the campaigns against April faction holdouts. In Lingshan County in 1966, for example, there were 5,779 members of these armed militia units under the direction of the PAD, organized into 22 regiments (*tuan*) at the district level and 390 battalions (*ying*) at the administrative village level. Half of them were demobilized veterans of the PLA.[72] An administrative village in the county on average would have roughly 15 of these armed militia members at their disposal, though they could also call up additional armed militias at the district level or mobilize members of unarmed militia units in the village.

When leaders in administrative villages drew up death lists, they consulted household registers that were kept at that level on families under their jurisdiction.[73] They then ordered militia units to go to the natural villages where the targeted individuals lived and take them back to the headquarters of the administrative village for a mass rally and execution, or to a remote location for summary execution. The structure of militia forces, together with the settlement patterns of natural villages, imply that few if any of the militia squads that carried out rural killings were members of the same natural village from which the victims were extracted. They came in from outside, at the command of the higher levels.

There were nonetheless many reported atrocities during this period, beyond summary executions, that might breed the suspicion that ordinary residents may have been drawn into acts of violence against neighbors. There are a range of reported atrocities that seem possibly to have been acts by co-residents rather than members of rural militias. The most common are the killing of small children and the elderly, sexual violence and predation against women, and, most spectacular of all, the public mutilation and display of corpses and the public eating of body parts of those who were killed. None of these actions was mandated by county or district authorities who unleashed waves of killing in rural regions, but they nonetheless occurred with disturbing frequency. Because these acts have suggested to some analysts that the killings expressed community-level antagonisms, it is worth exploring descriptions of these events to understand why they occurred and who carried them out.

## Crimes of Opportunity

Descriptions of atrocities are almost always linked to activities by militia forces during the high tide of suppression campaigns. Some cases indicate local tensions that could have motivated them. One is the settling of personal scores. In one case, a district PAD commander in Binyang County, who was appointed as head of the district's Revolutionary Committee, took vengeance on individuals who had denounced him three years before during the Socialist Education Campaign. These individuals had accused him of hiding the fact that his father was arrested as a bandit in the early 1950s, which in fact made him a "four type element." After taking power in the district, the leader took revenge by falsely accusing his primary accuser, the former deputy head of the county's Propaganda Department, of leading an underground "Anti-Communist Salvation Corps." He sent a militia force to the man's home late at night, where they shot him to death in his bed. The militia displayed the corpse in the street with a placard reading, "Anti-Communist Salvation Corps Commander." Several associates of the murdered official, who all had earlier held leadership positions in the district and villages, were also executed. All of those killed had been underground party members or members of communist guerrilla units before 1949.[74]

## Sexual Violence and Predation

Another crime of opportunity followed the execution of male household heads during the suppression campaigns. Those executions created opportunities for sexual violence and predation against surviving females in the family, and such crimes appear to have been widespread.[75] One case, from Binyang County, occurred in July 1968, during the height of the killings. Several days after ordering and personally participating in the beating death of a "four type" counter-revolutionary and his brother, the deputy head of a production brigade visited their home on the pretext of borrowing a farming tool. He offered to provide the widow with material compensation from the commune coffers if she would have sex with him. After she refused, he raped her and then told her that if she reported the act, he would have all surviving members of her household killed.[76]

In Rong County, the suppression campaign targeted a local family headed by a returned overseas Chinese. The commander of the village militia personally escorted the adult son back home after a denunciation rally and found his unmarried adult sister at home along with his father and mother. He insisted that the sister accompany him on a house search, and took her into another room, where he told her, "Your pussy can save your elder brother and father from being beaten to death, otherwise your whole family will be killed." After she refused, her assailant tied her to the bed and raped her. After this act, the militia commander wanted to continue to force himself on the sister, but he feared that if her brother and father found out, they would seek revenge. At a subsequent meeting to designate targets for execution, he accused her brother of having explosives and insisted that he be killed. At the mass denunciation rally, he personally killed the brother, clubbing and knifing him to death. After this act, he feared that the father might take revenge in the future, so he immediately dragged the father to view his son's corpse and beat him to death on the spot. Several days later, the militia commander went to the family's home, and again raped the sister at knife point.[77]

Yet another example is the case of Wang Detang, the PAD official whose violent proclivities in Lingyun County were described earlier in this chapter. Wang turned into a sexual predator shortly after establishing himself as head of the county's Revolutionary Committee. According to the investigation report, "from September 1968 to May 1969, taking advantage of people's precarious positions, and using his powers of office, employing coercion and offering of favors, on nine occasions he sexually violated the wives of cadres and teachers who were killed, the daughters of cadres who were subjected to struggle sessions, and female students. Moreover, he sexually harassed or molested five other young women."[78]

In He County in early January 1968, a militia member who had taken part in the killing of a group of nine people went to the home of one of the victims and raped his daughter. He then conspired with another member of the militia to commit a series of rapes of women in the households of men whom they had killed.[79] In Mengshan County in June 1968, after beating a woman to death during a struggle session, the militia platoon leader in one of the communes went to the family home. There he confronted the sole surviving family member, her twenty-two-year-old daughter, with a demand for sex. He told her that there would be further killings in the village, but if she "liked him," he could protect her. If not, she would be put on the death list. The daughter refused, at which point the militia head raped her at knife point. Several days later, the militia commander escorted her to a separate location, where he and six other militia members threatened her with a knife and gang-raped her for two hours, leaving her unconscious.[80]

In one district in Lingshan County, shortly after the execution of a former landlord, his widow was gang-raped by seven men; in another incident the militia battalion commander raped a teenage daughter after directing the execution of her father. After she reported it to two others, he had all three of them killed after they came to the police office to report his crime.[81] In Fusui County in late July 1968, the son of a landlord fled to another district to escape his fate, but he was tracked down by militia members who shot him in the back with a high-powered rifle as he attempted to escape. Three weeks later the head of the militia unit went to his home on the pretext of assessing a fine on his surviving family members, and raped his widow.[82]

In one district in Pubei County in April 1968, a thirty-person militia squad was formed to confiscate and distribute the possessions of the families whose male heads had been executed. The widows of those killed, along with their daughters, became part of the household property to be distributed. They were involuntarily married off to others, in some cases to the militia members who had killed their husbands and fathers. With the approval of the PAD commander and the head of one production brigade, marriage licenses were issued for two daughters and "marriage transfer certificates" were issued for four widows of those recently executed. In another production brigade, militia members who had killed the former landlord father of two teenage daughters went to the home and raped them both, threatening to kill them if they reported the crime. All the victimized women were married off, and in each instance, they were assessed large fees by the commune and production brigade for the service provided.[83]

During July and August 1968 in Shanglin County, longstanding animosities in a village due to earlier political campaigns led to revenge killings and rapes of the surviving spouses. A group of four brothers had denounced a commune leader during the 1957 antirightist campaign for keeping a concealed firearm, and in 1962 denounced him again for corruption. During the early months of the Cultural Revolution the commune leader and his relatives took revenge on the four brothers by attacking them as "rich peasants that had escaped the net". During a struggle session staged by the commune leader and several of his family members in July 1968, the four brothers were savagely beaten. Two died on the spot, and a third later committed suicide. In mid-August the commune leader called together supporters and told them that the July 3 Orders provided a window of opportunity to kill the surviving brother, but they needed to act fast. The surviving brother had been beaten so badly that he was bedridden, no longer able to walk. The commune leader led several of his followers to the family compound and ordered two surviving teenage daughters of the dead brothers, ages seventeen and nineteen, to carry the surviving brother on a stretcher to a ferry crossing. They told the two teenage girls to stand aside as they bound the surviving brother's hands with a rope, smashed his head with a club, cut his stomach open with a five-inch blade, and pushed him into the river.[84]

Several days later, one of the killers went back to their home and abducted the older of the two daughters, escorting her to a warehouse where more than ten others were waiting. They bound her hands, tied them to the roof beams, blindfolded her, and stripped off her clothing. The men proceeded to fondle and torture her, and then cut her down and gang-raped her. The next day, two of the attackers returned to the family compound and raped two other young women in the household. After the killing of the four brothers and the rapes of the surviving daughters, the home was looted, and the surviving family members scattered to other locations.[85]

Fewer than twenty cases of rape were described in any detail in the investigation reports. Summary statements in many of the reports indicate that sexual violence and predation was far more widespread than the individual case descriptions. A typical example is in the report on Wuxuan County: "Extremists showed contempt for the law, losing any sense of humanity, doing whatever they wanted. Some killed husbands and raped the wives, some killed fathers and raped the daughters, and even some underage girls were violated."[86] Surely in this setting, as elsewhere in the world, most sexual assaults went unreported.

*Cannibalism*

The most spectacular and infamous of the reported atrocities were cases of cannibalism. These cases were described in elaborate detail in publications that appeared almost three decades ago.[87] This was surely much less common than sexual violence, but many more cases were described in the investigation reports. The act differed from the cannibalism frequently reported during the famine that followed the Great Leap Forward six or seven years before. This was not a response to starvation, but instead the eating of selected body parts of individuals who had been recently killed. The practice often reflected folk beliefs about the medicinal or spiritual benefits of eating specific human body parts, in particular the heart and liver.[88]

The investigation reports describe a total of 84 instances of cannibalism.[89] These were scattered across 30 localities, all but one in rural counties. Even in these places it was rare: 17 reported only 1 case, and 6 reported only 2. Most of the cases occurred in 7 counties that reported a total of 55, and half of these were in only two counties: Lingshan (11) and Wuxuan (16). Lingshan and Wuxuan had little in common. Almost all the residents of Lingshan, on the northern border of Qinzhou Prefecture, were Han Chinese, and its death rate of 5.1 per thousand was far above the provincial average. Two-thirds of the residents of Wuxuan, on the southern border of Liuzhou Prefecture, were ethnic minorities, primarily Zhuang, and its death rate of 2.5 per thousand was only half of Lingshan's and well below the provincial average. The only thing the two counties had in common was that each had a significant Hakka minority (14 percent for Lingshan, 21 percent for Wuxuan).

In Wuxuan, cases of cannibalism were disturbingly frequent. A reported 75 corpses were cannibalized, some 14 percent of the people killed in the county.[90] Almost all the cases occurred during June 1968, at the height of the wave of mass killings. There is almost a casual quality to the descriptions, as if individuals were simply taking advantage of a rare opportunity to eat human flesh. In mid-May a villager was killed, and his assailants cut him open and removed his heart and liver. The organs were taken back to their home village and cooked for an evening banquet. More than twenty villagers at two tables took part.[91] On June 12, after a rally at the county seat to condemn several former landlords, one was beaten to death. The corpse and one of the survivors were taken to a different location, where their hearts and livers were removed—the survivor's organs were cut out by disemboweling him while he was unconscious but still alive.[92] The next day, in another district, five brothers from two "four type" families were paraded in the streets and were severely beaten. Afterward, the militia escorted them to their home, where another brother was detained, and all six of them were then shot to death. The hearts and livers of all six were removed.[93]

Perhaps the most gruesome case occurred in the county seat several days later, when a victim was paraded through the town's streets. When they reached the entrance to the town's bookstore, the victim was shot and wounded with a handgun. The assailants cut out his heart and liver while he was still alive, and then bystanders crowded around and began to carve out flesh from the freshly killed corpse for themselves. After almost all the flesh was removed, an elderly lady cut off the genitals and took them away, and an accountant from the county foodstuffs company cut off a leg and took it back for his co-workers as stew meat. Several cadres who were in town for a large leadership conference participated in the eating of body parts. A deputy head of the county Revolutionary Committee was at the scene, as was a deputy head of the county PAD. Neither of them said a word or did anything to stop the gruesome display.[94]

The investigation reports describe these incidents but never try to explain the behavior. The description of one case in Binyang County provides a hint that rural residents believed that the consumption of certain human organs had health benefits. After a commune Revolutionary Committee held a mass rally to denounce six "four type" individuals on their death list, the militia escorted them to the outskirts of the town and carried out the execution. Two bystanders, longtime asthma sufferers, said they had heard that their affliction could be cured by eating human liver. They asked for onlookers to carve up one of the victims. One of them pulled out a knife used for slaughtering pigs and cut open the corpse of a former landlord named Yan, and he gave slices to the two to take home.[95]

*    *    *

There is a clear connection between the accounts of mass killings in the first part of this chapter and the subsequent descriptions of sexual violence and cannibalism. The latter always occurred in the context of a wave of mass killings that were themselves atrocities, and these killings were carried out in an organized fashion by political authorities and their militia forces. Although the militia members were indeed residents of villages, they acted under the direction of superiors as part of a chain of command. What distinguished sexual violence and cannibalism from the killings is that the latter were mandated by local authorities, while the former were not. Sexual violence and cannibalism were crimes of opportunity, as individuals took advantage of extreme circumstances to commit acts that ordinarily would have brought legal sanctions and punishments. The descriptions of sexual violence suggest that leaders and members of militia units took advantage of the power of life and death that they held over the victimized families to violate women. The descriptions of cannibalism much more commonly portray uninvolved bystanders and spectators as seizing an opportunity for meals that folk beliefs endowed with special properties. Both types of atrocity were closely associated with waves of mass killings, and the killings in turn were organized by authorities and implemented by individuals under their command. However much these acts may appear to have expressed group hatreds in rural communities, the detail in the investigation reports shows that they were closely associated with activities directed by authorities.

The question is whether the mass killings or other atrocities were a manifestation of actors at local levels whose activities spiraled out of control. The weight of evidence in these descriptions, and the statistical materials presented in earlier chapters, indicates overwhelmingly that the actors who committed these atrocities were under the direction of local civil and military authorities. There are no descriptions in any of these case materials of crowds of villagers organizing themselves to attack "four type" households or members of rival factions. Mass rape and cannibalism were by no means mandated by provincial authorities or by Beijing's July 3 Orders.

There is evidence that the wave of mass killings was also unanticipated by provincial authorities who mandated local campaigns against nonexistent anti-Communist conspiracies. The provincial authorities on the Preparatory Committee may have been taken aback by the wave of killings touched off by their rhetoric. On May 12, 1968, they issued a directive that called for a halt to mass killings and demanded the end of casual killings of members of stigmatized families. The directive was duly distributed at all levels and widely ignored. The report on Mengshan County observed that "this directive was simply distributed by the Mengshan Revolutionary Committee to each of the districts and communes. In fact, it was never enforced, and consequently incidents of mass killing continued without interruption."[96] What spun out of the Nanning authorities' control was not rural communities, but their own military and civilian apparatus of repression, which reached deeply into villages.

## CHAPTER 8

# Analysis

I have presented a range of evidence to demonstrate that Guangxi's high death rates were not due to intergroup violence that targeted politically stigmatized "four type" households in villages. In as many as one-third of all counties, these rural households did indeed bear the brunt of suppression campaigns, largely where the April faction had not been active. However, there was an equally large number of counties where those associated with the April faction bore the brunt of the rural killings, in areas where they had been most active. In the remaining regions the killings focused variously on both categories of potential victims. The decisive evidence about intergroup violence is the identity of those who carried out the killings. The village militias under the command of PADs and newly established Revolutionary Committees were overwhelmingly responsible.

To this point I have set aside a range of arguments, outlined in chapter 1, about the distinctive regional characteristics that may have intensified Guangxi's violence. None of the analysis that I have presented so far addresses the possibility that the deadly suppression campaigns—and the factional conflict that preceded them—may have been intensified by features that distinguished Guangxi from other Chinese regions. One possibility is the heavy concentration of ethnic minorities. Another is the presence of the Hakka, which prior research has linked to high death tolls in Guangxi and neighboring Guangdong. Yet another is the economic backwardness and remoteness of many subregions in the province, which may have permitted killings to spiral out of control, going much further than provincial military authorities had anticipated.

The narrative accounts in the investigation reports, and the data extracted from them, contain no information about the ethnicity of the village communities or of the actors involved. There is no hint in these materials that the events may have expressed ethnic antagonism. It is possible that the investigators studiously ignored any ethnic dimension as a politically sensitive topic that would have complicated the official diagnosis of the entire episode as the product of an "ultra-left" political line. There is no mention of Guangxi's ethnic groups as actors in these materials, and the ethnicity of many individuals named as perpetrators or victims is unknown.

We can nonetheless examine this possibility in a systematic if indirect fashion. Despite the silence of the investigation reports, we can draw on data collected from a range of sources about the population characteristics of Guangxi's counties and cities. Wide local variations across the province can shed light on these issues. If Guangxi's ethnic composition was responsible for elevated death tolls, then the regions where both Han and ethnic minorities were present in significant numbers should have had higher death tolls than the regions whose populations were ethnically uniform. If, however, local death rates did not vary with ethnic profiles, it is doubtful that ethnic diversity was responsible for Guangxi's large death tolls relative to the rest of China.

Other potentially consequential characteristics are Guangxi's relative economic backwardness and the geographic and political remoteness of many of its subregions. The province had very low levels of urbanization and economic development, and correspondingly low levels of education. Reports of cannibalism are considered by some observers as an indicator of cultural backwardness. Limited rail and highway networks and mountainous terrain meant that many subregions were remote from centers of political authority. Prior publications have argued that intergroup violence spun out of control in regions where the state's reach was weak.

I have cast doubt on the idea that rural killings expressed intergroup violence. Instead, I have argued that it was not ordinary villagers whose actions spun out of control, exaggerating death tolls far beyond what authorities in Nanning had anticipated, but instead the actions of local security forces and village militias. There

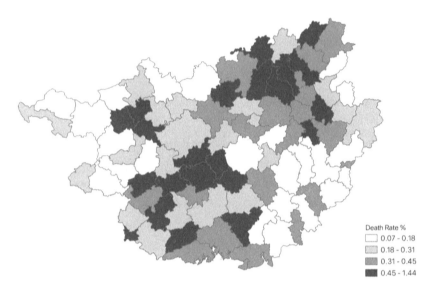

Death Rate %
☐ 0.07 - 0.18
☐ 0.18 - 0.31
▨ 0.31 - 0.45
■ 0.45 - 1.44

MAP 8.1.   City- and County-Level Death Rates, by Quartile

are several plausible measures of development, and of the remoteness of a locality, that permit us to look at these questions directly.

In earlier chapters I have employed data about the distribution of political events across regions and over time in a descriptive fashion, searching for patterns by examining averages, counts, and time trends. In this chapter I will connect a range of information about local characteristics with data about local events and look more closely at statistical patterns that might otherwise have been obscured in the descriptive analyses in previous chapters. There is wide variation in local death rates, as illustrated by map 8.1, which divides Guangxi's counties and cities into four quartiles of approximately equal size, ranging from the lowest to the highest death rates. The jurisdictions in the bottom quartile, indicated by white, had death rates far below the Guangxi average (0.7–1.8 per thousand), and indeed were all below the national average of 2.1 deaths per thousand. The top quartile, indicated by black, were all far above the provincial average of 3.6 (4.5–14.4 per thousand).[1] Between these two extremes are localities with death rates that range from a low of 1.8 per thousand, still below the national average, to a high of 4.5 per thousand, well above Guangxi's average. The analysis to follow will examine the features of these local jurisdictions to search for characteristics related to local death rates. This will require the use of regression models that subject some of the ideas expressed in previous chapters a more rigorous examination.

## Ethnicity

Prior research, based on published local histories from Guangxi and Guangdong, reported that large ethnic minority populations were associated with fewer deaths, while large Hakka populations were associated with more.[2] These findings supported an analysis that identified a regional history of migration and group antagonisms as a distinctive feature of the region. Whatever the merits of such an argument as an explanation for violence in specific communities, we need to be clear that we are asking not whether violence may have expressed local group antagonisms, but why death rates were *higher* in Guangxi than elsewhere. If death rates in Guangxi were higher due to its mixed population of ethnic and subethnic groups, then these differences should also be apparent *within* Guangxi. It should be precisely in those subregions where these groups existed in mixed communities that the violence was most intense. If this was not the case, or if death rates did not otherwise vary by local ethnic profiles, then the reasons for Guangxi's high death rates must rest elsewhere, even if local violence in some regions did reflect ethnic tensions or prior historical conflicts.

If ethnic conflict was associated with the presence of non-Han ethnic minorities, it would have been with the Zhuang, by far the largest such group in the province, constituting one-third of its population.[3] There are good reasons to doubt that ethnic antagonism, or ethno-nationalist aspirations, can be linked to the presence of the Zhuang. Unlike in Inner Mongolia during this period, there was no explicit campaign that targeted ethnic minorities for alleged political disloyalty, and there was no adjacent state like Mongolia that could have vied for their loyalty. One prominent analyst of Inner Mongolia interprets the campaign against an alleged "Inner Mongolian People's Party" not as an expression of ethnic antagonism, but as a deadly political purge that targeted Han and ethnic Mongols alike.[4] There were several large rebellions in Tibetan regions after 1955 in reaction to their incorporation into a new Chinese nation-state intent on transforming traditional religious, economic, and political institutions. It is therefore more plausible to suspect that violence in Tibet might have expressed ethno-nationalist resistance.[5] Even in Tibet, however, this interpretation is disputed by specialists who argue that, unlike earlier rebellions in Tibetan regions, the bloody 1969 rebellion in Nyemo County was factional warfare, with ordinary Tibetans, and Tibetan and Han cadres on both sides.[6]

The Zhuang, by contrast, were incorporated into Chinese states in a process that had begun many centuries before. Most Zhuang were largely assimilated into Han culture by the twentieth century, with language being the primary remaining marker of their identity. Provincial annals compiled in the 1930s noted that the older Zhuang customs had largely disappeared. One analyst of the region, referring to the early twentieth century, noted that "few of these people are really distinct from the Han. The majority of the Zhuang were absorbed by successive waves of Han immigrants and did not maintain a separate identity. Those few Zhuang who kept a distinctive Zhuang identity lived in the hills in the north and west of the province; they identified not with the sinicized Zhuang, but with other peoples living in the same areas, the Miao and the Yao."[7] The 1938 census counted the Zhuang as Han.[8] Chinese nationalist thinkers at the time advanced the questionable claim that the Zhuang were descendants of the earliest Chinese settlers in distant centuries.[9] Contemporary local annals, when discussing the struggles of ethnic minorities for equal rights earlier in the modern era, refer to the struggles of Yao, but not Zhuang.[10] Unlike Tibetans, Mongols, and Uighurs, the Zhuang were not marked off by pronounced cultural and religious differences, or by aspirations for political autonomy or statehood in the twentieth century.[11]

There are also reasons for doubting that the presence of the Hakka subgroup can account for elevated death tolls in Guangxi. Prior research that implicated Hakka communities in elevated death tolls was based on evidence that considered Guangxi together with Guangdong.[12] Whatever the evidence regarding Guangdong, the Hakka are far less prevalent in Guangxi. Even if Hakka were prone to more intense and violent group conflict, they could only marginally have inflated Guangxi's overall death rates. An additional problem is that Guangxi's death rates were much higher than Guangdong's, while the proportion of Hakka in Guangdong was almost four times larger.

There are wide variations in the distribution of Zhuang and other officially recognized minority groups across Guangxi's prefectures and prefecture-level cities. Minority populations were highly concentrated in Bose, Hechi, Nanning, and Liuzhou prefectures, where the Han constituted an average of only 35.2 percent of the

TABLE 8.1.  Average Death Rates (per thousand) by Population Characteristics

| Population Features | Percent Han | Deaths/ 1000 | Maximum | Minimum | N |
|---|---|---|---|---|---|
| Autonomous Minority County | 50.0 | 3.8 | 7.7 | 1.5 | 8 |
| Significant Hakka Population (>20%) | 76.8 | 2.6 | 4.1 | 0.9 | 10 |
| Minority Dominant Population (>88%) | 6.3 | 3.6 | 14.4 | 0.8 | 17 |
| Non-Han Majority (12–29% Han) | 19.9 | 3.6 | 7.7 | 1.2 | 17 |
| Balanced Population (30–70% Han) | 47.2 | 3.7 | 13.6 | 0.9 | 17 |
| Han Majority (70–93% Han) | 86.4 | 4.2 | 8.0 | 1.6 | 17 |
| Han Dominant Population (>94%) | 97.3 | 3.0 | 7.6 | 0.7 | 18 |
| *Total* | *51.9* | *3.6* | *14.4* | *0.7* | *86* |

population. In Bose Prefecture, only 16.8 percent of the population was classified as Han.[13] At the opposite extreme are six prefecture-level jurisdictions where Han made up an average of 77–94 percent of the population. Nanning and Liuzhou were overwhelmingly Han, while their suburban counties were predominantly minority. Half of all localities had fewer than 44 percent Han.[14]

Table 8.1 shows mean death rates across localities with different ethnic profiles. Only three categories deviate substantially from the provincial average of 3.6 per thousand. The eight counties with relatively large Hakka populations (greater than 20 percent) have a much lower death rate than average—the opposite of expectations based on past research.[15] The other categories are defined as quintiles, based on the percentage of the population classified as Han Chinese. In the table they are listed according to the size of the minority population. Only two groups deviate from the provincial average. Localities that are almost entirely Han (greater than 94 percent), have average death rates well under the provincial average. Localities with a large Han majority, but with a minority population between 7 and 30 percent, have higher average death rates. Note that there is very wide variation within each of these categories in death rates. Not surprisingly, none of these categories comes close to standard levels of statistical significance when included in a simple regression equation (not shown) that controls for the size of the local population.[16] However, I will further consider the two categories that deviated from the provincial mean in a series of regression models that include a larger number of variables.

## Underdevelopment and Geographic Remoteness

In chapter 1, when considering regional characteristics that may have contributed to Guangxi's higher levels of deadly violence, I discussed two further features:

(1) Guangxi's low levels of urban development and education, and (2) the geographic remoteness of many localities. Prior research has not explicitly linked economic backwardness to violence, but it is implicit in some descriptive accounts. Reports of cannibalism have been interpreted by some writers as indicators of the region's low level of modern economic development.

Geographic remoteness, in contrast, can be considered a distinctive regional characteristic, but it can also be treated as an indicator of underlying political processes that generated high death tolls. In his study of rural killings in Guangxi and Guangdong, Yang Su argued that geographically remote regions (measured as distance from the provincial capital) would be more weakly monitored by party-state authorities, and that it would be precisely in these regions that intergroup violence would spiral out of control. He also offered a parallel measure of party-state capacity—the number of party members or government cadres in a locality. Lower numbers of party members or cadres should have had the same impact as geographic remoteness—presumably a weaker capacity to restrain community violence.

Yet, if rural killings were carried out by party-state authorities and their village militias, the prediction for both measures would be different. One possibility is that remoteness or the strength of local party-state structures had no effect: because death rates were carried out by militia structures that were present in every county, the death rates in remote regions should be just as high as elsewhere. A more dramatic possibility would be a *negative* effect, such that remote regions with weaker party-state structures would be associated with *lower* death rates. This would be even more convincing statistical evidence that the killings were organized and implemented by local political and military organizations: death rates were higher where these structures were strong, and lower where they were weak.

Let us first examine urban and economic development. Guangxi was overwhelmingly rural. In the median locality, only 6.7 percent of the population lived in urban settlements. The five largest cities were extreme outliers, averaging 73 percent urban.[17] Educational enrollments were also highly skewed: 20 percent of Guangxi's counties and cities had fewer than 1,200 students enrolled in junior and senior high school; at the upper end of the distribution, 20 percent had more than 5,000, and 10 percent more than 10,000. Enrollments as a percentage of the total population were also highly skewed; two-thirds of localities had enrollments that were less than 1 percent of the total population, and an average of 0.7 percent. The top 10 percent of localities had enrollment rates that averaged seven times larger, nearly 5 percent. With such skewed distributions there is virtually no correlation between rates of urbanization or school enrollment rates and death rates.[18] If these measures have any relationship with death rates, it should be as a contrast between the localities at the high end of the distribution and all others.

There are two measures of geographic remoteness, and two measures of the reach of party-state structures. Geographic remoteness can be indicated by distance from political centers, in this case distance of a locality from its prefectural capital. This measure varies from 0 (in the case of prefectural capitals) to 340 kilometers.[19] The correlation of this measure with local death rates is close to zero, so any relationship is not linear, and we should examine the most distant localities for differences from the provincial mean.[20] A second measure of remoteness is more straightforward—whether the jurisdiction is on a provincial land border. There are thirty-one counties and two cities that lie along Guangxi's borders with Vietnam and the provinces of Yunnan, Guizhou, Hunan, and Guangdong. Most of the counties are along mountain ranges and were poorly accessible by modern road networks. Regions along China's provincial borders have historically been associated with banditry and other measures of weak state control, and this remains a plausible indicator of remoteness.[21]

The strength of local party-state structures can be expressed as the number of party members or party-state cadres as a percentage of the local population. Numbers of party members and numbers of party-state cadres have subtly different implications. The number of party members reflects the extent to which the local party apparatus has recruited ordinary citizens into its political networks. The number of party-state cadres indicates staffing levels of government administration, essentially a measure of local state capacity. The rate of party membership ranges from a minimum of 1.0 percent to a maximum of 3.5 percent, and an average of 1.8 percent. The correlation of this measure with the local death rate is close to zero. Cadre numbers relative to local population range from a minimum of 0.09 percent to a maximum of 2.7, and average 0.9 percent. There is a small positive correlation between this latter measure and death rates (.152), but it is not statistically significant. Like the measures of urbanization and education, both percentages are skewed at the high end in a small number of localities, so any detectable differences are likely to be at the high end of the distributions.

TABLE 8.2.  Average Death Rates (per thousand) by Local Characteristics

| Jurisdiction Features | Deaths/ 1,000 | Maximum | Minimum | N |
|---|---|---|---|---|
| Cities | 3.7 | 4.2 | 3.0 | 6 |
| Most urbanized (top quintile, >11.1%) | 3.6 | 7.6 | 1.2 | 18 |
| Top school enrollments (top quintile, >1.7%) | 3.8 | 14.4 | 1.2 | 18 |
| Cadres per capita (top quintile, >1.33%) | 5.1 | 14.4 | 1.7 | 18 |
| Party members per capita (top quintile, >2.21%) | 3.4 | 8.0 | 0.9 | 18 |
| Distant from Prefecture (top quintile, >105km) | 3.4 | 6.9 | 1.4 | 18 |
| Border location | 2.7 | 7.4 | 0.7 | 33 |
| *Total* | *3.6* | *14.4* | *0.7* | *86* |

Table 8.2 displays differences across categories defined by the measures for development and remoteness just described. None of the measures of urbanization or educational development has any evident impact on death rates. The most developed localities in Guangxi had death rates very close to the provincial average. Only two types of jurisdictions show any substantial deviation from the provincial average, and both have the same implications. Localities with the highest numbers of cadres relative to local population—presumably a measure of the strength of local party-state structures—had average death rates (5.1) far *above* the provincial average. Guangxi's border regions, presumably where the reach of the party-state was relatively weak, had average death rates (2.7) well *below* the provincial average. These figures are what we would expect if party-state agents in localities mobilized harsh suppression campaigns, and they are the opposite of what we would expect if intergroup violence in villages spun out of government control.

Note that once again there are wide variations within each of these categories in death rates. As a result, regression models that control for population size (not shown) find very few of these categories to have any significant impact on death rates. The one exception is the estimate for border regions, which had net death rates close to 40 percent lower than other regions. The confidence level in the estimate is very high (p > .001). Localities with the highest number of party-state cadres had estimated death rates 28 percent higher than others, but the estimate does not reach minimum levels of statistical significance. I will reconsider these two measures of local party-state strength in the context of regression models that contain larger numbers of variables.

## Political Processes

The analysis in previous chapters relied heavily on observations of trends over time, and it documented intensifying levels of repression after February 1968. The process was one in which the April faction developed an insurgency against the Guangxi Military District after the complete breakdown of the November 1967 agreement imposed on the parties in Beijing. As the April faction mobilized, the Preparatory Committee and Military District mobilized PADs, and the rural militias at their command, to crush any local resistance, real and imagined. As suppression campaigns escalated with the drive to establish Revolutionary Committees, the April faction was increasingly defined by Nanning as a subversive counterrevolutionary movement rather than as a legitimate if aggrieved rebel faction. The July 3 Orders validated this definition and removed remaining constraints on the use of deadly force.

The narrative accounts suggest a time trend of increasing repression over time as the drive to establish Revolutionary Committees progressed. This implies escalating levels of organized violence over time, reaching a crescendo during July and August that finally pushed Guangxi's overall death rates far above those observed elsewhere in China. This distinctive political process—the province-wide alignment of local PADs and rural militias with the Allied Command faction, the urgent push to quell provincial disorders in the context of massive American military escalation across the border in Vietnam, and the issuance of the July 3 Orders focused specifically on the "Guangxi Problem"—set Guangxi apart from other regions of China, none of which had this same combination of features.

This narrative implies a time trend of escalating death tolls. Suppression campaigns were related to efforts to establish and consolidate Revolutionary Committees. A plausible measure of this time trend would be the timing of a local Revolutionary Committee's establishment, and this measure should be expected to predict ultimate local death rates. Localities that established Revolutionary Committees earlier would suffer lower death rates than localities where suppression campaigns began later. The timing of a local Revolutionary Committee, measured as the time lag before it was established, might be considered an indicator of the political processes that narrative accounts in prior chapters have identified as responsible for higher death rates.

TABLE 8.3. Average Death Rates (per thousand) by Timing of Local Revolutionary
Committee

| Date of Revolutionary Committee | Average Death Rate | Local Maximum | Local Minimum | Number of Jurisdictions |
|---|---|---|---|---|
| March 1968 | 2.9 | 7.8 | 0.8 | 46 |
| April 1968* | 3.8 | 14.4 | 0.7 | 31 |
| August 1968 | 6.5 | 13.6 | 3.0 | 9 |

* Includes one county (Quanzhou) whose Revolutionary Committee was established May 8.

Table 8.3 examines death rates by the month that a Revolutionary Committee was established, and it shows a large increase over time. The jurisdictions where one was established in March 1968 had average death rates of 2.9 per thousand— well above the death rate elsewhere in China (2.0) but also well below the provincial average. In the thirty-one localities where this occurred by April, the average death rate was 3.8. When a Revolutionary Committee was delayed until August, after the July 3 Orders, the average death rate reached 6.5 per thousand, more than triple the national average.

Before we pursue this idea further, we need to consider more carefully the logical relationship between levels of deadly violence and the timing of a Revolutionary Committee. I am suggesting that death rates are a consequence of timing— the later a Revolutionary Committee was established, the more deadly force was employed, and the higher the local death rates. However, the reverse may be true: Revolutionary Committees may have been established later in localities that were already suffering the worst violence. If so, later timing of Revolutionary Committees could be a consequence of deadly violence, not the other way around. This is essentially a question about *when* high death tolls occurred. If they were already high in the months before a Revolutionary Committee was established, then this might have delayed the committee's establishment.

Figure 8.1 compares monthly death tolls from January to October 1968, across the three groups of localities as defined in table 8.3, the period when almost all of Guangxi's deaths occurred. Because there are wide differences in the number of localities and in the total numbers of deaths recorded, the numbers are indexed with the largest monthly death count as 1, with other numbers expressed as a proportion of that number.[22] The three graphs show clearly that the death tolls were

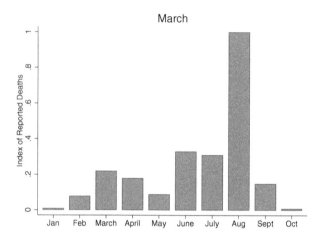

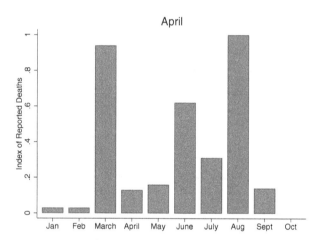

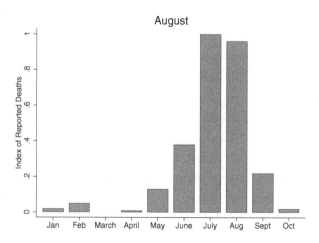

FIGURE 8.1. Index of Monthly Death Tolls by Month of Revolutionary Committee, 1968

highly concentrated later in time in the localities where Revolutionary Committees were established in August. This group suffered their highest death tolls by far during two consecutive months of July and August, with very little deadly violence prior to June. The localities with March and April Revolutionary Committees both experienced sharp spikes in death tolls during August, also reflecting the impact of the July 3 Orders. However, both groups suffered far more deaths in the period from February through June than did the August holdouts. The second wave of killings in the places where Revolutionary Committees were established much earlier is what pushed them, and the rest of Guangxi, to death rates far above the national average.

This leaves us with the question of what delayed the establishment of a Revolutionary Committee. The most likely reason is the scale of conflict between the April and Allied factions. But recall that factional conflict, whether armed or not, did not generate a high percentage of the death tolls. In an earlier chapter we found that actions by authorities accounted for more than 85 percent of all recorded deaths (table 6.5). Conflict between civilian factions, and armed resistance by the April faction, generated relatively few deaths. As one might expect, the localities that established Revolutionary Committees late reported more activity by the April faction over the entire period from March 1967 to the end of 1968. In the group of localities that established a Revolutionary Committee in March, there was an average total of 10 reported actions by the April 22 faction; in the April group, the average total was 15; and in the August Group, it was 24. Although these numbers are surely inflated where the suppression campaigns were delayed, we can be confident that previously high death rates did not delay a Revolutionary Committee.

At this point we will consider the time trend together with some of the regional features examined earlier and try to draw more confident overall conclusions. Table 8.4 displays negative binomial regression results that examine the joint impact of ethnic composition, levels of development, remoteness, and the political time trend. All the models include the local population, measured as units of 100,000, as a control variable, which turns the other coefficients into measures of a variable's impact on local death rates. The urban population, in units of 10,000, is a direct measure of the level of economic development (it is almost perfectly correlated with the number of nonagricultural workers in a locality). It is also included as a control variable because it is correlated with the strength of party and government organizations as well as with location in a border region. The regression models

TABLE 8.4. Negative Binomial Regression Estimates of Local Deaths (incident rate ratios; z-scores in parentheses)

|  | (1) | (2) | (3) | (4) |
|---|---|---|---|---|
| Total Population/100,000 | 1.26*** | 1.15+ | 1.20* | 1.20* |
|  | (5.1) | (1.7) | (2.3) | (2.4) |
| Urban Population/10,000 | .995 | .957* | .957** | .950** |
|  | (−0.35) | (−2.3) | (−2.6) | (−2.8) |
| Han Majority (70–93 percent Han) | 1.34 |  |  | 1.21 |
|  | (1.5) |  |  | (1.0) |
| Significant Hakka Population (>20 percent) | .822 |  |  |  |
|  | (−0.85) |  |  |  |
| Distance to Prefecture Seat/100 kilometers |  | 1.12 |  |  |
|  |  | (0.9) |  |  |
| Number of Cadres/1000 |  | 1.28** | 1.25** | 1.27*** |
|  |  | (3.2) | (3.1) | (3.3) |
| Number of Party Members/1000 |  | .980 | .975 | .967 |
|  |  | (−0.4) | (−0.6) | (−0.8) |
| Border Location |  | .504*** | .529*** | .521*** |
|  |  | (−4.8) | (−5.0) | (−5.1) |
| Lag Days to Revolutionary Committee |  |  | 1.005*** | 1.005*** |
|  |  |  | (3.6) | (3.2) |
| Constant | 442*** | 470*** | 285*** | 292*** |
|  | (42.1) | (33.4) | (27.3) | (27.4) |
| Number of Observations | 85 | 82 | 82 | 82 |

Note: + p<.1, * p<.05, ** p<0.01, *** p<0.001.

also consider two of the variables for local ethnic populations, and they include all four measures of party-state strength and geographic remoteness. The time trend illustrated in table 8.3 is defined as the number of days after January 1, 1968, that the local Revolutionary Committee was established. It ranges from 66 (March 7) to 239 (August 27). The variable "lag days to revolutionary committee" is designed to capture intensifying repression over time.

The results indicate that the only characteristic of local populations that has a significant impact on death rates is level of urbanization, which is a direct measure of nonagricultural development. The more urbanized the population, the lower the death rate. In the full equation estimated in column 4, each increment of 10,000 in urban population is associated with a 5 percent lower death rate (.95). This means that a county with an urban population of 30,000 at the 75th percentile would have a predicted death rate that is only 85.7 percent as high as a county with 10,000 urban residents at the 25th percentile ($.95^3$ = .857). A city with an urban population of 100,000 (at the 95th percentile) with ten times more urban residents, would have a predicted death rate that is 60 percent as high ($.95^{10}$ = .599). Other things being equal, less developed rural regions had higher death rates.

If the killings were an expression of intergroup violence, more remote communities with weaker party-state structures should have had higher death rates. If, however, they were part of an organized campaign, death rates should either be unaffected by these features, or be measurably lower. In addition, if Guangxi's violence was driven by political processes that contributed to the intensification of violent suppression over time, the areas where a Revolutionary Committee was delayed should have the highest overall death rates.

The estimates in table 8.4 indicate that geographic remoteness and the strength of party-state structures both have a large impact on local death rates.[23] In the full equation in column 4, the incident rate ratio of 1.27 indicates that for each additional 1,000 government cadres, the predicted death rate increases by 27 percent. A locality at the 77th percentile with 3,000 cadres would have a predicted death rate 61 percent higher than one at the 10th percentile with 1,000 cadres ($1.27^2$ = 1.61). The better staffed the political apparatus, the higher the death rate.

The estimate for location in a border region has the same implication. Border regions had predicted death tolls close to 48 percent lower than the interior of the province. A remote location cut the predicted death rate almost by half. These two results indicate that stronger local party-state structures generated higher death tolls, while location in a border region spared the residents the worst violence. The confidence levels for these estimates are very high.[24]

The timing of the local Revolutionary Committee also had a large impact on death rates. I proposed this as a measure of the escalating intensity of repression documented in the narrative descriptions in previous chapters. The incident rate ratio of 1.0053 indicates that each day after January 1 that a Revolutionary Committee was delayed added close to half of one percent (0.53) to the predicted death toll. This translates to an increase of 3.8 percent per week ($1.0052^7$ = 1.0377), or 17.2 percent per month ($1.0052^{30}$ = 1.172). A locality that established a

Revolutionary Committee on August 15 would have more than twice the predicted number of deaths compared to one established five months earlier, on March 15 $(1.0052^{150} = 2.21)$.

## Summary

The statistical analysis lends support to the argument developed with narrative accounts and descriptive statistics in prior chapters. Guangxi's large death tolls were a product of top-down mobilization of civilian and military structures that reached down into rural districts, and the levels of violent repression escalated over time. Localities where political structures were more fully staffed generated higher levels of violence, and remote border regions escaped the worst of the suppression campaigns. Localities where the April faction was able to delay the imposition of a Revolutionary Committee for long periods suffered the deadliest violence in the end. The story told in prior chapters is mirrored in statistical form in the regression models.

These results also indicate that Guangxi's ethnic diversity was not one of the reasons why its death rate was so much higher than those of other regions of China. There are virtually no systematic differences in death rates across regions with different ethnic profiles, whether these differences are defined by the presence of non-Han minorities or by the presence of the Hakka subgroup. Note that these results do not rule out the possibility that ethnic antagonisms played a role in local killings. It is possible that they may have done so in ethnically diverse regions. Measurement at the subcounty level—districts, administrative villages, and "natural" villages—would be necessary to explore this more fully. Such data are not available, although a focused local study could shed considerable light on this possibility. Unfortunately, the investigation reports are completely silent about ethnicity. What we can conclude, however, is that there is no evidence at the county level that ethnic composition had a measurable impact on death rates. Another way of stating this conclusion is that death rates were unusually high across Guangxi, regardless of the local ethnic profile, and were instead driven by political processes that distinguished the province from the rest of China. Violence in ethnically diverse regions may have been motivated by group antagonisms, but if so, it was no more severe than the violence in regions with little or no ethnic diversity.

# Epilogue

In a broad sense, the events in Guangxi followed a pattern that was common across most other regions of China: widespread factional warfare was followed by suppression campaigns that generated far higher death tolls than the disorders they were intended to quell.[1] Why, then, were the death tolls so much higher in Guangxi? Official histories published in China, and the investigation reports that are the primary foundation for this book, offer a straightforward explanation. Its essence is that Beijing's July 3 Orders unleashed unbridled repression, ostensibly targeting the April faction, leading to waves of killings carried out by civilian and military authorities.

These orders did accelerate the killings, but they simply intensified a trend that was already under way. The chain of events began with the collapse of the Guangxi Preparatory Committee near the end of 1967. Until then, Guangxi had avoided the violent factional warfare that swept across China during the summer of 1967. Scattered massacres in rural counties by PADs, designed to consolidate their power, precipitated the collapse of the November agreement. In Nanning and other cities, the April faction reacted to the first rural massacres by rearming and repudiating the Preparatory Committee of which they ostensibly were a part. They mobilized widespread armed resistance, causing the Allied faction to rearm and mobilize for armed combat.

To deflect attention from their loss of control over the situation, and their obvious failure to implement the November agreements in an equitable fashion, the Preparatory Committee and Guangxi Military District submitted reports to Beijing that grossly misrepresented what was happening. These misrepresentations led Beijing to issue the July 3 Orders, which in turn accelerated a wave of massacres in rural districts that were already escalating out of control. A truncated explanation that stops with a condemnation of the July 3 Orders and places blame on military officers and militia commanders does little more than restate the puzzle in more pointed form. It avoids two key questions: why were the PADs in rural counties so motivated to massacre unarmed civilians, even before the July 3 Orders? And why did they focus on politically stigmatized households that were largely uninvolved in factional conflicts? The investigation materials contain ample evidence, largely ignored by the investigators, that bears on these questions.

These materials do contradict one explanation for Guangxi's violence—that it expressed a conflict between those with vested interests in preserving the existing system of power and privilege, against a rebellion that challenged the status quo. For those who claim to see a conflict between reputedly "conservative" and "radical" forces, Guangxi represents the deadly extremes to which the powerful and privileged were willing to go to defend a system that benefited them. This is certainly the way that the April faction sought to portray their struggle. The counterargument by the Allied Command and their military allies—that the April insurgency was a barely concealed conspiracy to overturn China's socialist system—lends support for this idea. Both portrayals were falsehoods, rhetoric crafted for purposes of political struggle.

The narratives compiled by investigators suggest a fundamentally different type of conflict. They describe splits in civilian power structures and interventions by military forces that hardened new identities, sharpened their conflicts, and raised the stakes for all sides. They portray a shift of power from civilian to military actors and the intense militarization of the Chinese political system, as former civilian leaders were cast aside. They also reveal that military actors had different stakes in these conflicts: main force army units had different stakes than regional garrisons in cities and PADs in counties. Unlike PLA combat divisions deployed in Guangxi, the regional garrisons and PADs were embedded in local power structures and would remain there afterward. In short, the political "status quo" burst apart, and subsequent conflicts pitted fragments of former civilian and military structures against one another, along with rebel groups aligned with them.

The fragmentation of civilian power structures was evident from the outset, and at the very top. After the imposition of military control and the controversial appointment of Wei Guoqing to head the effort, two factions among Guangxi's ranking party leaders emerged: one was aligned with the Allied Command and pledged to support Wei Guoqing, while the other supported the April faction rebels, opposed Wei, and pledged support for Wu Jinnan. Both leaders were PLA veterans and had served in the top reaches of Guangxi's power elite since the mid-1950s, and both rebel factions therefore pledged support to bureaucratic insiders. The question was not whether the status quo would be preserved, but which parts of it would survive.

These splits were echoed at all levels of government, as seen in the crucial role of cadre rebels in the power seizures that spread across Guangxi. Cadre rebels were highly active in the events that led to the provincial power seizure, and they were a key part of the rebel coalition that carried it out. Some gravitated toward the Allied faction, and others toward the April coalition. This pattern was replicated throughout Guangxi, as power seizures spread rapidly to other cities, prefectures, and counties. The narrative accounts are impossible to square with an interpretation of these conflicts as bureaucratic insiders defending their privileges against a radical insurgency. These were fundamentally internecine conflicts that pitted insiders against one another, accelerating the collapse of civilian party and government structures.

In this process the military wing of the party-state thrust aside civilian leaders, a trend that was most pronounced at the county level. Beijing's late January 1967 orders for the military to "support the left" in power seizures made the heads of the PADs the only local leaders who were immune to overthrow. They were almost always ranking members of county-level party committees. While immunizing them against overthrow, Beijing's orders also turned them into the sole actors with authority to adjudicate local rebel disputes. This injected the PADs into factional disputes, eventually placing them at the head of what would become the Allied Command faction. This also meant that village militias under the command of the PAD backed the Allied Command, giving factional conflicts across Guangxi a clear organizational structure patterned by the surviving military branch of the party-state. This power shift became evident in the Revolutionary Committees that emerged at the end of this period. Political settlements imposed in the counties left PADs in command of local governments, marking a drastic decline of the civilian party elite.

The main force PLA combat units, by contrast, were not so uniformly aligned with the Allied faction. They did not have the same stakes in local conflicts as did the commanders of permanent garrisons and the county PADs. They were not directly under the command of the Guangxi Military District, headed by Wei Guoqing after March 1967. They were not under an obligation to support the Allied Command faction. The most visible and consequential example was the PLA unit in Guilin that supported the power seizure by anti-Wei rebels in that city who were at the core of the province-wide April 22 alliance. In addition, in August 1967, when it seemed that Beijing would come down on the side of the April faction, several main force PLA units in Nanning, Liuzhou, and other cities publicly repudiated their prior support for the Allied faction. This led to otherwise inexplicable efforts by the April faction in February 1968 to protest the transfer of a sympathetic PLA unit out of Nanning, fearing (justifiably, as it turned out) that this would clear the way for their suppression by more hostile local military units.[2]

Even if one were to insist that these conflicts somehow still represented a struggle between "conservatives" and "rebels" with different political orientations, this interpretation does not address the unusually widespread victimization of politically stigmatized "four type elements." Yang Su's analysis of mass killings correctly placed this question firmly at the center of attention.[3] In his estimation, it was the unusually widespread attacks on "four type elements" that pushed Guangxi's death tolls far above those of other regions of China. The evidence that I have presented in this book fully justifies this claim. Killings of "four type elements" and their family members were unusually widespread in Guangxi. Our best estimate is that close to half of all those killed during this period were members of these households. This was more than enough to have pushed Guangxi's death rates far above those in other regions of China. The violence unleashed against these households was far worse than their fate in the violent land reform and suppression of "counter-revolutionaries" in the early 1950s, which left their surviving members with stigmatizing political labels. If it were not for the massacres of individuals in these categories, Guangxi's death tolls would not have been exceptional.

The abundant detail in the investigation reports, however, leads us to a different understanding of the processes leading to the victimization. Based on chronologies in published county annals, Su found little evidence of factional conflict in rural regions. Published annals described factional conflict in cities, and to some extent in the towns that served as county seats, but rarely in rural districts and villages. Yet most deaths occurred in rural districts, where mass killings were concentrated. This led to the conclusion that the killings in rural districts were largely disconnected from the factional struggles in urban areas.

What, then, touched off the waves of killings in rural districts? The apparent absence of factional activity in rural regions made it appear that the harsh rhetoric against class enemies put out by the Guangxi Military District, coupled with widespread publicity about the July 3 Orders, inadvertently touched off waves of collective violence in villages that targeted "four type" households. This seemed to be a variety of the genocidal intergroup violence observed in other settings. Provincial military authorities periodically issued calls for mass killings to stop and did not appear to view them as necessary to consolidate military control. Moreover, it seemed clear that the killings were carried out by people who lived in the same rural districts, if not the same villages. It appeared that intergroup animosities were inadvertently stimulated by rhetoric emanating from Nanning, leading to massacres of households long identified with historical class enemies. Something went badly wrong in rural regions, perhaps signifying that community-level behaviors spun out of Nanning's control.[4]

The investigation materials alter this picture in several ways. First, the April faction was very active in around half of all counties, and their activity penetrated deeply into rural districts and villages in no fewer than a third of them. Rural killings hit April faction affiliates very hard in these places, but in regions where the April insurgency was less active, or largely absent, "four type elements" bore the brunt of suppression campaigns. Second, while the people who did the killings were indeed residents of the same rural districts and villages, in almost all cases the killers were members of regular militias or hastily organized "picket corps," essentially death squads, under the command of district-level PADs. They acted under urgent orders from their superiors, who mandated the drawing up of death lists, and who often had to pressure village leaders to either have their militia do the killings or turn the victims over to the district or county headquarters to carry out death sentences. Suppression campaigns were typically carried out via the same bureaucratic mobilization as in past political campaigns, although with a level of violent intensity not seen since the revolutionary foundations of the state. The waves of mass killings were not mandated by Nanning, but instead were pushed energetically by county-level authorities. These authorities were dominated by PADs that were themselves parties to local conflicts, and they were anything but a neutral force in the restoration of order. It was not local communities that spun out of control, but the lower reaches of military and security networks that reached deeply into rural districts, and that were largely intact and closely identified with the Allied Command.

There is very little evidence that Guangxi's distinctive history of migration and intergroup conflict or the presence of a large population of ethnic minorities served to intensify deadly violence. The investigation reports were completely silent about Guangxi's complex ethnic makeup and did not examine variation in the intensity of local violence. If certain local features were even partly responsible for Guangxi's elevated death rates, then the highest rates should have been in localities that had these distinctive features. By linking local death rates with data collected from other sources, we found virtually no discernible differences across regions with different ethnic profiles, and this applied equally to the Hakka subgroup, which was associated historically with violent intergroup conflict in Guangdong, the neighboring province to the east. We did find that more urbanized regions had lower death rates, but this simply confirmed the already evident fact that mass killings were located almost exclusively in rural districts. We also found that more remote regions along Guangxi's borders, and localities where the party-state structures were less fully staffed, had considerably *lower* death rates than localities in the interior, where the party-state's presence was stronger. This is the opposite of what we would expect to find if mass killings were the result of local communities that had spun out of the authorities' control.

Why, then, was Guangxi different? The answers flow from the unfolding of local politics, the organizational structure of military forces that were integrated into the party-state, and the location of Guangxi on the border of Vietnam precisely during the escalation of the American military effort. The last of these was especially relevant because Guangxi was the staging area for material and military support to North Vietnam during the same period when Beijing was urging the Vietnamese to refuse peace talks and fight on to victory.

The highly unusual retention of Wei Guoqing to head Guangxi's military control forces set in motion the train of events that led to the mass killings of 1968. No other long-serving top provincial official in China survived the wave of power seizures in early 1967. It was doubly unusual for a provincial leader who had been the target of all wings of local rebel movements to survive to head military control forces. The more radical members of the CCRG dissented strongly from this decision and from the outset actively sought to undermine Wei. They were never able to reverse this decision, but their active support of the April faction created deep splits among Guangxi's rebel forces and permitted the April faction to flourish through much of 1967. The surprising purge of these radical figures in September of that year robbed the April faction of their sponsors and set the stage for their eventual victimization.

Wei Guoqing's retention was undoubtedly a product of the rapidly escalating war in Vietnam. The Cultural Revolution was an assault on "revisionist" power holders across China, but it was also part of China's militant support for the struggle against global imperialism—a contrast with the revisionist USSR's recent espousal of peaceful coexistence. As Guangxi's longstanding party boss, Wei Guoqing was targeted as a revisionist by all rebel groups, especially after his early blunders in denouncing radical students in Guilin in the first stages of the Red Guard movement. Yet Mao Zedong was keenly aware that Wei had very close ties with Vietnam's leaders and had made historic contributions to their struggle against the French. As the Cultural Revolution unfolded, the American military campaign escalated beyond all expectations. Yet Mao was urging Vietnam's leaders to fight to victory and ignore Soviet advice to negotiate with the Americans.

If Wei had been purged along with other provincial leaders, it would have called into doubt China's commitment to Vietnam, and if disorders in the province had disrupted the flow of military supplies, this would further have undercut China's position in its rivalry with a "revisionist" Soviet Union. Mao appears to have decided early on to retain Wei, likely for this very reason. This would explain Wei's sudden "promotion" out of his position as the party boss of Guangxi only days after his missteps in handling the radical Guilin students. The surprising choice of Wei to head military control forces in Guangxi created a dilemma for rebel groups pre-viously hostile to him, and his appointment irrevocably split the already fractious rebel movement.

Further evidence is found in the pleas of Zhou Enlai and others that Wei had made great contributions in the struggle against imperialism and that support for him was essential in the ongoing war with the Americans. The April faction was unmoved by these arguments, surely due to backstage urgings by radical mem-bers of the CCRG, who were engaged in a speculative effort to get the "Center," essentially Mao, to change his mind about Wei. He never did, and the July 3 Orders, which explicitly mentioned the struggle in Vietnam as a justification for extreme measures, were the final piece of evidence for this interpretation.

Wei Guoqing inherited a situation in which Nanning's rebels had already split in the wake of their bungled power seizure. He had played no role in the events prior to late March 1967, when local military commanders had alienated one wing of the rebel movement. His appointment crystallized emerging factional align-ments in Nanning, and with the assistance of figures from the CCRG, the April faction was born.

Although Wei's unique position in the context of the escalating war in Vietnam was a key feature that distinguished Guangxi from other regions of China, it only set the context for the series of actions that led to the massacres of the summer of 1968. The key to the process were the wildly false reports about an underground anti-Communist movement throughout the province that the Preparatory Com-mittee and the Military District submitted to Beijing in the spring of 1968. These reports set in motion the sequence of events that pushed Guangxi's death tolls above those of all other regions of China.

We have seen that the actual situation at the time was one in which rural massacres of local April factions and noncombatants in "four type" households by PADs were escalating out of control, leading to a more militant response by a rearmed April faction and large-scale factional warfare in the cities. Instead of reporting accurately about the reasons why they were losing control of the situa-tion and failing utterly in their mission to enforce the November 1967 agreement reached in Beijing, the Nanning authorities submitted a wholly false and danger-ously inflammatory diagnosis to their superiors. They concocted a conspiracy theory that attributed the deteriorating situation in Guangxi to a massive covert movement to overthrow Communist Party rule by an "Anti-Communist Salvation Corps" spread throughout the province. This conspiracy, they charged, was aided by China's external enemies, in particular the Nationalist regime on Taiwan, and it allegedly activated remnants of historically reactionary forces that remained in the province—the "four type elements" who were designated as class enemies at the time of the Communist takeover.

As evidence for this conspiracy, PADs in counties also submitted false reports about local opposition to the forced imposition of Revolutionary Committees. The most egregious example was the unusually powerful April faction insurgency in Fengshan County, which in fact was headed by veterans of the Red Army. The Nanning authorities claimed that the strong resistance there was a revival of a real "Anti-Communist Salvation Corps" formed by defeated Nationalist Party loyalists that had operated in the county in the early 1950s. This utterly false portrayal of the situation denied any possibility that the April faction was a legitimate rebel faction with real grievances against the Preparatory Committee and local PADs. Instead, the group was portrayed as a front for an insurgency that sought to overthrow Communist Party rule in coordination with historical class enemies of the regime (the "four types") that were seeking to make a comeback.

Beijing ultimately accepted this false definition of the situation when it issued the July 3 Orders, with the tragic results described in earlier chapters. There are several reasons why they did so. There is ample evidence that Mao was already frustrated by his inability to curtail factional fighting, whether in Beijing's universities or in distant regions. By July 1968 Guangxi was one of the last regions that had yet to impose a Revolutionary Committee. The violence there was actually intensifying, despite the priority that Beijing had long given to resolving the conflicts there. Again, the urgency of pacifying the province as the American military campaign against North Vietnam escalated to its highest levels surely played a central role in Beijing's decision-making. In addition, there were potentially real security implications for China if there was any possibility that reports of active anti-Communist forces in the region were real.

The result was a harshly worded directive that focused specifically on Guangxi. To understand why the directive had such a drastic impact, however, we need to understand the organizational structure of factional conflict in the province. PADs in the counties, where the death tolls accelerated to the levels that distinguished

Guangxi from all other regions, were themselves parties to the factional conflict. Their networks of district and village militias were still intact. Their collapse in Fengshan County, where the PAD was decisively defeated for a period, was highly unusual, and stands in sharp contrast to other counties. The close association of the PAD with the Allied faction essentially made their networks of rural militias an instrument for the suppression of any locally active April factions, but, more important, it turned them into a machine that prosecuted a renewed class war against "four type" households, whom their superiors in Nanning had defined as part of a conspiracy to overthrow Communist Party rule. We do not know whether PAD and militia commanders believed this conspiracy theory, but their superiors certainly pressured them to act as if they did.

The underlying explanation involves a centralized bureaucratic machinery of oppression that was prone to internal escalation processes. The impact of the false narrative put forward by the Nanning authorities was exemplified in miniature by the events in Shangsi County, which generated the highest death rates of any jurisdiction in Guangxi.[5] A false report submitted by the county about local "bandits" reverberated in the provincial hierarchy and led its superiors to mandate a county-wide bandit extermination campaign. After a major effort, the authorities were unable to find any of the nonexistent bandits. Instead of admitting failure, or admitting that their original reports of banditry were false, they instead charged that villagers were hiding bandits. There followed a brutal campaign to coerce villagers to reveal the location of nonexistent bandits. This doubled the death toll that had already been racked up in the violence earlier applied to form the local Revolutionary Committee, giving the county the highest death rate of any locality. The parallels with local campaigns against "hiding grain" during the famine conditions at the end of the Great Leap Forward—which escalated death rates in Fengshan and Lingyun counties to close to 10 percent only a few years before—are unmistakable.

What ultimately distinguishes Guangxi from superficially similar incidents of mass killing in other settings is the highly organized nature of the process— a military-bureaucratic machinery that was intact despite the political disorders that had disabled civilian government. Notorious examples of ethnic cleansing in other settings, however, were the product of intergroup violence that followed the collapse of nation-states and the redrawing of national boundaries, spurring the mobilization of distinct groups marked off by religion, language, or other markers

of ethnic or national identity. A clear example was the partition of India and Pakistan in 1947, which spurred fighting among Hindus, Muslims, and Sikhs in the Punjab, East Bengal, and other regions, as local police forces disintegrated and sometimes joined in the violence.[6] Another is the collapse of Yugoslavia, which left Serb,
Croat, and Bosnian Muslim communities on the wrong side of new national borders, leading to mobilizations by breakaway leaders and paramilitary forces that
sparked intergroup violence in the form of ethnic cleansing. The explicit objective
was to drive groups out of a territory and create a more ethnically uniform population.[7] There was no comparable process in Guangxi, despite its highly diverse
population. The lines of conflict were instead defined by political factions that
were structured around networks of rural militias that extended into villages and
remained intact despite the collapse of civilian political institutions. This occurred
almost everywhere, regardless of local ethnic profiles.

   Although the Guangxi killings more closely resembled counter-insurgency
campaigns in other settings that victimized large numbers of noncombatants,
their distinctive organizational structure also sets them apart. The alleged 1965
coup attempt in Indonesia by Communist-affiliated military officers that led to
the murder of six generals set off a wave of mass killings of Communists and other
leftists, generating death rates that surpassed those in Guangxi. These events differed, however, in several ways. First, the local targets of these organized killings
were primarily people associated with major political parties. Indonesia had the
world's largest Communist Party outside of China, and an array of other leftist
groups were organized locally and in competition with nationalist and religious
parties.[8] The "conspiracy" of these groups and their alleged support for a coup attempt was more firmly rooted in longstanding political divisions than in an entirely fictional anti-Communist conspiracy as in Guangxi. Second, the killings
were organized by regular army units that operated through civilian militias and
youth groups associated with local political parties.[9]

   Indonesia did not have the militarized political structures of 1960s China, in
which regular militia forces were integrated into single-party rule down to the village level. Regular army units had to mobilize civilian political and religious organizations that were otherwise hostile to leftists. As a result, the mobilizations for massacres took place over a much longer period in Indonesia, and ultimately had much
higher death tolls.[10] In Guangxi, by contrast, the killings were highly organized and

completed in a very short and intensely violent period by local actors who were integrated into existing militia networks. They ended abruptly after the formation of the provincial Revolutionary Committee in August 1968. The organizational structure of Guangxi's mass killings also differs from deadly counter-insurgency campaigns in many other settings, which typically are carried out by regular military units that intervene in villages whose political loyalties are largely unknown to them, and which are suspected of harboring underground insurgencies.[11]

The distinctiveness of the Chinese setting from these superficially similar cases is what makes the upheavals of the Cultural Revolution so enigmatic, and what makes the conflicts of the period so difficult to understand. China was ruled by a highly centralized hierarchy that had both civilian and military components. It reached downward into local communities in ways that were unprecedented in China's long history, and which are replicated in few other modern states. These features permitted unusually high levels of political control, but when threatened with disintegration, they could unleash conflicts and death tolls of surprisingly sudden intensity. During the late 1960s, these structures disintegrated from within due to interventions from above by one unusually radical supreme leader. They had deadly consequences as the political order was rebuilt across China in 1968, but they found their most tragically intense expression in Guangxi, which found itself at a deadly conjuncture of domestic and international politics.

# The Sources and Data Set

The primary foundation for the narrative accounts and statistical analysis in this book is an eighteen-volume collection of materials, classified as "organizational secrets" (*jimi*), compiled in the 1980s by investigation teams sent out by China's central government. The background to the compilation of these reports is described in an article authored by a retired official from the Ministry of Public Security, published in the monthly magazine *Yanhuang chunqiu*, which before its forced closure in 2016 was well known for publishing articles about sensitive topics in Communist Party history.[1] The author was assigned by his ministry to take part in a joint investigation initiated by the Central Discipline Inspection Commission, the office of the Central Committee, the Ministry of Public Security, and other legal departments.

The investigations were conducted in two waves. The first, from April to June 1981, was a preliminary inquiry into "problems left over from the Cultural Revolution in Guangxi." The second wave, from April 1983 to January 1984, was a much larger effort under the supervision of a central party investigation team. A recent doctoral dissertation, based on extensive analysis of a broad range of official documents and interview sources, has deepened our understanding of these materials and how they were generated.[2]

## How and Why the Materials Were Compiled
The investigations had a clear political motivation. China's post-Mao leadership was engaged in a several-year-long campaign to "completely repudiate the Cultural Revolution." The trial of the "Gang of Four" and others implicated in Mao's remarkably destructive schemes took place in 1981.[3] China's mass media were filled with stories of political persecution and oppression during the Cultural Revolution, and the new party leadership sought to enforce the idea that all sides in the factional warfare of that period were to blame for the persecutions of that era. The disastrous results were attributed to the influence of an "ultra-left" political

line attributed to Mao's radical associates and generals linked to the long-since-disgraced marshal Lin Biao.

The investigation into Guangxi had a dual motivation. Well before Mao's death, the province had a reputation for brutally violent suppression of rebel insurgents, yet reports submitted by provincial officials did not reflect this. Wei Guoqing, no longer Guangxi's leader, had directed military forces in the province and served as head of the Revolutionary Committee established in 1968, the period when the killings occurred. Subordinates who were closely aligned with him were still in charge of Guangxi and, like Wei, had been aligned with the Allied Command faction and the Guangxi Military District at the time. They initially denied culpability for the events of the period and insisted that they had never done the bidding of the "Gang of Four" or Lin Biao.[4] The post-Mao leadership in Beijing viewed them as resisting the new trend in national policy and suspected that they were obscuring the death tolls and the causes.

In April 1981 the Central Committee sent a research team of twenty officials to Guangxi to conduct a preliminary investigation. For two months they interviewed individuals in the provincial leadership and consulted the provincial archives. They conducted similar research in several cities and selected counties, interviewed inmates of prisons and labor camps and more than 700 ordinary citizens, and collected some 3,000 written statements from witnesses. Local authorities were stubbornly uncooperative, limiting access to materials and interviewees.[5]

The investigation team returned to Beijing in June. They reported that local authorities had long hidden the true scale of the carnage and had obscured its causes. Back in October 1972, in the wake of the Lin Biao affair, the central authorities ordered Guangxi to account for its harsh repression campaign. Wei Guoqing directed the Guangxi Party Committee to report that 44,000 people had been killed in Guangxi, with the vast majority (33,000), coming from politically stigmatized "four type" households. The report attributed the killings to violent warfare between political factions and to popular animosity toward class enemies in "four type" households and absolved civilian and military authorities of any responsibility.[6] The report submitted by Beijing's investigation team, however, concluded that the true death toll was much higher, surely more than 100,000. Moreover, it concluded that very few of the deaths were the result of armed battles between civilian factions, and that most of those killed were executed by civilian and military authorities.[7] Some officials interviewed by the investigation team estimated that the true death toll was as high as 200,000. In a private conversation in 1981 with the deputy head of the Supreme People's Court, Wei Guoqing reportedly stated that the number was 150,000.[8]

The report was harshly critical of the Guangxi authorities, both their actions at the time and the subsequent effort to conceal and distort. One week after the report was submitted to CCP General Party Secretary Hu Yaobang, Guangxi's First Party Secretary Qiao Xiaoguang admitted that there were 70,400 "abnormal" deaths.[9] The Guangxi authorities nonetheless drafted a detailed refutation of the report, claiming that the death toll was inflated and that officials in Guangxi were not culpable. Wei Guoqing, who left Guangxi in 1976 and was at the time director of the PLA's General Political Department, submitted a lengthy letter to Hu Yaobang, denouncing the investigation report.[10]

Given these findings and the defensive reaction by figures from Guangxi, the central authorities were even more determined to document Guangxi's recent history. The second investigation began in April 1983 and lasted for nine months. It was overseen by Song Renqiong and Xi Zhongxun, both Politburo members, who outranked the leaders of Guangxi. They directed a forty-person investigation team led by Zhou Yifeng, Li Rui, and others, that was given authority over the Guangxi Party Committee. Now compelled to cooperate fully, the Guangxi Party Committee formed an investigation team of more than one hundred people, sending them to all twelve prefectures and cities and to the larger enterprises and universities. The prefectures and cities, in turn, sent investigation teams to each of the counties. The investigators assigned to Nanning alone interviewed more than 8,000 people and examined more than 20,000 written statements.[11]

This second investigation documented a total of 89,810 "abnormal" deaths during this period.[12] Its primary finding, beyond documenting a more complete death count, was that almost all the deaths were organized by provincial authorities during 1968, and they were carried out systematically by rural militias under PADs. The provincial authorities still insisted as recently as 1981 that most of the deaths were due to armed battles between factions or to massacres carried out by the victorious rebel faction. They had further asserted that most of the deaths occurred when government authority had collapsed and "the masses" got out of control. The investigation reports found something very different: civilian and military authorities had carried out killings in an organized way.

There remains considerable uncertainty about the reported death toll, which is likely an undercount. The investigators initially counted close to 20,000 people who had disappeared, and whose deaths could not be documented—the reason why their initial 1981 report expressed confidence that the actual death toll was more than 100,000.[13] Tabulations from the detailed city- and county-level materials contained in the eighteen-volume compilation yield totals closer to 82,000. Summary reports submitted to the Central Committee contained numbers that ranged from 84,000 to 87,000.[14] It is possible that the second investigation report decided to focus primarily on killings for which direct responsibility could be attributed, even though information about suicides and the missing was collected to verify compensation claims.[15]

Uncertainty about the final death toll raises questions about how the investigations were conducted. We know the number of investigators dispatched by Beijing, and we have an overall understanding of the large number of local investigators mobilized for the task. The eighteen volumes of investigation materials do not contain a "methodological appendix," but there are extant copies of the forms that investigators were required to fill out, and the instructions that accompanied them, and they shed some light on how investigators proceeded.[16]

The forms and accompanying instructions indicate an effort akin to a census, in which enumerators visit households to identify deaths related to the events of the period. Unlike a census, however, the enumerators did not need to visit every household in a locality. It is not clear what procedures were used to identify eligible households. The standard forms indicate that lists of individuals who were killed or missing were compiled for the "units" where the deceased individuals were employed or in residence at the time of death. This included government offices, schools, factories, and in rural areas the production brigade (or administrative village). Investigators in these units were expected to compile a complete list of all qualifying casualties. Each line contains information about one household: the number of people currently in the household; the occupation of the person killed and whether they were a "four type element" or a descendant of one; whether the victim was killed, committed suicide, disappeared, or died in armed combat; and the time period when the death took place (before or after the local Revolutionary Committee was formed, or before or after the July 3 Orders). Presumably, if more than one person was killed in a household, more than one line would be filled out on the form. The forms do ask how the individual was killed or who was responsible. This apparently was a line of investigation separate from documenting the total death count.

The instructions make clear that the forms were filled out through interviews with surviving family members. While the enumerators' job was like that of a census taker, it was also like that of an insurance adjuster. Interviewers were instructed to explain the party's determination to fully account for the wrongs committed during the period and to properly compensate the survivors. They were to show seriousness of purpose and have a sympathetic attitude. If the survivors made "excessive" demands for compensation (presumably, more than what was offered), the interviewers were instructed to carefully explain the party's policy. Standard forms state the monetary compensation for each person killed.

There are also detailed instructions about handling the forms: they are to be filled out with ink pen in triplicate, distributed to specific offices, and collated and stapled into booklets, and the numbers aggregated at each level of government as they are passed upward. The instructions also provide criteria for determining what kinds of deaths qualify for compensation (e.g., deaths that result from personal feuds or animosities do not qualify; deaths must follow within six months of a severe beating or injury). The instructions convey the ambiguity of the category of "missing"—the survivors must "affirm" (*queren*) that the missing person is dead. This seems primarily to be a legal declaration required to receive compensation.

It seems likely, although this is not stated, that investigators visited every household in a town or village known to have suffered a death. It is not known how they were identified. The household registration system at the time certainly made it possible to contact nearly every household. Those familiar with survey methodology will wonder what quality checks assured that all eligible households were visited and that forms were filled out accurately. They will also wonder about the identity of the interviewers. Given the responsibility of local authorities for the killings, this might inhibit a full reporting by surviving family members. We do not know how investigators were selected, or who they were. Most of those implicated in killings were still in residence, and many of them had risen to positions of authority. Even if they did not interfere with investigations, surviving household members might be wary of retaliation. The instructions to interviewers indicate that the designers of the survey understood that this was a potential problem. It is hard to imagine that there were not efforts by local officials who were threatened by this effort, especially those in rural areas, to prevent a full accounting. A well-known writer and investigative journalist who visited some of the most violent rural districts in 1986 was disturbed to find that people who had engaged in killings were still living in the same locations, and some were in positions of authority. He had heard that some of them had threatened revenge against individuals who reported on them, making people hesitant to speak up. He strongly suspected that the true scale of the carnage had yet to become fully known.[17]

Another source of undercounting is that some households did not survive intact and no longer existed. Narrative accounts in the investigation materials make clear that there were some households where everyone was killed, where the children were orphaned and sent to live with others, where only the elderly survived (and perhaps subsequently died), or where the females in the household were married off to others after the deaths of male household heads. Unless separate arrangements were made, these deaths would escape detection.

There may also have been internal debate about how to tabulate and report the totals on the forms that reached Nanning. The final number given in the 1983 report appears to have focused more narrowly on killings that could be confirmed. If the report that 20,000 people were "missing" is accurate, then this number clearly was not included in the final tabulations. Whether the final number was 83,000, 89,800, or even 110,000 was largely beside the point—death tolls in Guangxi were unusually high by any standard, and the question that really mattered to Beijing was who was responsible. The enumeration of deaths was a relatively small part of the overall effort to collect data. The final compilation of materials includes detailed descriptions of political events that could only have been collected from local government archives, as well as interviews and oral histories. Again, we have only a general idea of how these additional materials were collected, but they turn out to be the most valuable parts of the final compilation.

The investigations led to the transfer or removal of large numbers of provincial leaders. As the central government gained greater clarity about the obscured history of the province, Guangxi's Party Committee was "reorganized" repeatedly in the early 1980s, with each reorganization removing officials implicated by the investigations and restoring to leading posts those who were wrongfully purged. Guangxi's leading bodies were reshuffled in December 1980, March 1983, and June 1985, to deal with "lingering problems" left over from the Cultural Revolution.[18] Wei Guoqing, Qiao Xiaoguang, and four other top Guangxi officials were forced to admit their guilt and confess to responsibility in self-criticisms offered at central party meetings during 1983. Despite evidence of their direct responsibility and later efforts to cover it up, Wei Guoqing and the others were permitted to confess only to a failure to rein in the killings once they were under way. They were transferred to other posts, and some were forced to retire, but none was punished, although all were charged with grave political errors.[19]

More than 53,000 lesser-ranking individuals were punished because of the investigations, including more than 18,000 party and government officials. The minimum punishment, applied to more than 25,000, was expulsion from the Communist Party, usually followed by demotion or removal from leading posts. A small minority were sentenced to prison terms that often seemed light given the nature of the charges. An even smaller number received the death penalty.[20] Widespread retribution was avoided, and many were able to escape with a sincere confession and expulsion from the Communist Party. To avoid further destabilizing the party and risk yet another round of factional strife, Beijing's approach was to reveal the truth while showing leniency toward those who made sincere and full confessions.[21]

## The Scope and Reliability of the Materials

The final eighteen-volume compilation contained 12,237 pages of material about political events in the province from mid-1966 to the end of 1976. Most of the material concentrated on the years of greatest upheaval, 1967 and 1968. Volumes 1–6 contain detailed accounts of "major incidents" (*da shijian*) in each city and county, and volume 7 contains similar accounts that affected the entire province. Volumes 8–15 contain chronologies of political events in each city and county, along with summary statistical material and long lists of individuals who were punished for criminal acts documented in the investigations. Volumes 16 and 17 contain separate chronologies for 73 provincial departments and bureaus, universities, and other agencies. Volume 18 contains an overall chronology for the province, focusing primarily on developments in the provincial capital and on interactions with

Beijing.[22] The volumes have been reproduced as 36 searchable digital files (2 per volume) and are available through online subscription, CD-ROMs, or print copies.[23] I have obtained originals or photocopies of the original eighteen volumes, and I cite them by volume and page numbers in this book.

It is very rare to have access to materials of such comprehensive coverage and detail about political movements and state repression. Students of political conflict usually build databases of political events by tabulating press accounts from national or local newspapers, or they utilize routine data compiled by governments or police agencies. All these sources have potential biases, and these materials are no different. Their extraordinary level of evidentiary detail lends them considerable authority, but the fact remains that the results were a product of a politically motivated investigation, one that was designed to reveal atrocities in China's recent history that had been denied or concealed prior to the death of Mao Zedong.

The analysis presented in this book echoes the primary conclusion of the investigation: a large majority of the deaths inflicted on citizens were the product of coordinated suppression campaigns mandated by provincial authorities and carried out by local civilian and military hierarchies. There are so many different types of evidence presented in these materials that it is difficult to imagine that this conclusion was seriously distorted by the political objectives of the investigators and their sponsors in Beijing. It is possible that the investigators focused so single-mindedly on uncovering wrongdoing by people in positions of authority that similar acts by ordinary citizens were neglected to a certain degree in compiling case detail. Only half of those punished were expelled from the Communist Party, which suggests that most of the others were neither party members nor party-state cadres. Many of them are likely to have been members of rural militias or ordinary residents who cooperated with them or took advantage of opportunities for personal revenge or plunder. Summary statistics derived from narrative accounts about the identity of the actors implicated in the killings so overwhelmingly name grassroots authority figures that even if the percentages are exaggerated, it is hard to imagine that many ordinary citizens acted independently of their direction.

There are other reasons for doubting that the investigation's conclusions were seriously distorted by its political objectives. The full report contains a rich trove of data that the investigators collected but never analyzed. Some of the most valuable information is entirely unrelated to the objectives of the investigation. The main example concerns the detailed chronological narratives of local rebel movements, how city and county governments were overthrown, how they interacted with military units, how and when rebel factions formed, how local factions became affiliated with April 22 or the Allied Command, and how the course of conflict between them evolved over time. These local narratives provide historical detail that is not needed to determine how many people were killed and who was responsible. Yet they provide an unprecedented window onto politics at the provincial, city, and county levels that permits an analyst to sort out how factions developed and how conflict between them escalated. The accounts for the provincial capital of Nanning, combined with the province-level chronology in volume 18, also provide highly revealing detail about the involvement of emissaries from Beijing in the creation of the April faction and its subsequent survival.

Another example is information about the timing and scale of events in different localities. However incomplete the overall death counts may have been, and however obscure the methodology used by the investigators in counting the deaths, there are thousands of events recorded in these materials that permit us to track different kinds of political activity and associated deaths over time and place. None of this information was essential for the main purposes of the investigations, and it was compiled without undergoing any analysis. Yet the patterns of variation exhibited in these materials provide important clues about the processes that made Guangxi so much more violent than other regions of China.

These materials uncover statistical patterns that more convincingly support the investigators' conclusions. One is that very high death counts were generated over very short periods. These death counts correlated very closely with orders issued by provincial and local authorities. And at the local level, death rates spiked around the time that a local Revolutionary Committee was created, showing the impact of repression by military and civilian authorities. It is hard to imagine that death tolls of such magnitude that exhibited this pattern were generated by collective action at the local level that was not coordinated by civil and military networks.

Event data extracted from these materials, when combined with data from other sources, permit us to explore questions that the investigators never considered, but which reinforce their broad conclusions. An example is the statistical analysis in chapter 8, where regression models indicated that death rates were higher in localities where party-state structures were more fully staffed, and lower in remote border regions where the reach of provincial authorities was presumably weaker. These findings are based on unobtrusive measures at the county level that circumvent potential biases. They are what you would expect to find if actors under party-state authority carried out killings and are the opposite of what you would find if killings were the result of community actions that spun out of authorities' control.

### Extracting Data from Detailed Narratives

Two separate data sets were extracted from the narrative accounts and other sources.[24] The first is cross-sectional, with the 86 counties and cities as the unit of observation.[25] It includes a wide range of variables: demographic and social data (total population, urban population, minority population, Hakka population, school enrollments, number of nonagricultural workers, and so forth); political and geographic data (number of party members, number of salaried state cadres, distance from the seat of the prefecture, location along provincial or international borders, and so on); summary data about casualties (total numbers killed, total numbers victimized in other ways); and dates of key local political events (a rebel power seizure and collapse of civilian government, first intervention by the armed forces, first appearance of rebel factions, the formation of local factions identified with the April 22 faction or the Allied Command, the formation of a revolutionary committee, and so on). The data about the counties were extracted from published material: statistical yearbooks, histories of local Communist Party organizations, and local annals. Data about the timing of key political events and their impact were extracted from the investigation reports. The resulting cross-sectional data set contains very little missing information.

In the second data set, the unit of analysis is 4,937 events identified by location and time. It contains data about the type of action, the actors and harmed parties, and associated casualties. This event-based data set can be linked to the cross-sectional data set on counties and cities by using a jurisdiction code. While the cross-sectional data set is more comprehensive and complete than what I have been able to compile from published local annals in past research, the event-based data set represents an extraordinary advance in scope of coverage and level of detail.

While the abundant detail about events in the investigation reports makes them unusually valuable, it also presents new challenges for the compilation of a data set. The descriptions in the chronologies of major events in published annals that I have used in past research contain far less narrative detail. Large numbers of events are noted with little if any narrative description. This permitted relatively simple coding schemes that identified the type of an event in a typology of 11 categories, defined by whether the action was one of rebellion or suppression, conflict between rebel factions, or part of an organized campaign by authorities.[26]

The abundant detail in these investigation materials requires a complete rethinking of how to code them. The simple codes used in earlier research would ignore large quantities of valuable information. These materials typically provide specific detail about the actors involved. When military or civilian authorities are involved, the investigation reports describe a wide array of different actors: PLA units, PADs, rural militias, organized village "picket corps," Revolutionary Committees, village governments, or individual government officials or military officers. This requires a much more elaborate coding scheme. Regarding the nongovernment actors, "insurgents" or rebels, the narrative accounts similarly describe a wide array of different actors: the Allied Command faction, April 22 faction, Red Guards, unspecified "masses" or "rebels," and so forth. The accounts also provide detail about the target of the action, or the "harmed parties": members of the stigmatized "four type" households, one or the other rebel faction, unspecified "masses," government officials, military units, and so forth. To preserve this valuable detail, we devised more elaborate coding categories for both "actors" and "harmed parties." An additional complication is that for many events, several actors and several harmed parties are named. To capture this detail, up to three categories of each were recorded for an event. In the present case, this proved valuable in charting the joint actions of one or another rebel faction alongside military or government actors. It also proved valuable in charting the harmed parties that were the objects of their action.

There are several difficulties in defining an "event." The first is time duration and location. Narrative accounts are sometimes dramatic descriptions of individual battles, but they are just as often summary statements about a range of similar actions in a single location over several days, weeks, or even months. All this information is highly valuable, especially the information associated with these events—actors, harmed parties, numbers killed or wounded, and so forth. However, the descriptions of narrowly defined individual events might overlap with summary statements that cover many similar actions in the same locality in a specified period. The more narrowly defined individual events, usually given as examples of more broadly defined summary statements, are a subset of the overall activity described in these accounts. To add clarity to the nature of the "event" in the data set, the starting date (or month) and ending date (or month) for each are recorded. In addition, a separate code is added to identify the more narrowly defined cases that are also included in summary information about events from the same place and time. To use the resulting information to chart trends in types of events or associated casualties over time, it is necessary to restrict the analysis to events that are defined as occurring within a single month or two adjacent months, and which are not also coded as overlapping with more narrowly defined events in the same location. The data set thus preserves all potentially valuable information, but the analyst must exercise care in defining and selecting the cases to be used to address specific questions.

A second complication is defining the action that characterizes an event. The simple coding scheme used for the sparse descriptions in published annals permitted the classification of an event into a small number of general action types (for example, armed battle between factions, rebel attacks on authorities, suppression of rebels by authorities, or one of three specific political campaigns). To capture the more abundant detail in these materials, more fine-grained categories had to be devised. For example, an action by rebels could be a protest march or demonstration, an attack on a government compound, an attack on another rebel group, an attack on a military compound, a raid on an arms depot to seize weapons, a raid on a warehouse to seize material or food, a kidnapping or imprisonment of an opponent or government official, or a killing or summary execution. To accommodate the greater detail, the typology of 11 types used in coding the published annals was expanded into 27, more detailed categories.

The more detailed typology, however, proved difficult to implement in practice, because highly detailed descriptions could fall into several categories at once. For example, a raid by a rebel group on a building held by their opponents could start with a protest march and sit-in, which subsequently evolved into a violent but unarmed clash, which later involved calling in armed reinforcements for a full-scale "armed battle." The description could also include the taking of prisoners, the summary execution of one or more captives, mass meetings to denounce and abuse prisoners, and so forth. How to code such an event? Should instances of each of these actions be coded as separate events? Or should coders be forced to choose a single action type and ignore the other action types that are described? If so, which single type should the coder choose? The decision rule that we adopted, after much discussion and trial and error, was that the action should be coded into the broadest category that characterizes the event. In this example, the action should be classified as an "armed battle" between factions, with the understanding that a range of more narrow action types are typically included in that type of event. The narrow action types were reserved for smaller-scale, less complex events—for example, when a protest march does not evolve into something else, or when a rebel group simply captures prisoners from another faction (or executes them), or when captives are subjected to public struggle sessions during which they are brutalized. The rule of thumb used in coding was that the broadest category that "best characterizes" the event in question should be used, even if more narrow action categories are also evident as part of the broader event.

The extraordinary level of detail provided in many of these volumes was therefore both an opportunity and a challenge. It afforded the opportunity for a much higher-resolution picture of a larger range of political activity, but it also injected both ambiguity and imprecision into any coding scheme. This required a long process of devising workable coding categories and decision rules, and a long trial-and-error process of training coders, implementing the coding schemes, and engaging in continual discussion of particularly complicated cases as the compilation of the database proceeded. It also requires that anyone who analyzes the event data must understand how the categories were constructed and be clear about how to select a subset of specific events that are appropriate for the questions being asked.

The result is a multifaceted coding scheme that preserves as much information as possible, while providing an analyst several different ways to define events of interest. Events can be characterized by action type, by the actor or actors involved, by the harmed party or parties, or some combination of these features. Ambiguities in the definition of an action type can be bypassed by collapsing similar categories, or by focusing solely on the actors or harmed parties. This flexibility is useful in characterizing one of the most common action types in the dataset—instances of group killings, which were primarily responsible for the accumulation of the high death tolls. One can use information about the actors to answer key questions that we address in this book: which actors were responsible for the high death tolls, and whether factional opponents were killed in villages, which would indicate that factional conflict was not restricted to urban settings. Another useful distinction is when the actor is identified as local militia and the harmed parties as members of a losing civilian faction, or alternatively when the actors are local "masses" and the harmed parties are members of stigmatized class categories. The first would indicate a coordinated campaign; the second would indicate collective behavior at the community level. If the description permitted, each event was coded based on whether the location of the event is in an urban settlement (city or town) or a rural district or village.

The least difficult decision to make in coding events is recording their impact. For each action the numbers killed, injured, or otherwise harmed are recorded, if such numbers are provided in the account. If no figures are provided for these categories, zero is entered. In this book I have used the event data and associated casualty counts in two separate ways: to describe trends over time and place by charting different types of nonoverlapping events, and to answer questions about the causes of Guangxi's high death tolls by examining the actors and harmed parties.

The statistical analysis of data extracted from the narratives permits a much closer and more systematic look at this rich body of evidence, which from a social-science perspective has gone almost completely unanalyzed. It permits us to trace events and related killings over time and place. The multivariate analyses in chapter 8, which link this data with separate information from other sources, provide an independent check on the broad conclusions that the investigators drew from these materials. In addition, the database provides leverage over questions that were never asked by the investigators, and that were never raised in the conclusions that they submitted to authorities in Beijing. They did not address variation in the intensity of violence across localities. We found, for example, that half of Guangxi's counties were not much more violent than the rest of China, and that high death rates were concentrated in a minority of counties. We also found that the April faction was spread unevenly across Guangxi, but in a large minority of regions they penetrated deeply into rural communities. This finding lent more plausibility to the notion that the repression of the April faction was an important motivation for rural killings, and that stigmatized households were swept up as collateral damage or were treated as scapegoats in communities where the April faction was absent.

The analysis of local variation permits us to address additional questions that were never considered by those who compiled the reports, such as whether there were ethnic or other group antagonisms that might have elevated death rates, or whether there is independent evidence to support the contention that the deaths were organized by local authorities and carried out by militias under their direction. Our discovery that ethnic diversity did not appear to exaggerate the intensity of violence casts doubt on suspicions that Guangxi's diverse populations may have generated more intense violence than was the case in other regions of China. Even more telling, the finding that death rates were considerably higher in regions where the reach of the party state was strongest was not a question that the investigators even considered, but it strongly reinforced their conclusion that the killings were organized by local authorities and carried out primarily by rural militias under their command. Further analysis of the material therefore goes well beyond the questions asked by the investigators and provides independent support for the broad conclusions that they drew from the materials they collected.

It was once customary to provide extensive tabular material in the appendices of publications about the variables in a data set, their definitions, and the coding rules that were followed in compiling them. Following current practice, I have instead made this information, along with the data sets themselves, available through a link on my current faculty webpage.[27] Those who have questions about my analysis can examine these materials themselves. In subsequent years this material will be transferred permanently to a public data repository. I invite those interested in the details of my analysis, or who can devise more creative ways to analyze this information, to utilize this material. As is often the case in projects such as this, I have explored only a fraction of the questions that might be addressed with the data collected.

# CHRONOLOGY

**1966**

**August 7.** Fight breaks out at Guangxi Normal College between students who had opposed the work team sent by the Guilin Party Committee and students who supported the work team. This became known as the "August 7 Incident."

**August 10.** Red Guards from Guilin Normal College send a delegation to Beijing to protest the "August 7 Incident" and actions by Guilin's party secretary. The delegation demands that Wei Guoqing come to Guilin to handle the situation and remove the party secretary from his post for obstructing the Cultural Revolution.

**August 13.** Wei Guoqing is in Beijing for the meetings of the Central Committee's 11th Plenum. Wei takes a flight to Guilin and convenes a meeting there of the provincial leadership. On August 17 they accede to the student demands and remove Guilin's party secretary and a deputy party secretary from office.

**August 18.** Mao Zedong holds massive Tiananmen Square rally in support of the Red Guards. Students from Guangxi Normal College seize and humiliate Guilin's deputy party secretary; the first party secretary flees the city to escape them. Red Guard groups begin to form in Nanning and other cities.

**August 19.** Outraged by students' seizure of the Guilin official, Wei Guoqing denounces them as "rightists" and orders a tightening of security forces to prevent a recurrence.

**August 24.** Wei Guoqing is removed as first party secretary of Guangxi and replaced by the second-ranking party secretary, Qiao Xiaoguang. Wei is moved to a nominally higher-ranking post as second party secretary of the Central Committee's Central-South Bureau, a position that normally would not require him to vacate his provincial post.

**September 3.** To repair relations with rebellious students, Wei Guoqing issues a "wall poster" welcoming students to criticize him, declaring his firm support for the student rebellion.

**September 9.** Guilin Red Guards from Guangxi Normal College stage a protest at the Guangxi Party Headquarters in Nanning to protest Wei Guoqing's denunciation of them as "rightists." This develops into a prolonged sit-in hunger strike that rallies support from large numbers of Red Guards from Nanning.

**September 20.** Red Guards put up wall posters attacking Wu Jinnan, the provincial official in charge of conducting the Cultural Revolution in Guangxi.

**Early October.** Wu Jinnan is forced to attend a series of mass struggle sessions where he is abused and made to apologize for his political errors. Wu resigns as head of Guangxi's Cultural Revolution Committee.

**October and November.** The rebel campaign grows in Nanning, as students and workers form a variety of alliances, all of them targeting Wei Guoqing and other top provincial officials.

**December 3.** First organization of rebel workers is formed. Others follow in subsequent weeks.

**December 4.** *Guangxi Daily*, the official party organ, publishes an article declaring that the party leadership has committed a series of mistakes in their initial response to the growing student campaign. The same day, Wei Guoqing issues a self-criticism for his responsibility in carrying out the "bourgeois reactionary line" in Guangxi.

**December 8.** Mass rally organized by 27 rebel groups and attended by more than 50,000 followers denounces the "bourgeois reactionary line" of the Guangxi and Nanning party leadership. Except for Wei Guoqing, most of the top leaders are in attendance. Qiao Xiaoguang gives a speech apologizing for their errors.

## 1967

**January 7.** Rebels on the staff of *Guangxi Daily* announce their takeover of the newspaper and rename it the *Daily Bulletin*. The first issue denounces the newspaper for carrying out an erroneous political line for the previous nine years under Wei Guoqing.

**January 15.** A large alliance of rebel cadres in Nanning forms a coalition with worker and student rebels known as the "Rebel Army."

**January 19.** Wei Guoqing is taken hostage by rebels at the Guilin Air Force hospital, where he had taken refuge. With other provincial officials, he is subjected to three successive days of abusive mass struggle sessions at Guilin Stadium. The officials are forced to kneel and wear black placards and dunce caps, while they are harangued by the rebels. After each session they are paraded through the streets of Guilin on the back of trucks. Wei Guoqing, on the first truck, is pelted with stones and spat upon by the crowds.

**January 21.** Guangxi's Party Secretariat issues a statement welcoming the seizure of power by the Rebel Army.

**January 23.** At 3 a.m., twenty-six rebel groups affiliated with the Rebel Army, led by the Workers' Headquarters, invade the provincial offices, and take power. The Guangxi Military District expresses its support.

**January 26–28.** The Rebel Army requests that PLA officers be sent to key offices and enterprises to back up their power seizure.

**January 29–February 5.** Wei Guoqing issues three more wall posters apologizing to rebel groups for his political errors.

**February 4.** Wang Li, an emissary from Beijing's Central Cultural Revolution Group (CCRG), criticizes the Rebel Army for failing to unite with other rebels and attacking too many leading cadres. He counsels a second power seizure to unite with selected provincial leaders.

**February 8 and 9.** Wang Li meets with cadre rebels in the provincial offices about joining with rebel groups to form an anti–Wei Guoqing coalition along with former provincial leaders.

**February 11.** The Rebel Army withdraws its representatives from provincial offices, ceding control to the Military District.

**February 11 and 16.** At two leadership meetings in Beijing, military figures express anger about the impact of the Cultural Revolution, leading to a backlash against allegedly "conservative" military officials and suspicion of the motives of army commanders in the provinces. This becomes known as the "February Adverse Current."

**February 12 and after.** Wei Guoqing and other provincial leaders are forced to attend a series of eight mass struggle sessions attended by more than 50,000 people.

**February 14.** Guangxi Military District withdraws its support for the Rebel Army and designates rebel groups that had withdrawn from its power seizure coalition and others as the "genuine revolutionary left."

**February 19.** A dozen ranking provincial leaders issue a proclamation repudiating Wei Guoqing.

**February 22.** Rebels from *Guangxi Daily* drag Wei and Qiao Xiaoguang to their offices for a struggle session, and afterward circulate material accusing them of political crimes.

**March 1.** Mass rally organized by defectors from the Rebel Army, encouraged by the Military District, denounces the errors of the Workers' Headquarters. Several groups call for "smashing" that rebel group, while supporters demonstrate at the Military District Headquarters to protest its stance.

**March 12.** Rebel cadres from the Guangxi Party Committee offices coordinate with more than 100 rebel organizations to hold a mass struggle session attended by 40,000 rebels to criticize Wei Guoqing and Qiao Xiaoguang.

**March 13.** Zhou Enlai telephones Wei Guoqing and informs him that to aid the effort to support Vietnam and resist American imperialism, Guangxi will be put under military control and that he will be appointed as head. He orders the

Guangzhou Military Region to provide him an army uniform and has the PLA 7th Air Force division fly him to Guangzhou the next day.

**March 17.** Wei Guoqing receives instructions from Zhou Enlai and flies to Beijing. Commanders of the Guangxi Military District set up a committee to convince local rebels to accept Wei as "standing forward" for the revolution. They hold a series of meetings to convince rebel groups to reverse their stances and support Wei.

**March 19.** Guilin Red Guards issue a call to "overthrow Wei Guoqing and liberate Guangxi."

**Mid- to late March.** The CCRG's emissary to Guangxi, Wang Li, coordinates with rebel groups to oppose Wei Guoqing and confers with his superiors in Beijing, who encourage efforts to undermine Wei and the Guangxi Military District.

**March 23.** The imposition of military control under Wei Guoqing is publicly announced.

**End of March.** Large public demonstrations and parades are held by rebel groups, some expressing their determination to overthrow Wei Guoqing and others expressing their support for him. Street confrontations follow. Sensing a shift in Beijing's position regarding Wei, more than 50 provincial cadres and 150 mass rebel groups shift toward support for Wei.

**Mid-April.** Rebel groups hold rallies and demonstrations in support of the Workers' Headquarters. They demonstrate at *Guangxi Daily* offices and demand that the military control group withdraw; counter-rallies in support of the military control group are held.

**April 19.** A proclamation is issued by Wu Jinnan and a large group of provincial leaders in support of rebel groups that oppose Wei Guoqing and actions of the Guangxi Military District.

**April 22.** A mass rally is held by anti-Wei rebels at Chaoyang Stadium to declare support for the "April 19 Proclamation." Protest marches to the offices of *Guangxi Daily* follow. Reinforced by others, they invade the newspaper's building and take it over on April 27. They withdraw on May 3 on orders from Beijing. This rallies anti-Wei groups across Nanning under a new rebel alliance that adopts the name "April 22 Revolutionary Action Headquarters," which becomes the April 22 faction.

**April 24.** During meetings in Beijing, the CCRG's emissary Wang Li consults with his superiors about "the Center's" attitude toward Wei Guoqing, and he is told that for the time being Wei cannot be overthrown, but that mass opposition might eventually succeed.

**April 29.** Anti-Wei petition group from Guangxi presents their accusations against Wei Guoqing and the Guangxi Military District in Beijing.

**April 30.** Beijing orders representatives from pro- and anti-Wei factions to come to the capital to negotiate their differences. While in Beijing, the anti-Wei rebels meet repeatedly with CCRG representatives, who encourage their continued opposition to Wei.

**May 3.** Anti–Wei Guoqing delegation of twelve members, headed by Wu Jinnan, boards train for Beijing.

**May 11.** Pro–Wei Guoqing rebels form an alliance called the "Nanning Region Proletarian Revolutionary Allied Command," which becomes the province-wide faction known as "Allied Command."

**Late May.** The April faction again invades and takes over *Guangxi Daily*; counterattacks by Allied Command rebels and harsh warnings by military commanders follow.

**May 26.** April faction delegates and supporters stage a demonstration in Beijing at the hotel where Wei Guoqing is staying, planning to take him into custody. They remain on site until May 31, when the CCRG orders them to stop.

**June 1.** First meeting of the Guangxi delegations in Beijing with Premier Zhou Enlai and other leaders.

**June 14.** Train service along route to Vietnam is blocked by factional conflicts. A second meeting of the Guangxi delegations takes place in Beijing with Zhou Enlai, who expresses anger about the blockage of the railway system. Subsequent meetings are held on June 15 and 29. Zhou orders a halt to factional clashes.

**July 4.** "Ten-point agreement" to halt factional conflict, blocking railways, and seizing arms is signed by delegates in Beijing. It has little effect, and arms seizures by the two factions increase during July.

**Mid-July.** Qi Benyu meets with the April 22 delegation in Beijing. Representing the CCRG, he makes statements that indicate the April faction is their favored side in the Guangxi conflicts.

**August 9.** April 22 activists in Beijing, reinforced by local Beijing Red Guards, make a second attempt to seize Wei Guoqing at his Beijing hotel. They are unable to take him hostage, but Wei is beaten severely and hospitalized for several weeks with serious injuries.

**August 11.** Violent clashes continue at the offices of *Guangxi Daily* in efforts to dislodge April 22 forces that occupied the premises.

**Late August.** Representatives of the CCRG meet with April faction delegates in Beijing to ask for their final demands in the negotiations, leading them to believe that a decision in their favor is imminent.

**August 24.** In meeting with delegations in Beijing, Zhou Enlai calls April 22 a genuine rebel organization, while the Allied Command is simply a "mass organization." The statement is widely interpreted as clear support for the April faction, demoralizing Allied Command leaders, spurring defections to the April faction, and causing several PLA units stationed in Guangxi to withdraw their support for the Allied Command.

**Early September.** Mao Zedong reverses his support for rebel attacks on military forces and orders the arrest of the CCRG's Wang Li and Guan Feng for "wrecking the Cultural Revolution." He delays until January 1968 an order for Qi Benyu to be arrested for the same reasons. This removes the April faction's most active supporters in Beijing.

**October.** First mass killings of "four type elements," organized by People's Armed Departments (PADs), occur in rural counties in Guilin Prefecture, along the border with Hunan Province.

**November 8.** Delegations in Beijing sign a formal cease-fire agreement, which is celebrated in Nanning by a mass rally of 120,000 people at Chaoyang Stadium.

**November 12.** Mao Zedong approves the plan for an alliance of rebel groups under Wei Guoqing and a Preparatory Committee to create a new government in the form of a Revolutionary Committee in Nanning.

**November 18.** Beijing issues its final decision on Guangxi. Wei Guoqing and the commanders of the Guangxi Military District issue self-criticisms for "supporting one faction and suppressing another," while Wu Jinnan issues self-criticism for his role in promoting factional conflict.

**November 19.** In his final meeting with the Guangxi delegations in Beijing, Zhou Enlai warns the Allied faction against further mass killings of the kind that occurred the previous month in Guilin Prefecture.

**November 23.** The two Guangxi delegations take a flight back to Nanning, where they are welcomed and applauded by a crowd of more than 1,000 at the airport.

**November 27.** Wei Guoqing convenes the first meeting of the Preparatory Committee. It orders the return of arms by both factions, the end of factional fighting, the return of all fighters to their home counties, and the resumption of military control over *Guangxi Daily.*

**Late November.** Killings of April faction members and "four type elements" by Allied Command forces and local militia begin to spread in rural counties.

**Mid-December.** Preparatory Committee urges end to armed battles outside of Nanning.

**December 19.** Sit-in protest over mass killings, by more than 200 people from 10 rural counties, occurs at the Military District Headquarters in Nanning. The April faction forms an antimassacre committee to demand that the Preparatory Committee immediately send armed troops to stop killings in rural counties.

**December 20.** Representatives from outside Nanning demand that authorities telephone local PADs to halt suppression campaigns and local massacres.

**December 24.** Preparatory Committee and Military District issue a directive calling a halt to arrests and killings in rural regions, and an end to factional battles, but they do not dispatch troops to enforce the orders.

**December 26.** April faction rally is held at Military District Headquarters to demand a halt to mass killings.

## 1968

**January 5.** Students affiliated with the Allied Command stage a rally of more than 1,000 at the entrance to the Military District Headquarters, demanding punishment for Wu Jinnan. Students from Guangxi University seize Wu and drag him to an athletic field where he is insulted and physically abused for two hours. Zhou Enlai sends a telegram denouncing the actions, and the April faction stages a massive demonstration to protest.

**January 18 and 20.** Rebels from Hechi Prefecture stage demonstrations at the Military District Headquarters to protest killings in Lingshan County. The Military District agrees to send officers to deal with the problem.

**Late January.** Armed fighting escalates; rural militias step up killings of "bandits" and "counter-revolutionaries."

**February 2.** Preparatory Committee issue orders against armed battles.

**Early February.** Disputes within the Preparatory Committee lead to a collapse of cooperation between the leaders of the two factions. The April faction accuses the Military District of complicity in rural massacres, while military officers blame the April faction for continued fighting. The April faction mobilizes for self-defense, while the military commanders become more closely aligned with the Allied Command and PAD forces.

**Early February.** April faction rebels in the Liuzhou Railway Bureau repudiate the cease-fire, which they argue is forcing them to surrender to an aggressive Allied Command faction, and they call for armed resistance. This leads to a split within the April faction leadership over whether to withdraw from the alliance agreement.

**February 12.** More than 5,000 members of the April faction protest at the Military District Headquarters to demand that PLA unit 6984 refuse transfer orders out of Nanning.

**February 18.** The Military District denounces April faction efforts to block the transfer of sympathetic PLA units and orders the accelerated formation of city and county Revolutionary Committees.

**February 22.** The Guangxi Military District sends a report to Beijing claiming that "class enemies" are attacking the Preparatory Committee, occupying military offices, violating central directives, seizing weapons, and kidnapping officials.

**February 27.** The Preparatory Committee issues an urgent directive to form local Revolutionary Committees as fast as possible. This leads to an upsurge of mass killings that accompany their formation in March and April.

**February 28.** The April faction forms "field armies" to stop local massacres and support the April faction in rural regions.

**March 2.** Large April faction rally demands the return of PLA unit 6984 to Nanning, charging that the transfer was in preparation for their suppression.

**March 15.** The Military District sends a report to Beijing claiming the discovery of a counter-revolutionary organization in Ningming County headed by a former landlord; they send another report to Beijing the next day that denounces the April faction's "field armies" as preparing for large-scale warfare.

**March 18 and 19.** The April faction sends a petition delegation of 400 to Beijing to protest their victimization at the hands of the Preparatory Committee.

**March 29.** Leaders of the April faction split over the field armies. Those who refused to denounce them are removed from the Preparatory Committee.

**April 3.** April faction leaders in Nanning declare their opposition to the formation of the Guangxi Revolutionary Committee and organize a large protest at the Military District Headquarters. The Allied Command responds that the formation of a Revolutionary Committee is a victory over counter-revolutionaries.

**April 9.** Mass meeting is convened by the Preparatory Committee to celebrate the formation of the Nanning City Revolutionary Committee. Speakers denounce those who oppose the Revolutionary Committee, and claim they are planning massacres of Communists like those carried out by Chiang Kai-shek in 1927.

**April 11.** *Guangxi Daily* calls for a "force 12 typhoon" of fierce suppression against those who are resisting the formation of Revolutionary Committees and allegedly plotting to carry out mass killings across Guangxi. The Military District reports to Beijing that April faction fighters in Wuzhou are out of control, fighting against PLA and PAD forces. Several days later another report charges that the April faction is working together with former class enemies to oppose Communist Party rule.

**April 19.** April faction delegation in Beijing lodges protest at the CCRG offices about false reports submitted by the Guangxi Military District.

**Mid-May.** Allied Command forces seize arms and ammunition from PLA units. Zhou Enlai orders them to stop arms seizures and return the weapons.

**May 17.** The Preparatory Committee and Military District submit a report to Beijing that claims the discovery of an underground organization linked to the Nationalist Party that has branches throughout Guangxi. They claim that its headquarters is a building on Liberation Road in Nanning that is the headquarters of the April faction.

**May 20.** The Military District and Preparatory Committee issue a detailed directive calling for an offensive against this subversive organization, which has links to historical counter-revolutionaries in "four type" households in collaboration with the April faction. In a report to Beijing, they claim that an armed anti-Communist movement has formed in Fengshan County, led by counter-revolutionaries and traitors.

**End May.** After the withdrawal of PLA unit 6984 from Nanning, Allied Command forces attack remaining April faction bases in the city; the Preparatory Committee reports to Beijing that large-scale armed battles are imminent in the city. Beijing orders Wei Guoqing to come to Beijing and report personally on the worsening situation.

**Early June.** Armed warfare escalates in Guilin, and militias in 12 counties in the region prepare for a battle that will be fought over the next two months. Allied Command forces stage a series of large arms seizures in Nanning to prepare for the final battle with the remaining April faction forces.

**June 9.** Preparatory Committee and Military District order county Revolutionary Committees to stop sending militia forces to engage in armed battles in Nanning, Guilin, and Liuzhou.

**June 13.** Nanning Revolutionary Committee claims to have discovered an "Anti-Communist Salvation Corps" headquarters in the city, linked to "five type elements," traitors, and secret agents. The Allied Command uses an anti-aircraft gun to attack an April faction base at the city's department store, setting it ablaze.

**Mid-June.** April faction protest delegation in Beijing stages sit-in at the hotel where Wei Guoqing is staying. They try to invade the premises but are arrested by PLA troops.

**June 17.** The Preparatory Committee and Military District send out a notice directing a coordinated, province-wide effort to extinguish a reputed "Nationalist Anti-Communist Salvation Corps," which is allegedly coordinating resistance to the formation of Guangxi's Revolutionary Committee.

**June 19.** Allied Command fighters attack a building held by the April faction and massacre 62 of the defenders, dumping the corpses into the Yong River.

**June 23.** Allied Command attacks a wharf controlled by the April faction on the Yong River, destroying or damaging 40 boats.

**July 1.** The Nanning Garrison Command holds a conference to plan for final attacks on April faction strongholds in Nanning; six companies of PLA troops from the Military District and militias from nine counties would be mobilized for the offensive.

**July 3.** Beijing issues the "July 3 Orders," unleashing any remaining constraints on the use of armed force; this accelerates mass killings in rural counties across Guangxi.

**August 26.** After remaining April faction resistance is crushed by armed force in Nanning, Guilin, and Liuzhou, and following an unprecedented surge of mass killings in rural districts, the Guangxi Revolutionary Committee is established. Military control of the province is consolidated after sporadic executions of captured insurgents during September. Killings are finally curtailed.

**Guan Feng** (关峰). Younger member of the Central Cultural Revolution Group in Beijing; supporter of the April 22 faction who during 1967 worked to undermine Wei Guoqing in Guangxi and encouraged rebel attacks on military commanders across China. He was purged and imprisoned in September 1967 for "wrecking the Cultural Revolution."

**He Ximing** (贺希明). Third-ranking party secretary of Guangxi prior to the rebel power seizure in January 1967; supporter of Wu Jinnan and the April 22 rebel faction.

**Hu Yaobang** (胡耀邦). Chairman and then general secretary of the Chinese Communist Party from 1981 to 1987 who authorized the investigations of the Cultural Revolution in Guangxi and otherwise pushed for the liberalization of China's political system. He was removed from office after his policies were blamed for encouraging a wave of student prodemocracy protests near the end of 1986. His death in April 1989 touched off another wave of student protests that were eventually crushed by military force.

**Huo Fan** (霍泛). Sixth-ranking party secretary of Guangxi prior to the rebel power seizure in January 1967; supporter of Wu Jinnan and the April 22 rebel faction.

**Li Rui** (李锐). As vice director of the Central Organization Department and member of the CCP Central Committee, he was one of the leaders in charge of the investigation team sent to Guangxi. He spent almost twenty years in labor camps and prisons after making critical comments about Mao and the Great Leap Forward at the Lushan Plenum in 1959. He was rehabilitated after Mao's death and elevated to the Central Committee in 1982. Forced to resign from his positions in 1984, he later became a leading critic of the party and advocated for fundamental political reforms.

**Qi Benyu** (戚本禹). Younger member of the Central Cultural Revolution Group in Beijing; supporter of the April 22 faction who during 1967 worked to undermine Wei Guoqing in Guangxi and encouraged rebel attacks on military commanders across China. He was purged and imprisoned in January 1968 for "wrecking the Cultural Revolution."

**Qiao Xiaoguang** (乔晓光). First party secretary of Guangxi after Wei Guoqing's transfer to a new post in the Central-South Bureau of the Central Committee in August 1966; supporter of Wei Guoqing and aligned with the Allied Command faction.

**Song Renqiong** (宋任穷). As head of the Central Committee's Organization Department, was one of two Politburo members who oversaw the Guangxi investigations of the early 1980s.

**Wang Detang** (王德堂). Political commissar of the Lingyun County People's Armed Department. He took control of the county after a rebel power seizure and later became the head of the county Revolutionary Committee. Removed from that post as a serial rapist in 1969, he was sentenced to death for murder and rape, and executed in 1985.

**Wang Li** (王力). Younger member of the Central Cultural Revolution Group in Beijing; supporter of the April 22 faction who during 1967 worked to undermine Wei Guoqing in Guangxi and encouraged rebel attacks on military commanders across China. He was purged and imprisoned in September 1967 for "wrecking the Cultural Revolution."

**Wang Li** (王荔). On the staff of the "Reporter's Station" of the Central Cultural Revolution Group. Served as envoy to Guangxi, where he encouraged opposition to Wei Guoqing, helping to form the April 22 faction and subsequently encouraging its stand.

**Wei Guoqing** (韦国清). Guangxi's longstanding top party official. His appointment as head of military control forces was supported by the Allied Command faction and opposed by the April 22 faction. He became head of Guangxi's Revolutionary Committee in 1968 and served in that post until 1975.

**Wu Jinnan** (伍晋南). Second-ranking party secretary of Guangxi prior to the rebel power seizures in January 1967; highest ranking official to oppose Wei Guoqing as head of military control forces. He was aligned with the April 22 faction, which supported him as an alternative to Wei Guoqing.

**Xi Zhongxun** (习仲勋). Politburo member with liberal and proreform sympathies; was imprisoned during the Cultural Revolution but freed and placed in charge of Guangdong Province in 1978, where he helped to pioneer early economic reforms. As a Politburo member in 1982 was one of two leaders who oversaw the Guangxi investigations. Father of Xi Jinping, who became China's leader in 2013.

**Xiong Yijun** (熊一军). Nanning rebel leader involved in the Guangxi power seizure who led a large worker rebel alliance opposed to Wei Guoqing. He was arrested by Military District forces in February 1967 and released on Zhou Enlai's orders in August.

**Zhou Enlai** (周恩来). China's premier who worked to blunt the more destructive impulses of Mao and members of the Central Cultural Revolution Group. Directed negotiations between the Allied Command and April 22 in Beijing from May to November 1967.

**Zhou Yifeng** (周一峰). Official in charge of the Guangxi investigation team in 1983; at the time he was deputy governor of Jiangsu Province.

# NOTES

## Prologue

1. This account of the battle of Nanning draws on two sources: Guangxi Cultural Revolution Chronology (1990, 106–16), and Guangxi Party Committee (1987, 13:106–11).

2. Photographs of the devastated neighborhood, ranks of marching prisoners, and the summary executions were included in a publication that has long since been withdrawn in China (Guangxi Cultural Revolution Chronology 1990). Several of the photographs are reproduced in Walder (2015).

3. This account is based on Guangxi Party Committee (1987, 3:647–55, 6:242–60 and 297–306).

4. This account is based on Guangxi Party Committee (1987, 2:31–63).

5. Guangxi Party Committee (1987, 2:62).

6. For example, Sutton (1995); Zheng (1996); Su (2011); Song (2002).

7. This account is based on Guangxi Party Committee (1987, 2:40–41).

8. One well-documented example was a month-long battle in the Yangzi River port city of Luzhou, in Sichuan Province, in July 1968, which engaged some 24,000 fighters and claimed 2,000 lives (Walder 2019, 169–70; drawing on Luzhou City Annals 1998, 38; and Sichuan Province Annals 1999, 139–40).

9. Walder (2019, 178–87).

10. Two widely reported instances were in Changping and Daxing counties, in the Beijing suburbs, and in Dao County, Hunan, and several surrounding counties in Lingling Prefecture (Song 2002; Tan 2010; 2017).

11. This is based on a detailed examination of numbers reported in published and unpublished local accounts from more than 2,200 local jurisdictions, which yielded estimates that tally closely with reports of an internal Central Committee investigation conducted in the 1980s (Walder 2014; 2019, 188–90).

12. Guangxi Party Committee (1987, 7:127).

13. Yan (2012). The total death toll of 89,810 in the official report was said to include an unspecified number of "missing." It is possible that some of the missing were included in the final official tally, which is higher than the results of

tabulations mentioned in the previous paragraph. The separate reports for cities, counties, and organizations only rarely provide totals for the missing. Yan appears to refer to information about the missing that was excluded from the final report.

14. Fengshan County's death rate was 1.36 percent; Shangsi County's was 1.44 percent.

15. Of the 2,246 counties and cities for which officially published or unpublished data are available, 52 localities had death rates above 4.0 per thousand. Of these, 30 were in Guangxi, and the next largest number were in Inner Mongolia, where 3 counties reported death rates greater than 10 per thousand, or 1 percent (Walder 2019, 192).

16. Ball, Kobrak, and Spirer (1999, 119); Robinson (2018, 120–21).

17. For Bosnia, Zwierzchowski and Tabeau (2010). Syria's prewar population was close to 21 million, slightly below that of Guangxi in 1966. The United Nations and other sources estimate a range of 400,000 to 500,000 dead in the Syrian upheavals.

## Chapter 1

1. Walder and Su (2003); Walder (2014; 2019, 173–87).

2. For example, Guangxi Cultural Revolution Chronology (1990).

3. Central Committee, Chinese Communist Party (1968); and the account in Bu (2008, 707–15).

4. Walder and Su (2003); Walder (2014; 2019).

5. The term, and the interpretation, was first developed by Lee (1978). Variants of the argument are Chan, Rosen, and Unger (1980) and Rosen (1982). It has been widely influential, although it has often appeared in modified form (e.g., Andreas 2002; 2009).

6. For example, Liu Guokai (1987), who was aligned with the defeated Red Flag faction in neighboring Guangdong.

7. For example, Yang (2021).

8. Hua Linshan (1987; 1996). Hua was a native of Guilin and sympathized with the April 22 faction.

9. This is the highly original approach offered by Su (2011).

10. Unger (1984); Walder (2015, 108–12).

11. For example, Strauss (2006, 65–121) on Rwanda; Brass (2003), Copland (1998; 2002) and Khan (2007) on the Indian subcontinent; Bećirević (2014, 54–143) and Naimark (2001, 139–84) on Yugoslavia.

12. Strauss (2006, 1 and 96).

13. Bećirević (2014, 85 and 88). Similar cases of extreme intergroup violence come from 1941, in war-torn Europe: Bosnia (Bergholz 2016) and Poland (Gross 2002).

14. The widely cited cases were Dao County, Hunan, in late 1967, and neighboring counties in Lingling Prefecture, and two rural counties in the Beijing suburbs in late 1966 (Song 2002; Tan 2010; 2017; Yang 2021, 346–54).

15. In the 1964 census there were 8.4 million Zhuang, 90 percent of whom lived in Guangxi (Mackerras 1994, 158 and 238). Guangxi was also home to smaller ethnic groups, which constituted another 7 percent of the population, the most important of which were the Yao, Miao, and Dong. Mullaney (2010) shows that there is considerable ambiguity and inconsistency in the official categories applied to widely varied indigenous populations.

16. Schafer (1967, 1).

17. Shin (2006, 20–53).

18. Schafer (1967, 14–15). I have altered Schafer's older rendition of the terms for Guangxi (Kwangsi) and Zhuang (Chuang).

19. Marks (1998, 54–55).

20. Marks (1998, 55).

21. Li (1960, 958).

22. Barlow (1987).

23. Shin (2006, 56–105).

24. Marks (1998, 93–95); Shin (2006, 106–37).

25. Marks (1998, 93).

26. Shin (2006, 138–83).

27. Wang, Wang, Hartmann, and Luo (2012).

28. For the sake of brevity, throughout this book I refer to Guangxi as a province rather than an "autonomous region."

29. Bu (2008, 644–51) provides a concise overview. The true magnitude of the death tolls remains uncertain. The officially acknowledged death toll is 16,222; researchers at Inner Mongolia University reported a figure of 27,900; and an émigré Mongol scholar has claimed 50,000 (Yang 2014, 323). The first estimate yields a death rate of only 1.2 per thousand and the last, 3.8 per thousand, which would place it close to Guangxi's. Published annals for eight counties in Inner Mongolia report death rates above 4 per thousand, with the three highest ranging from 14 to 17 per thousand (data set employed in Walder 2019).

30. Yang (2014). Wu (2010) dissents from this interpretation, and views this as a political campaign that targeted ethnic Mongols and Han cadres alike.

31. Ngagpo (1988) and Smith (1996) both interpret the violent rebellion in Nyemo County as nationalist resistance. Goldstein, Jiao, and Lhundrup (2009), however, argue that, in distinction to earlier rebellions in Tibetan regions, this was instead a form of factional warfare that divided Tibetans against one another.

32. Su (2011, 79–94).

33. Cohen (1968); Hashimoto (1973); Constable (1996); Leong (1997).

34. Roberts (1969). "Punti" is Cantonese for "locals," *bendi* in standard dialect.

35. See the maps in Guangxi Organization Department (1995). Qinzhou Prefecture was not permanently transferred from Guangdong to Guangxi until 1965 (Beihai City Organization Department 1993, 101; Qinzhou Prefecture Organization Department 1996, 90–96).

36. Kuhn (1978). Spence (1996, 126–57) mentions Wuxuan, Quanzhou, and Xing'an, which were parties to the battle for Guilin described briefly in the prologue, and all of which had large death tolls.

37. Su (2011, 79–86).

38. Describing Guangxi early in the twentieth century, Lary (1974, 23) noted that "relations between recent Hakka immigrants and established Han immigrants . . . were very bad. Persistent feuding between the two groups led to the formation of many para-military groupings."

39. Su (2011, 233–35).

40. This is based on contemporary sources that put the Hakka population at 21 million out of a total provincial population of 59 million, and it assumes that the proportion has been stable in recent decades: https://baike.baidu.com/item/广东民系/3782255, accessed January 18, 2021.

41. This is an estimate. Data on the percentage of Hakka in the population of Guangxi's counties and cities are from http://www.360doc.com/content/11/0109/17/164198_85241080.shtml, accessed January 11, 2021. The figures are largely consistent with less complete data in other sources and coincide with the historical lists compiled by Hashimoto (1973). These percentages were applied to the population of each county and city, and summed to yield a total Hakka population of 2.4 million in 1966, out of a total provincial population of 25 million.

42. Guangxi Local Annals Editorial Committee (1995, 438 and 441–45); Walder (2009, 20, 23).

43. Guangxi Local Annals Editorial Committee (1995, 209).

44. Zheng (1996) suggested the former, Sutton (1995) the latter.

45. In support of this argument, Su (2011, 236–39) offered evidence that killings were more prevalent in counties that were more distant from provincial capitals and had fewer party members and party-state cadres.

46. Guangxi Party Committee (1987, 1:1); Song (2020); Yan (2012).

47. These volumes have been transcribed and published as 36 searchable electronic files, 2 per each of the original 18 volumes (Song 2016). I have copies of the original volumes (Guangxi Party Committee 1987). Despite occasional errors in transcription and the omission of some of the tabular material, the electronic versions correspond almost exactly to the originals. However, the materials on Beihai

City—the last locality covered in volume 15—were omitted from the electronic collection. Page citations in this book are to the original volumes.

48. Walder and Su (2003).

49. Su (2011).

50. Publications based on the national data set include Walder (2014; 2019); Walder and Lu (2017); and Walder and Chu (2020).

51. See Ball, Kobrak, and Spirer (1999); and Robinson (2018).

**Chapter 2**

1. See Walder (2019, 108–26).

2. The only other surviving provincial leader was in Heilongjiang Province, bordering the Soviet Far East, where First Party Secretary Pan Fusheng became the head of a Revolutionary Committee that was quickly approved by Beijing in January 1967. Pan had been transferred into the province in October 1965 (Organization Department, CCP Central Committee 2000, 9:403). He won the support of Mao and the Beijing radicals by publicly supporting, almost from the outset, the rebel campaign against his longer-serving colleagues in the provincial leadership (Bu 2008, 390–92).

3. Chen (2001, 131–32).

4. Chen (1995; 2001, 124–38); Li (2019, 48–50, 108–29); and Zhai (2000, 45–49).

5. Organization Department, CCP Central Committee (2000, 9:653–56, 15:419–21).

6. Lary (1974, 103–7).

7. Guangxi Organization Department (1995, 514).

8. Lewy (1978, 42–50); https://history.army.mil/html/reference/army_flag/vn .html, accessed January 28, 2021.

9. Lewy (1978, 375–81).

10. Chen (2001, 226–27).

11. Chen (2001, 207–12).

12. Chen (2001, 213–14).

13. For example, during this period Zhou Enlai met repeatedly with North Vietnam's prime minister, Pham Van Dong, to persuade him to ignore the USSR's advice to negotiate. He recalled Stalin's 1948 advice to Mao that he halt the PLA's advance at the Yangzi River, but the CCP pushed on to victory, knowing that the Americans would be unwilling to take over a sustained war effort from a collapsing Nationalist regime (Zhou Enlai Chronology 1997, 143). China's support for Vietnam's war effort was central to its competition with the Soviet Union over influence with North Vietnam (Chen 2001, 226–27).

14. Guangxi Cultural Revolution Chronology (1990, 2).

15. Guangxi Party Committee (1987, 11:150, 17:115–17).

16. Most notably, Liu Shaoqi and Deng Xiaoping, who were demoted at those meetings and would become the two highest-ranking victims of the Cultural Revolution (MacFarquhar and Schoenhals 2006, 86–92).

17. Guangxi Cultural Revolution Chronology (1990, 5–6); Guangxi Party Committee (1987, 17:117).

18. Guangxi Party Committee (1987, 6:237–39).

19. Guangxi Party Committee (1987, 11:150).

20. Guangxi Cultural Revolution Chronology (1990, 6–7); Guangxi Party Committee (1987, 17:117–18, 18:15–16).

21. MacFarquhar and Schoenhals (2006, 106–10).

22. Guangxi Party Committee (1987, 18:17); Guangxi Organization Department (1995, 92 and 514).

23. Guangxi Party Committee (1987, 11:151).

24. Guangxi Party Committee (1987, 18:21).

25. Guangxi Party Committee (1987, 18:21); and Guangxi Cultural Revolution Chronology (1990, 8–9).

26. Guangxi Cultural Revolution Chronology (1990, 10); Guangxi Party Committee (1987, 13:70–71).

27. MacFarquhar and Schoenhals (2006, 136–40); Walder (2009, 164–67); and Walder (2015, 222–24).

28. Guangxi Party Committee (1987, 18:26); Guangxi Cultural Revolution Chronology (1990, 14).

29. Guangxi Party Committee (1987, 6:241–42, 18:33–35).

30. Accounts of events in each of the provincial party and government departments describe widespread internal rebellions by their own staff from December through January 1967 (Guangxi Party Committee 1987, 16:1, 13–16, 35, 45–46, 55, 105–6, 136–37, 167, 492–93).

31. Guangxi Cultural Revolution Chronology (1990, 14).

32. Guangxi Cultural Revolution Chronology (1990, 13–14); Guangxi Party Committee (1987, 16:17–18).

33. Guangxi Party Committee (1987, 13:74).

34. The rise of the Third Headquarters and its role in Beijing's elite Red Guard movement is chronicled in Walder (2009, 155–71).

35. Guangxi Party Committee (1987, 13:74–75).

36. Guangxi Cultural Revolution Chronology (1990, 16).

37. Guangxi Party Committee (1987, 13:77).

38. The Central Cultural Revolution Group maintained a large staff that eventually grew to more than 1,000, including a network of reporters who acted as intelligence agents for Beijing and as advisors to local rebel groups (MacFarquhar

and Schoenhals 2006, 100; Walder 2009, 15–17, 169–70). This envoy, Wang Li, was a reporter from *Liberation Army Daily* who worked in the CCRG's "reporter station" (*jizhe zhan*). He submitted regular reports and traveled back and forth from Nanning to Beijing. Wang Li's name (王茘) has the same pronunciation as, but uses a different character for "Li" than, the name of a more senior and more famous Wang Li (王力) who was a radical member of the CCRG until his purge as a traitor in September 1967. To add to the confusion, the senior Wang Li was the person to whom the junior Wang Li reported about events in Guangxi. An intimate account of how the CCRG operated was provided by a set of interviews with a former staff member (Li Chuanjun 2012). The article includes a photograph of the "entire staff" of the CCRG as of December 1967, arrayed in 8 rows of 50 people.

39. Guangxi Cultural Revolution Chronology (1990, 17).

40. Guangxi Cultural Revolution Chronology (1990, 17).

41. Guangxi Party Committee (1987, 18:45).

42. Guangxi Party Committee (1987, 18:45).

43. Guangxi Cultural Revolution Chronology (1990, 17).

44. Nonetheless, this alliance was later listed as one of the rebel groups that supported the April faction (Guangxi Party Committee 1987, 13:82).

45. Guangxi Party Committee (1987, 18:46–48). The full name of the "Proletarian Alliance" was the Allied Headquarters of the Proletarian Revolutionary Rebels (*wuchan jieji geming zaofan pai lianhe silingbu*); the full name of the "Red Alliance" was Guangxi Proletarian Red Rebels Allied Headquarters (*wuchan jieji hongse zaofanzhe lianhe silingbu*) (Guangxi Party Committee 1987, 13:76). The account in Guangxi Cultural Revolution Chronology (1990, 11, 17), confusingly refers to the latter group as the "Proletarian Alliance" and omits reference to the formation of the former group. It is clear from other details in the two accounts that the latter group's shortened name was misspecified.

46. Guangxi Cultural Revolution Chronology (1990, 18).

47. Guangxi Party Committee (1987, 18:49–50, 53).

48. Guangxi Cultural Revolution Chronology (1990, 19–20).

49. Guangxi Cultural Revolution Chronology (1990, 20); and Guangxi Party Committee (1987, 13:78).

50. Guangxi Cultural Revolution Chronology (1990, 21).

51. Guangxi Cultural Revolution Chronology (1990, 22–23); Guangxi Party Committee (1987, 13:79); Zhou Enlai Chronology (1997, 135).

52. Guangxi Party Committee (1987, 18:56). This was the charge, also false, leveled against Ulanfu, the leader of Inner Mongolia, who was dismissed from his posts in August 1966 (MacFarquhar and Schoenhals 2006, 43).

53. Guangxi Party Committee (1987, 18:59).

54. Guangxi Party Committee (1987, 18:59, 61).

55. Guangxi Party Committee (1987, 18:61–62).

56. MacFarquhar and Schoenhals (2006, 180–82).

57. Central Military Commission (1967a; 1967b; 1967c).

58. Xiong appears to have remained in custody until Zhou Enlai ordered his release during a negotiation session on August 24 (Guangxi Cultural Revolution Chronology 1990, 20); and Zhou Enlai (1967e).

59. These were the Construction Workers' Rebel Headquarters and the Auto Workers' Rebel Headquarters (Guangxi Party Committee 1987, 18:63–64).

60. Guangxi Party Committee (1987, 18:64–65).

61. Guangxi Cultural Revolution Chronology (1990, 22–25); Guangxi Party Committee (1987, 13:79).

62. Guangxi Party Committee (1987, 18:72–73).

63. Guangxi Organization Department (1995, 514).

64. Guangxi Party Committee (1987, 13:81–83).

65. Guangxi Party Committee (1987, 18:75).

66. Guangxi Cultural Revolution Chronology (1990, 27–29).

67. Guangxi Party Committee (1987, 18:76–80, 83).

68. Guangxi Party Committee (1987, 13:83–84).

69. The classic early statement is Lee (1978). The interpretation was applied to Guangxi by Hua (1987; 1996).

70. The rebel student representatives from the Beijing Third Headquarters in fact criticized the Workers' Headquarters for continuing to attack the former Scarlet Guards and for "not believing that the great majority of the former 'Scarlet Guards' (*chiwei dui*) and 'Shield Guards' (*zhipai bing*) genuinely want revolution" (Guangxi Party Committee 1987, 18:44). Interestingly, the rebel organization formed by former Scarlet Guards on February 3 and referred to as the "Red Alliance" (*hong lian*) was listed among the rebel groups aligned with the April 22 faction at its founding rally (Guangxi Party Committee 1987, 13:82).

71. Wu was never a member of the CCP Central Committee, so he is not included in published biographies of national leaders. There are several online biographies of Wu Jinnan that differ only in their level of detail. For example, see https://zh .wikipedia.org/wiki/伍晋南, accessed March 8, 2021.

## Chapter 3

1. Wu Jinnan first joined the Provincial Party Committee in 1954 as the second -ranking deputy party secretary, two years before Wei Guoqing arrived in Guangxi (Guangxi Organization Department 1995, 313, 316).

2. *Red Flag* (*Hongqi*) was a biweekly periodical that was the mouthpiece of the Central Cultural Revolution Group. It issued authoritative editorials and directives throughout this period. Its most important articles were often distributed via newspapers and radio prior to their publication.

3. Walder and Lu (2017) analyze the process statistically with national-level data; Walder (2019, 79–107) provides a more descriptive historical account.

4. Guilin City and Guilin Prefecture, Wuzhou City and Wuzhou Prefecture, and Yulin Prefecture. These dates are all recorded in the investigation materials and published local annals.

5. Liuzhou City, Liuzhou Prefecture, and Nanning Prefecture had power seizures on January 25; Bose and Qinzhou Prefectures had power seizures on January 26.

6. In Xilin County meetings among county administrative staff to organize a power seizure began on January 20. The wording in the account is vague about the exact date of the power seizure, but it may have been before the Bose Prefecture power seizure on January 26 (Guangxi Party Committee 1987, 15:449–51).

7. Walder and Lu (2017); Walder (2019, 79–107).

8. The latter number includes employees in manufacturing and services but excludes administrative staff in government offices. The mean is skewed by a small number of more industrialized suburban counties; the median county had only 3,698 salaried workers.

9. These figures, and similar factual statements in this chapter, are tabulated from the chronologies in the investigation reports.

10. The investigation reports often provide considerable detail about the formation of cadre rebel groups in the county administration near the end of 1966. For example, in Lingchuan County there were 19 separate rebel organizations in the county party and government agencies (Guangxi Party Committee 1987, 10:350); in the 29 offices and departments in Lingui County, there were more than 50 small fighting groups with a membership of 520 out of the county's 883 cadres and staff (Guangxi Party Committee 1987, 6:328); Fusui County had 22 rebel organizations in various party and government offices (Guangxi Party Committee 1987, 2:234); in Tiandong County, cadres and staff organized a cross-department alliance with more than 100 members (Guangxi Party Committee 1987, 10:350). A full discussion of the significance of rebel cadres and their motivations is in Walder (2016).

11. This is described in the materials on Luzhai County (Guangxi Party Committee 1987, 4:492–96). Cadres from the county who observed a power seizure in Liuzhou Prefecture rushed home and argued that failing to act quickly would risk power seizures by others.

12. Central Military Commission (1967a).

13. Nelsen (1972; 1981).

14. Nelsen (1972).

15. Guangxi Party Committee (1987, 6:239–40, 11:152–54).

16. Military units stationed in Guilin were the 47th Army's 141st Division, the Guangzhou Military Region Logistics Department's 20th Branch, the 5th Reconnaissance Division of the Air Force, the 41st Army's 127th and 123rd Divisions, and the Air Force Bomber Division—all stationed in Guangxi to assist Vietnam. All these units sent personnel to "support the left" in January. A total of 470 officers took part (Guilin Municipal Party Committee 1996, 192).

17. Guangxi Party Committee (1987, 11:154–55).

18. Guangxi Party Committee (1987, 10:20).

19. The air force units stationed at Guilin's large air force base were among the forces assigned to "support the left" activities, but they are not mentioned as playing a support role regarding the original power seizures (Guilin Municipal Party Committee 1996, 191–92). It was not unusual elsewhere in China for officers from different PLA units to give support to opposed rebel factions; see Dong and Walder (2018; 2021).

20. Guangxi Party Committee (1987, 11:156–57).

21. Guangxi Party Committee (1987, 11:158–61).

22. Guangxi Party Committee (1987, 11:5, 4:214–17).

23. Guangxi Party Committee (1987, 11:7).

24. Guangxi Party Committee (1987, 11:8).

25. Guangxi Party Committee (1987, 9:665–68).

26. Guangxi Party Committee (1987, 9:669–71).

27. Guangxi Party Committee (1987, 9:672–73, 674–79).

28. As "county-level" cities, Beihai and Pingxiang were under the administration of prefectures (Qinzhou and Nanning, respectively) and were parallel in rank to a county.

29. This account is based on Guangxi Party Committee (1987, 12:591–94).

30. Beihai was part of Hepu County, in Guangdong Province, until it was first designated a separate city in 1951. Its status changed several times in the 1950s, shifting back and forth between Guangdong and Guangxi province. It was designated a county-level city in 1964 before its transfer to Guangxi in 1965 along with Qinzhou Prefecture, providing previously landlocked Guangxi with a seacoast (Beihai City Organization Department 1993).

31. This account is based on Guangxi Party Committee (1987, 2:386–91, 8:615–19).

32. This account is based on Guangxi Party Committee (1987, 10:12–21).

33. This account is based on Guangxi Party Committee (1987, 8:170–74).

34. This account is based on Guangxi Party Committee (1987, 2:234–40, 8:540–48).

35. This account is based on Guangxi Party Committee (1987, 13:252–53, 309–13).

36. This account is based on Guangxi Party Committee (1987, 3:339–41, 15:534–38).

37. During the investigations of the 1980s, the PAD political commissar was investigated and executed as one of the most notorious criminals of the period. His activities as head of the Allied Command are described in chapter 7.

38. This account is based on Guangxi Party Committee (1987, 3:514–18, 15:121–25).

39. The same dispute occurred in neighboring Tianyang, where cadre rebels also declared a unilateral power seizure and rebels outside the county administration who were excluded protested the act. In the subsequent debates, however, the PAD took the opposite stance of its counterpart in Tiandong and argued that power seizures could only be carried out by those who worked *within* an organization (Guangxi Party Committee 1987, 15:72–74).

40. This account is based on Guangxi Party Committee (1987, 6:327–40).

41. Described as "Red Army veterans," these individuals probably joined Communist military units when the county was part of a short-lived local base area on Fengshan's border with Lingyun County that was active from 1929 to 1932. It had its own detachment of the Red Army, which retreated to the Jiangxi Soviet base area in 1932. Local guerrilla forces affiliated with the Red Army were also briefly active in the region during 1943 (Fengshan County Annals 2008, 529–30, 556–80). These local military veterans appear to have obtained administrative posts across the county and into the districts and villages in the 1950s.

42. Guangxi Party Committee (1987, 14:431–33).

43. This death toll reportedly included 4,783 deaths from "unnatural causes," a term that is not defined, but appears to cover those who were deliberately denied food supplies as punishment along with those who were beaten and tortured to death in the campaign to force farmers to reveal hidden grain (Fengshan County Annals 2008, 379–80, 678). Deaths due to torture, beatings, and suicides are not directly described in this source, but they have been documented in detail during the campaign against "hiding grain" in other regions (Yang 2012, 28–37, 224–29, 335–38; Zhou 2012, 18–19, 25–36). This episode is covered in extensive detail in two investigation reports issued by the Prefecture and Provincial Party Committees in June and July 1961, part of a national rectification campaign to uncover local abuses that led to the famine. They are reproduced as an appendix in Fengshan County Annals (2008, 805–12). The two officials deemed responsible were promoted to positions outside the county by 1966.

44. Walder (2015, 164).

45. Fengshan County Annals (2008, 382); Guangxi Party Committee (1987, 14:434).

46. Guangxi Party Committee (1987, 14:435).

## Chapter 4

1. These totals include only descriptions of events that take place within a two-month period, and that do not duplicate summary counts of the same type of event in the same location within this two-month period.

2. Zhou Enlai (1967a; 1967k).

3. Zhou Enlai Chronology (1997, 159).

4. Both delegations included members of the Guangxi Party Secretariat, the top six ranking officials in the province. The pro-Wei delegation included Qiao Xiaoguang and An Pingsheng, who left on May 1 as part of a fourteen-person delegation. Wei Guoqing was already in Beijing. The April 22 delegation departed for Beijing two days later, and included Wu Jinnan, He Ximing, and Huo Fan (an alternate member of the Secretariat) (Guangxi Cultural Revolution Chronology 1990, 30; Guangxi Organization Department 1995, 514).

5. Yang (2004).

6. For example, Zhou Enlai (1967d), in which he heatedly rebuts the April faction's insistence that Wei Guoqing is somehow directing the Allied Command forces in Guangxi.

7. See Binyang County Organization Department (1996, 143); which contains an unpaginated map for 1958 at the front of that volume. A photograph of the railway junction, probably dating from the mid-1980s, shows a major switching yard with dozens of separate sets of tracks (Binyang County Annals 1987, front matter).

8. Zhou Enlai (1967b); Zhou Enlai Chronology (1997, 161).

9. Guangxi Party Committee (1987, 9:519–20); Guangxi Cultural Revolution Chronology (1990, 36–37).

10. Zhou Enlai (1967c).

11. Zhou Enlai (1967e).

12. Zhou Enlai (1967e); Zhou Enlai Chronology (1997, 182).

13. Zhou Enlai (1967f).

14. Walder (2019).

15. See the analysis in Walder (2019, 152–71); and Walder and Chu (2020).

16. The involvement of military units, not surprisingly, elevated the death tolls from factional conflicts. When events that involve the participation of military units are included in such a graph—almost exclusively during July 1968—the number of deaths for July increases from fewer than 700 to more than 4,500, dwarf-

ing all of the other months in the figure. This primarily reflects the battles in Nanning and Guilin, described in the prologue.

17. The narrative account for Beihai gives the clear impression that these battles led to the total defeat of the April faction, which appears to have been unable to recover (Guangxi Party Committee 1987, 12:593–606).

18. Guangxi Cultural Revolution Chronology (1990, 28–30).

19. Guangxi Party Committee (1987, 18:84).

20. Guangxi Cultural Revolution Chronology (1990, 32–33).

21. Guangxi Cultural Revolution Chronology (1990, 48).

22. Guangxi Party Committee (1987, 18:85).

23. Guangxi Party Committee (1987, 18:87).

24. Guangxi Party Committee (1987, 18:87–88); Guangxi Cultural Revolution Chronology (1990, 33–34).

25. Guangxi Party Committee (1987, 18:121–23; 7:69–72); Guangxi Cultural Revolution Chronology (1990, 47–48).

26. Wei attended every session with Zhou until the August 24 meeting (Zhou Enlai 1967e). He did not again appear as a participant until September 22 (Zhou Enlai 1967g).

27. Guangxi Party Committee (1987, 11:158–60).

28. Guangxi Cultural Revolution Chronology (1990, 40–41).

29. Guangxi Party Committee (1987, 18:113); Guangxi Cultural Revolution Chronology (1990, 44).

30. Guangxi Cultural Revolution Chronology (1990, 49).

31. Zhou Enlai (1967e); Guangxi Military District (1967a; 1967b).

32. Guangxi Cultural Revolution Chronology (1990, 49–50).

33. Zhou Enlai Chronology (1997, 182); Mao Zedong Chronology (2013, 113–14); MacFarquhar and Schoenhals (2006, 229).

34. See Schoenhals (2005).

35. MacFarquhar and Schoenhals (2006, 229–30); Mao Zedong Chronology (2013, 114).

36. Quoted in Zhou Enlai Chronology (1997, 175).

37. Zhou Enlai Chronology (1997, 231–33).

38. Walder (2015, 250–56). The dramatic impact this had in a province where the military commander had been under severe pressure during the summer is illustrated in Dong and Walder (2011, 435–38).

39. Zhou Enlai (1967f); Zhou Enlai Chronology (1997, 189).

40. Zhou Enlai (1967g).

41. Zhou Enlai (1967i); Zhou Enlai Chronology (1997, 200).

42. Zhou Enlai (1967k).

43. Guangxi Military District (1967c).

44. Central Committee, Chinese Communist Party (1967b; 1967c).

45. Central Committee, Chinese Communist Party (1967d).

46. Zhou Enlai (1967h; 1967i; 1967j); Zhou Enlai Chronology (1997, 201).

47. Zhou Enlai (1967j). Mass killings of "four type elements" in politically stigmatized households began in Quanzhou County, where seventy-six people were executed in one production brigade over two days in early October (Guangxi Cultural Revolution Chronology 1990, 53).

48. Guangxi Cultural Revolution Chronology (1990, 57).

## Chapter 5

1. Ethnic minorities constituted only 5 percent of the prefecture's population; almost all of them were Yao, who made up close to half of the population of the Jianghua Yao Autonomous County (Lingling Prefecture Annals 2001, 91–92, 146, 1540).

2. Tan (2017, 20).

3. Zhou Enlai (1967j).

4. Tan (2017, 20–21). The published annals for the prefecture do not provide these figures, but they describe the events and state that they "shocked the entire nation" (*zhendong quanguo*) (Lingling Prefecture Annals 2001, 208–10).

5. Tan (2017, 30–32), Lingling Prefecture Annals (2001, 209).

6. Tan (2017, 35–46).

7. Tan (2017, 357–74).

8. Tan (2017, 118).

9. Guangxi Party Committee (1987, 10:604).

10. Guangxi Party Committee (1987, 10:295). The narrative states that the killings occurred under the influence of Hunan's Dao County.

11. Guangxi Party Committee (1987, 11:789). The narrative states that the killings occurred under the influence of Dao County, along with the two Hunan counties in Lingling Prefecture that shared a border with Fuchuan—Jianghua and Jiangyong.

12. Guangxi Party Committee (1987, 12:493–94); Guangxi Cultural Revolution Chronology (1990, 58).

13. Guangxi Cultural Revolution Chronology (1990, 57–58).

14. Guangxi Party Committee (1987, 10:559).

15. Guangxi Party Committee (1987, 12:281–87).

16. Guangxi Cultural Revolution Chronology (1990, 61–62).

17. Guangxi Cultural Revolution Chronology (1990, 62–63).

18. Guangxi Party Committee (1987, 13:520).

19. Guangxi Party Committee (1987, 13:16–24, 327–32, 656–61). Dongxing County was renamed Fangcheng County in 1979 (Qinzhou Prefecture Organization Department 1996, 253).

20. Guangxi Cultural Revolution Chronology (1990, 67–68).

21. Guangxi Cultural Revolution Chronology (1990, 70–72).

22. Guangxi Cultural Revolution Chronology (1990, 71).

23. Guangxi Cultural Revolution Chronology (1990, 73–74).

24. Guangxi Cultural Revolution Chronology (1990, 75–78).

25. Guangxi Cultural Revolution Chronology (1990, 80–81, 84).

26. Guangxi Cultural Revolution Chronology (1990, 86–87).

27. Guangxi Party Committee (1987, 12:602–6).

28. Based on monthly tabulations of events in the data set.

29. Based on summary statistics provided for each locality, recorded in the data set.

30. Guangxi Cultural Revolution Chronology (1990, 88–89, 95–96). Not surprisingly, this source states that the report was later found to be entirely false.

31. Guangxi Cultural Revolution Chronology (1990, 90).

32. Guangxi Cultural Revolution Chronology (1990, 92). In fact there had been such an anti-Communist rebel movement in the county with the same name that was suppressed by PLA units in the early 1950s, although the leaders of this newly discovered anti-Communist insurgency were in fact veterans of the Red Army (Fengshan County Annals 2008, 13 and 382). The formation of Fengshan's April faction was described near the end of chapter 3, and the county's violent conflicts will be detailed in chapter 7.

33. Guangxi Cultural Revolution Chronology (1990, 96).

34. Guangxi Cultural Revolution Chronology (1990, 98).

35. Guangxi Cultural Revolution Chronology (1990, 95).

36. Guangxi Party Committee (1987, 3:652–54, 6:261–64).

37. Guangxi Cultural Revolution Chronology (1990, 96–98).

38. Guangxi Cultural Revolution Chronology (1990, 95).

39. Vietnam played a key role in the Sino-Soviet split, with China urging the Vietnamese to fight to victory rather than negotiate a compromise peace. See Lüthi (2008, 316–36); also Chen (2001, 236–37). The Vietnamese began negotiations in Paris in May 1968, and the talks continued until an agreement was reached in 1973.

40. Walder (2009, 246–47).

41. Central Committee, Chinese Communist Party (1968). The document is reprinted in full in Guangxi Party Committee (1987, 18:579–81).

## Chapter 6

1. Figure 6.1 assumes that the overall monthly distribution of deaths approximates that of the deaths that can be tied to specific months in the data set. It sets

the number reached in September at a final death rate of 4.0 and estimates the cumulative death rate based on the monthly death counts documented in the investigation reports.

2. Su (2011).

3. These numbers are derived by dividing the numbers in table 6.1 for cities by 6 and for counties by 80.

4. Tan (2017, 20–21).

5. These events are limited to those that describe actions that occur in one place within one or two months and in which the reported deaths do not overlap with other events of longer duration in the data set.

6. The alternative approach, used in table 6.3 for identifying victims, would be to exclude cases where more than one actor is named. Because so many more cases name more than one actor, this would reduce by more than half the total number of deaths that can be associated with actors.

7. These were events defined as having occurred within a two-month period and whose death counts did not overlap with deaths counted in other reported events.

8. There is some imprecision in allocating deaths to months: of the 1,468 unique events that report deaths that spanned no more than two consecutive calendar months, 1,385 occurred within a single calendar month and 83 (5.7 percent) report events for which the death counts span across consecutive months. I define the month as the last month, which is the end of the period where the count ends for this subset of cases.

9. The boundaries and names of rural jurisdictions changed frequently prior to and after the period examined here. Districts were previously called "communes" (*gongshe*), a name revived gradually beginning in late 1966. In the 1980s, after communes were abolished, they became "townships" and were given the name (*xiang*) previously used for "villages," which in turn became known as *cun*. The investigation reports consistently use the terminology of *qu* (district) and *xiang* (village) for these two levels of administration. These changes are described in detail in published county-level organizational histories of the Communist Party, and they are conveniently summarized in the front matter to Lingui County Organization Department (1996).

10. District-level PADs are detailed in published organizational histories, e.g., Luchuan County Organization Department (1992, 300–302); and Lingui County Organization Department (1996, 330).

11. Pingle County Annals (1995, 35).

12. In Pingle County, for example, there were 1,344 "natural villages" under the 13 district-level jurisdictions, an average of 12 smaller settlements clustered into each administrative village (Pingle County Annals 1995, 35–40). In Fengshan

County, there were 1,574 "natural villages" under 86 administrative villages, an average of 18 each (Fengshan County Annals 2008, 39–49).

13. The data cited in this paragraph and the next are extracted from published county-level "organizational histories of the Communist Party" (e.g., Binyang County Organization Department 1996), and are included in the data set. A handful of county-level volumes were unavailable. For these counties the same information was extracted from prefecture-level organization histories (e.g., Qinzhou Prefecture Organization Department 1996).

## Chapter 7

1. In the 1953 census, Zhuang constituted 65 percent of the population, Han Chinese 25 percent, and the Yao minority another 9 percent (Fengshan County Annals 2008, 700).

2. Fengshan County Annals (2008, 529); Lary (1972).

3. Deng Xiaoping was the political commissar of the base area and moved to Jiangxi with the troops in 1930. The base area was founded by a Zhuang activist and Donglan County native who was trained at the Canton Peasant Movement Institute, which during that period was directed by Mao Zedong (Lary 1972; Lary 1974, 103–7).

4. Wei Guoqing was a Red Army veteran from the region. A native of Donglan County, he joined the Red Army in this base area at age sixteen in 1929. He accompanied the Red Army to the Jiangxi Soviet, where he joined the CCP in 1931 (Organization Department, CCP Central Committee 2004, 805).

5. Fengshan County Annals (2008, 529).

6. Guangxi Cultural Revolution Chronology (1990, 90–92).

7. The county's death rate in 1959 was triple that of 1957, and in 1960 four times larger. The county's population, net of 8,508 births from 1958 to 1960, was nonetheless close to 8 percent smaller in 1961 than in 1957 (Fengshan County Annals 2008, 678–79).

8. Fengshan County Annals (2008, 380, 805–9).

9. Guangxi Party Committee (1987, 5:316–20).

10. Fengshan County Annals (2008, 383–84); Guangxi Party Committee (1987, 5:325–29).

11. Fengshan County Annals (2008, 384); Guangxi Party Committee (1987, 5:329–37).

12. Fengshan County Annals (2008, 385); Guangxi Party Committee (1987, 5:337–45).

13. Fengshan County Annals (2008, 386); Guangxi Party Committee (1987, 5:345–50).

14. Binyang County Annals (1987, 557, 561).

15. Guangxi Party Committee (1987, 8:175).

16. Guangxi Party Committee (1987, 8:176).

17. Guangxi Party Committee (1987, 8:177–78).

18. Guangxi Party Committee (1987, 8:181–82).

19. Guangxi Party Committee (1987, 8:182).

20. This term is not defined in the source, but it appears to be a version of the longer list of politically suspect categories, frequently referred to as "21 types," named in a January 1967 document known as the "Six Articles on Public Security" (Central Committee 1967a). The list includes seemingly anyone who had run afoul of the authorities since 1949, along with their family members. It explicitly mentions landlords, rich peasants, counter-revolutionaries, rightist elements, former inmates of labor reform camps and factories, former members of reactionary parties and groups, leaders and employees of reactionary religious sects, former officers in enemy and puppet armies, political organizations, police, military police, and intelligence agents, elements who have undergone labor reform but who have not reformed their thinking well, speculators and profiteers, and family members of those who have been executed, imprisoned, placed under observation, or have fled abroad and who persist in their reactionary views.

21. Guangxi Party Committee (1987, 8:182–83).

22. Guangxi Party Committee (1987, 8:183).

23. Guangxi Party Committee (1987, 8:183–84).

24. Guangxi Party Committee (1987, 8:185–86). Leadership praise for districts that killed large numbers, along with criticism of those that were slow, was a standard practice in the mobilization for mass killings. See also Guangxi Party Committee (1987, 14:468–69).

25. Guangxi Party Committee (1987, 8:191).

26. Binyang County Annals (1987, 158–59).

27. Guangxi Party Committee (1987, 2:62). In Lingshan County, which had the second-highest death toll overall (3,220), more than 75 percent of those killed were from "four type" households: 1,232 were individuals who had been given the label in the early 1950s, and 1,228 were their sons or daughters (Guangxi Party Committee (1987, 13:520).

28. Gongcheng was designated as a county for the Yao minority; Longsheng was designated as the home of "various minorities" (*gezu*), primarily Yao, Dong, and Miao. Both also had significant Zhuang populations.

29. Guanyang shared a border with Dao County, Hunan. While Zhou's denunciation and warning may have helped to curtail further organized killings there,

it certainly did not do so in the case of the other county that Zhou warned about, Quanzhou, which nonetheless generated the largest overall death toll in the region.

30. These are the percentages provided in the investigation reports for these counties.

31. Guangxi Party Committee (1987, 6:246–48).

32. Guangxi Party Committee (1987, 6:249–52, 3:647–50).

33. Guangxi Party Committee (1987, 11:222–27).

34. Guangxi Party Committee (1987, 11:229–32).

35. Guangxi Party Committee (1987, 11:233–37).

36. Guangxi Party Committee (1987, 11:237–39, quotation at 237).

37. Guangxi Party Committee (1987, 6:359–61).

38. Guangxi Party Committee (1987, 6:361).

39. Guangxi Party Committee (1987, 11:245).

40. Guangxi Party Committee (1987, 6:360).

41. Guangxi Party Committee (1987, 6:362).

42. Guangxi Party Committee (1987, 10:231–34).

43. Guangxi Party Committee (1987, 10:235–36).

44. This more accurately reflects the central document about public security work (Central Committee 1967a).

45. Guangxi Party Committee (1987, 10:239–40).

46. Guangxi Party Committee (1987, 10:241–43). The names of those executed are given without other identifying information. Presumably they were either April faction activists or "four type elements" and others targeted as "21 types."

47. Guangxi Party Committee (1987, 10:244–45).

48. Guangxi Party Committee (1987, 10:246–48).

49. Guangxi Party Committee (1987, 10:251).

50. Guangxi Party Committee (1987, 10:253–54).

51. Guangxi Party Committee (1987, 13:599). Cadres from Shangsi and Qinzhou counties protested at the Qinzhou Prefecture Headquarters for being forced to carry out the campaign, which they denounced as part of the reactionary line (Guangxi Party Committee (1987, 13:250–51).

52. Guangxi Party Committee (1987, 13:600).

53. Guangxi Party Committee (1987, 13:602).

54. Guangxi Party Committee (1987, 13:603).

55. Guangxi Party Committee (1987, 13:604–5).

56. Guangxi Party Committee (1987, 13:605–7).

57. Guangxi Party Committee (1987, 13:609).

58. Guangxi Party Committee (1987, 13:610).

59. Lingyun County Annals (2007, 166).

60. Guangxi Party Committee (1987, 3:209–10).

61. For example, Hangzhou (Gao 2004, 56–58) and Guangdong (Vogel 1969, 104–24, 211–16). Vogel (1969, 345–47) found that these tensions were revived during the first phase of the Cultural Revolution.

62. The large differences from standard northern dialect are shown in Lingyun County Annals (2007, 229–33).

63. Lingyun County Organization Department (1994, 39, 41–42, 44, 81, 231, 238).

64. During the Great Leap Forward, false reporting of output and a coercive campaign to extract "hidden" grain from starving peasant households led to 6,841 "unnatural deaths," 8 percent of the county's population at the time. As the famine spread, a harsh campaign against cadres who spoke out to avert disaster led to the abuse and purge of close to 20 percent of the county's cadres for "rightist tendencies." These individuals were described as "honest people who spoke the truth and reported the real numbers." They were eventually rehabilitated in 1961 and returned to office, coinciding with Wang Detang's demotion, which suggests that he likely was one of the "leftist" cadres pushing the disastrous policies and attacking colleagues who tried to limit the damage (Lingyun County Annals 2007, 159, 550–51).

65. Lingyun County Organization Department (1994, 81). Zhao was apparently transferred in from another county; he is not listed in any other post in the county prior to that date.

66. This account of the formation of Lingyun's factions is based on Guangxi Party Committee (1987, 3:339–41, 15:534–38).

67. This account summarizes events described in Guangxi Party Committee (1987, 15:538–52).

68. Guangxi Party Committee (1987, 3:335).

69. Guangxi Party Committee (1987, 3:335–36).

70. Binyang County Annals (1987, 8, 10, 558). For example, in Binyang there were 788 "production brigades" (*shengchan dadui*) that were created in 1962. These groupings changed frequently as the boundaries of "people's communes" were enlarged and contracted in the early years of collective agriculture. The terminology that describes these different levels shifted frequently over time, as administrative units were combined or subdivided. The term "commune" (*gongshe*) for a period was applied to districts (*qu*), at other times to administrative villages. The term *xiang* was applied to the former "districts" during the 1980s and is commonly translated as "township." However, in Guangxi during this period the term *xiang* was commonly applied to administrative villages, which were also at times referred to as "production brigades" (*shengchan dadui*).

71. Fengshan County Annals (2008, 39, 50, 678). For example, according to a survey of natural villages in the early 1980s, there were 983 Zhuang villages, 877 Han villages, 144 Yao villages, and only 163 with mixed ethnic populations (Fengshan County Annals 2008, 50).

72. Lingshan County Annals (2000, 435). Militia regulations in force at the time required all able-bodied men and women from eighteen to thirty-five years of age who were "politically reliable" to enroll in local militia platoons (*pai*) (members of "four type" households were ineligible). Men and women were enrolled in "core militia" (*gugan minbing*) when they reached age eighteen and appear to have been subject to occasional drills. When men reached twenty-eight and women turned twenty-three, they became "ordinary militia" (*putong minbing*) (Lingshan County Annals 2000, 434).

73. In Lingshan County in 1966, for example, there were an average of 373 households and 15,300 individuals in its 380 administrative villages (Lingshan County Annals 2000, 155).

74. Guangxi Party Committee (1987, 8:189–91).

75. Widespread sexual violence is frequently reported in other historical instances of mass killing, such as the former Yugoslavia (Naimark 2001, 167–70), Partition-era India (Khan 2007, 133–35), and Rwanda (Strauss 2006, 52). In these cases, systematic rape is part of the deadly assault on targeted groups. Instances described in the materials on Guangxi are almost entirely cases where individuals or small groups abuse their authority over surviving females in households where the male heads have been killed.

76. She nonetheless reported the rape, but the immediate consequences for the rapist are unclear. He was not imprisoned for this act until 1984 (Guangxi Party Committee 1987, 8:187).

77. Not until 1981 was the militia commander arrested for these acts; he was executed in 1985 (Guangxi Party Committee 1987, 12:494–95).

78. These offenses caused his removal as head of the Revolutionary Committee and expulsion from the party in May 1969. He was not further punished for his behavior until February 1985, when he was convicted of murder and rape, and was executed. (Guangxi Party Committee 1987, 3:209, 214).

79. The two were sentenced to more than twelve years in prison in 1984 (Guangxi Party Committee 1987, 11:591).

80. Guangxi Party Committee (1987, 11:484–85). The source makes clear that the seven rapists were convicted of the crimes during the early 1980s, but their punishments were not specified.

81. Guangxi Party Committee (1987, 13:540).

82. Guangxi Party Committee (1987, 8:563).

83. Guangxi Party Committee (1987, 13:396–97).

84. Guangxi Party Committee (1987, 8:237–38).

85. Guangxi Party Committee (1987, 8:238).

86. Guangxi Party Committee (1987, 9:187). One example given in that report was the gang-rape of a girl in her early teens by several men who had beaten her father to death at a public rally shortly beforehand (Guangxi Party Committee 1987, 9:201).

87. Zheng (1996).

88. The most extensive exploration of the cultural roots of these practices is Sutton (1995). Zheng (1996, 131–49) found ancient antecedents in both Zhuang and Han cultures, and notes that Guangxi had a reputation for cannibalism in Han regions in earlier centuries, but he did not find this adequate to explain the widespread nature of the phenomenon during the Cultural Revolution.

89. This is the number of incidents that involved cannibalism that were recorded by coders, not the number of people involved or the number of victims, which would be much larger.

90. Guangxi Party Committee (1987, 9:187).

91. Guangxi Party Committee (1987, 9:200).

92. Guangxi Party Committee (1987, 9:203).

93. Guangxi Party Committee (1987, 9:205).

94. Guangxi Party Committee (1987, 9:205).

95. Guangxi Party Committee (1987, 2:40–41).

96. Guangxi Party Committee (1987, 11:477).

**Chapter 8**

1. Recall that 3.6 per thousand is based on the numbers recorded in the investigation reports, which do not count the roughly 20,000 "missing" as deaths.

2. Su (2011, 237–38).

3. The smaller groups, such as the Yao, Miao, and Dong, constituted another 7 percent of the population and lived in isolated clusters.

4. Wu (2010).

5. Goldstein (2014; 2019); Weiner (2020).

6. Goldstein, Jiao, and Lhundrup (2009) argue that the factional conflict originated with discontent mobilized by dissatisfaction over unfavorable grain procurement policies and the anticipated imposition of collective agriculture.

7. Lary (1972, 127). In this passage I have altered the author's older spelling of Zhuang (Chuang).

8. Mackerras (1994, 130).

9. Shin (2006, 196–98).

10. For example, "because they had been deprived over many generations of equal rights with Han and Zhuang, minority groups revolted in order to defend their livelihoods." The paragraphs that follow this passage describe resistance by the Yao (Fengshan County Annals 2008, 702). Pockets of poor and unassimilated Zhuang persisted in Guangxi and existed well into the twentieth century. These "tribal" Zhuang lived in hilly districts in the western part of the province, and in fact were the foundation for the short-lived guerrilla base area that was established on the border of Fengshan and Donglan counties in the late 1920s (Lary 1972).

11. Mackerras (1994, 44, 130, 144, 266).

12. Su (2011, 221–41).

13. Bose Prefecture and Bose County are written in Chinese with a character for "hundred" (百), pronounced "Bai" and is often rendered as "Baise" in websites and dictionaries. Many local place names in Zhuang regions were given Chinese characters that only approximated the Zhuang pronunciation. In 1965 the provincial government designated a two-character term "Bai-se" to represent a four-syllable Zhuang term for the locality (Wang et al. 2012, 5). In 1988 the Guangxi government and broadcasting network decreed that the official pronunciation, and romanization, should revert to something closer to the Zhuang pronunciation, "Bo-se."

14. The average percentage is lower than the overall census figure of 60 percent Han because ethnic minorities were concentrated in a large number of counties with small populations.

15. The average death rate is 3.0 in the twenty counties with greater than 10 percent Hakka populations.

16. Because local populations range from 41,124 to 799,308, the total population is included as a control in all equations, as local death tolls will vary greatly due to the population at risk. Including this control variable turns the estimates for the other variables into a measure of their impact on local death rates. The regression estimates are based on negative binomial models, appropriate for this kind of count data.

17. Another possible measure of development is the number of nonagricultural workers in the population. This variable is in the data set, but it is almost perfectly correlated with the urban population of a locality (.961).

18. Log transformations of these variables do not change this statement.

19. This measure is preferred because the immediately superior political jurisdiction is the prefecture. This is linear distance calculated from GPS coordinates, the measure employed in a previous publication (Walder and Lu 2017, 1159–60). Su (2011, 239) used distance from the provincial capitals of Nanning and Guangzhou.

20. The correlation is not improved by a log transformation of the variable.

21. Lary (1974, 6) noted that historically, "border zones tend to be isolated and poverty-stricken . . . less amenable to government control than inner-provincial areas; they were often the locus of rebellion, the haunt of rebels and bandits."

22. The average number of reported deaths per locality at the high point of each is roughly comparable; it is 153 for the March group, 189 for the April group, and 141 for the August group. These are raw counts, not death rates.

23. Another model for count data is Poisson regression, which is appropriate only when the dependent variable is not highly dispersed, defined as a variance that is not much higher than its mean. The dependent variable here—total local deaths—is very highly dispersed, with a mean of 955 and a variance of 548,540. With highly dispersed counts, Poisson regressions underestimate the standard errors of the estimates and attribute erroneously high levels of statistical significance to explanatory variables, or "false positives" (Ryan, Evers, and More 2018). Su (2011) employed Poisson regression in his analyses, a primary reason for his different findings.

24. I had not anticipated such a large negative impact of location in a border region. My prior expectation was simply that border regions would have net death rates that were just as high as those of other regions. It is possible that political pressures to prosecute suppression campaigns with zeal were less intense in remote border regions. But it is also possible that this finding is the spurious result of less thorough enumerations of deaths in border regions during the investigations conducted in the 1980s. Even if this is so, the results still support the claim that militias under the direction of local political authorities carried out the killings.

### Epilogue

1. Walder (2014); Walder (2019); Walder and Chu (2020).

2. Recall the discussion in chapter 5.

3. Su (2006; 2011).

4. This argument appears only in Su's book-length treatment of the topic (Su 2011). It is absent from his earlier analyses (Su 2006), which place greater emphasis on the role of local authorities in organizing the killings.

5. Described in chapter 7.

6. Brass (2003); Copland (1998; 2002); Khan (2008, 122–42).

7. Silber and Little (1997, 92–104, 244–57); Naimark (2001, 159–67, 170–82). In Bosnia, "the nasty work of creating ethnically homogeneous Serb Territory was carried out primarily by paramilitary soldiers, who systematically beat, robbed, brutalized, and expelled the Muslim population, killing and raping as they moved from region to region. The paramilitaries were joined by local recruits, who operated close to their own towns and villages" (Naimark 2001, 159).

8. Robinson (2018, 32–53).

9. According to Robinson (2018, 21), "the army leadership mobilized an extensive network of civilian militia groups—like the NU [Council of Islamic Scholars] and PNI [Indonesian Nationalist Party]—and encouraged them to do the essential groundwork for the campaign of mass violence, such as identification, detention, transportation, and killing . . . It was through these officially sanctioned militia groups, moreover, that long-standing tensions were transformed into mass violence, that violence was sustained for long periods over wide stretches of the country, and that so many people became complicit in the crimes committed."

10. The killings began in October 1965 and continued into mid-1966 (Robinson 2018, 148–76). Robinson (2018, 120–21) states that the scholarly consensus is that the death toll was "somewhere around 500,000" (which he considers a conservative estimate). Cribb (2002, 557–59) provides a range of 400,000 to 800,000; based on a population of 104 million, this translates to a death rate ranging from 3.8 to 7.6 per thousand. A death toll of 500,000 would imply a death rate of 4.8 per thousand, somewhat higher than the death rate of 4.0, which was compiled in Guangxi in a much shorter period.

11. An example is the counter-insurgency campaign conducted by the military government against suspected leftists in rural Guatemala (Ball, Kobrak, and Spirer 1999).

## Appendix

1. Yan Lebin (2012). The journal's online archive of back issues no longer exists, but hard copies are still available in libraries.

2. Song (2020).

3. Cook (2016).

4. Song (2020) provides a careful analysis of their shifting attempts to justify themselves, which gave way to limited confession and self-criticism in the wake of extensive documentation compiled by the investigation teams.

5. Song (2020, 85–86) which corroborates Yan's (2012, 13–14) account of obstruction and provides additional detail from documentary and interview sources.

6. Yan (2012, 13); and Guangxi Party Committee (1987, 18:459). The latter source uses the term "five types" (landlords, rich peasants, counterrevolutionaries, bad elements, rightists). Song (2020, 65–72) provides an in-depth discussion of the preliminary efforts from 1972 to 1974 to document and interpret the death toll during the campaign to "Criticize Lin," which essentially blamed the "Lin Biao clique" for the excessively violent suppressions in the late 1960s.

7. Song (2020, 86–88); Yan (2012, 14).

8. Yan (2012, 14).

9. Song (2020, 30–31); Yan (2012, 14).

10. Song (2020, 87–89); Yan (2012, 13).

11. Yan (2012, 13–14).

12. Guangxi Party Committee (1987, 7:127).

13. Yan (2012, 13).

14. Song (2020, 32) tabulated numbers from all jurisdictions and organizations, and derived a total of 83,360. Our data set excludes all potentially overlapping organizations and includes only the totals provided for cities and counties, yielding a smaller total of 82,090.

15. The number of suicides during the period could be startlingly high. The number was provided in reports on death tolls for 23 of the 86 jurisdictions in the investigation reports. In this subset of jurisdictions, suicides constituted just under 40 percent of all deaths. This is unlikely to be representative, and the numbers were probably given in these reports precisely because they were so unusually high.

16. Guangxi Party Committee (1983).

17. Zheng (1996, 66–70, 114–19).

18. These changes are detailed in Guangxi Organization Department (1995, 631–44).

19. Song (2020, 118–23).

20. Guangxi Party Committee (1987, 1:1).

21. Song (2020, 95–117) provides a detailed analysis of the campaign to punish perpetrators and its rationale for leniency toward all but the most egregious criminal acts.

22. The chronology in volume 18 contains a great deal of information that was not included in one published in 1990, and which was withdrawn from circulation shortly afterward (Guangxi Cultural Revolution Chronology 1990).

23. Song (2016).

24. The data set was coded from the "chronicles of major events" for counties and cities included in volumes 8–15. To avoid double-counting, we did not code materials about individual organizations in volumes 16 and 17. We also excluded the accounts of "major incidents" in volumes 1–7, because they often repeated information in the chronologies.

25. There were 86 cities and counties at the time. The investigation reports also included material on Heshan City, a jurisdiction that was separated from Laibin County in 1981. The information from Heshan was consolidated with that for Laibin.

26. See Walder (2019).

27. https://sociology.stanford.edu/people/andrew-g-walder.

# REFERENCES

Andreas, Joel. 2002. "Battling over Political and Cultural Power during the Chinese Cultural Revolution." *Theory and Society* 31, no. 4 (August): 463–519.

Andreas, Joel. 2009. *The Rise of the Red Engineers: The Cultural Revolution and the Origins of China's New Class*. Stanford: Stanford University Press.

Ball, Patrick, Paul Kobrak, and Herbert F. Spirer. 1999. *State Violence in Guatemala, 1960–1996*. Washington, DC: American Association for the Advancement of Science.

Barlow, Jeffrey G. 1987. "The Zhuang Minority Peoples of the Sino-Vietnamese Frontier in the Song Period." *Journal of Southeast Asian Studies* 18, no. 2 (September): 250–69.

Bećirević, Edina. 2014. *Genocide on the Drina River*. New Haven: Yale University Press.

Beihai City Organization Department. 1993. *Zhongguo gongchandang Guangxi zhuangzu zizhiqu Beihai shi zuzhishi ziliao, 1926–1987* (Materials on the History of the Chinese Communist Party Organization in Beihai City, Guangxi Zhuang Autonomous Region, 1926–1987). Nanning: Guangxi renmin chubanshe.

Bergholz, Max. 2016. *Violence as a Generative Force: Identity, Nationalism, and Memory in a Balkan Community*. Ithaca: Cornell University Press.

Binyang County Annals. 1987. *Binyang xian zhi* (Binyang County Annals). Nanning: Guangxi renmin chubanshe.

Binyang County Organization Department. 1996. *Zhongguo gongchandang Guangxi zhuangzu zizhiqu Binyang xian zuzhishi ziliao, 1927–1987* (Materials on the History of the Chinese Communist Party Organization in Binyang County, Guangxi Zhuang Autonomous Region, 1927–1987). Nanning: Guangxi renmin chubanshe.

Brass, Paul R. 2003. "The Partition of India and Retributive Genocide in the Punjab, 1946–47: Means, Methods, and Purposes." *Journal of Genocide Research* 5, no. 1: 71–101.

Bu Weihua. 2008. *Zalan jiu shijie: Wenhua da geming de dongluan yu haojie* (Smashing the Old World: The Catastrophic Turmoil of the Cultural Revolution). Hong Kong: Zhongwen daxue chubanshe.

Central Committee, Chinese Communist Party. 1967a. *Zhonggong zhongyang, guowuyuan guanyu zai wuchan jieji wenhua da geming zhong jiaqiang gongan gongzuo de ruogan guiding* (Central Committee and State Council Regulations on Strengthening Public Security Work during the Great Proletarian Cultural Revolution). *Zhongfa* [67], 19, January 13. In Chinese Cultural Revolution Database (2013).

Central Committee, Chinese Communist Party. 1967b. *Zhonggong zhongyang, zhongyang wen'ge xiaozu pizhuan Wei Guoqing tongzhi 'Guangxi wenhua da geming zhong suo fan fangxiang luxian cuowu de jiantao'* (Central Committee and Central Cultural Revolution Group Approves and Forwards Comrade Wei Guoqing's "Self Criticism for Errors of Orientation and Line Committed During the Cultural Revolution"). *Zhongfa* [67], 342, November 12. In Chinese Cultural Revolution Database (2013).

Central Committee, Chinese Communist Party. 1967c. *Zhonggong zhongyang, guowuyuan, zhongyang junwei, zhongyang wen'ge guanyu Guangxi liangpai cujin geming da lianhe shitiao xieyi de piyu* (Instructions by the Central Committee, State Council, Central Military Commission and Central Cultural Revolution Group on the 10-point Agreement to Promote an Alliance of the Two Factions in Guangxi). *Zhongfa* [67] 343, November 12. In Chinese Cultural Revolution Database (2013).

Central Committee, Chinese Communist Party. 1967d. *Zhonggong zhongyang, guowuyuan, zhongyang junwei, zhongyang wen'ge guanyu Guangxi wenti de jueding* (Decision of the Central Committee, State Council, Central Military Commission and Central Cultural Revolution Group on the Guangxi Problem). *Zhongfa* [67] 353, November 18. In Chinese Cultural Revolution Database (2013).

Central Committee, Chinese Communist Party. 1968. *Zhonggong zhongyang, guowuyuan, zhongyang junwei, zhongyang wen'ge bugao* (Proclamation of the Central Committee, State Council, Central Military Commission, and Central Cultural Revolution Group). *Zhongfa* [68] 103, July 3. In Chinese Cultural Revolution Database (2013).

Central Military Commission. 1967a. *Zhongyang junwei batiao mingling* (Eight Orders of the Central Military Commission), 28 January. In Chinese Cultural Revolution Database (2013).

Central Military Commission. 1967b. *Zhongyang junwei shitiao mingling* (Ten Orders of the Central Military Commission), 6 April. In Chinese Cultural Revolution Database (2013).

Central Military Commission. 1967c. *Zhongyang junwei guanyu buren quanxian he chuli cuobu, qudi de qunzhong zuzhi wenti de liangge wenjian* (Two Documents of the Central Military Commission on the Authority to Make Arrests and Handling the Problem of Those Wrongly Arrested and the Suppression of Mass Organizations), 3 May. In Chinese Cultural Revolution Database (2013).

Chan, Anita, Stanley Rosen, and Jonathan Unger. 1980. "Students and Class Warfare: The Social Roots of the Red Guard Conflict in Guangzhou (Canton)." *China Quarterly* 83 (September): 397–446.

Chen, Jian. 1995. "China's Involvement in the Vietnam War, 1964–69." *China Quarterly* 142 (June): 356–87.

Chen, Jian. 2001. *Mao's China and the Cold War.* Chapel Hill: University of North Carolina Press.

Chinese Cultural Revolution Database. 2013. Song Yongyi, ed. Universities Service Centre for China Studies, Chinese University of Hong Kong. http://ccrd.usc .cuhk.edu.hk.

Cohen, Myron L. 1968. "The Hakka, or 'Guest People': Dialect as a Sociocultural Variable in Southeastern China." *Ethnohistory* 15, no. 3 (Summer): 237–92.

Constable, Nicole. 1996. "What Does It Mean to Be Hakka?" Pp. 3–35 in *Guest People: Hakka Identity in China and Abroad*, ed. Nicole Constable. Seattle: University of Washington Press.

Cook, Alexander C. 2016. *The Cultural Revolution on Trial: Mao and the Gang of Four.* Cambridge: Cambridge University Press.

Copland, Ian. 1998. "The Further Shores of Partition: Ethnic Cleansing in Rajasthan 1947." *Past & Present* 160 (August): 203–39.

Copland, Ian. 2002. "The Master and the Maharajas: The Sikh Princes and the East Punjab Massacres of 1947." *Modern Asian Studies* 36, no. 3 (July): 657–704.

Cribb, Robert. 2002. "Unresolved Problems in the Indonesian Killings of 1965–1966." *Asian Survey* 42, no. 4 (July–August): 550–63.

Dong Guoqiang and Andrew G. Walder. 2011. "Local Politics in the Chinese Cultural Revolution: Nanjing under Military Control." *Journal of Asian Studies* 70, no. 2 (May): 425–47.

Dong Guoqiang and Andrew G. Walder. 2018. "Forces of Disorder: The Army in Xuzhou's Factional Warfare, 1967–1969." *Modern China* 44, no. 2 (March): 139–69.

Dong Guoqiang and Andrew G. Walder. 2021. *A Decade of Upheaval: The Cultural Revolution in Rural China.* Princeton: Princeton University Press.

Fengshan County Annals. 2008. *Fengshan xian zhi* (Fengshan County Annals). Nanning: Guangxi renmin chubanshe.

Gao, James Z. 2004. *The Communist Takeover of Hangzhou: The Transformation of City and Cadre, 1949–1954.* Honolulu: University of Hawai'i Press.

Goldstein, Melvyn C. 2014. *A History of Modern Tibet, Vol. 3: The Storm Clouds Descend, 1955–1957.* Berkeley: University of California Press.

Goldstein, Melvyn C. 2019. *A History of Modern Tibet, Vol. 4: In the Eye of the Storm, 1957–1959.* Berkeley: University of California Press.

Goldstein, Melvyn C., Ben Jiao, and Tanzen Lhundrup. 2009. *On the Cultural Revolution in Tibet: The Nyemo Incident of 1969.* Berkeley: University of California Press.

Gross, Jan. T. 2002. *Neighbors: The Destruction of the Jewish Community in Jedwabne, Poland.* New York: Penguin.

Guangxi Cultural Revolution Chronology. 1990. *Guangxi wen'ge dashi nianbiao* (Chronology of the Cultural Revolution in Guangxi). Nanning: Guangxi renmin chubanshe.

Guangxi Local Annals Editorial Committee. 1995. *Guangxi tongzhi: jiaoyu zhi* (Guangxi Comprehensive Annals: Education). Nanning: Guangxi renmin chubanshe.

Guangxi Military District. 1967a. *Guangxi junqu guanyu huifu Guangxi gongren geming zaofan zongbu mingyu de shengming* (Declaration of the Guangxi Military District on the Withdrawal of Charges against the Guangxi Workers Revolutionary Rebel General Headquarters). September 10, 1967. In Chinese Cultural Revolution Database (2013).

Guangxi Military District. 1967b. *Guangxi junqu gonggao* (Proclamation of the Guangxi Military District). September 10, 1967. In Chinese Cultural Revolution Database (2013).

Guangxi Military District. 1967c. *Guangxi junqu zhizuo zhong suo fangxiang luxian cuowu de jiancha baogao* (Self-criticism of the Guangxi Military District for Errors of Orientation and Line Committed during Support the Left Work). November 8, 1967. In Chinese Cultural Revolution Database (2013).

Guangxi Organization Department. 1995. *Zhongguo gongchandang Guangxi zhuangzu zizhiqu zuzhishi ziliao, 1925–1987* (Materials on the History of the Chinese Communist Party Organization in the Guangxi Zhuang Autonomous Region, 1925–1987). Nanning: Guangxi renmin chubanshe.

Guangxi Party Committee. 1983. *Guanyu yinfa wo qu 'wen'ge' zhong bei dasizhe yishu jingji shanhou gongzuo shouxu, baobiao shixiang yiji shuoming de tongzhi* (Notice regarding Procedures for Properly Handling and Filling Out Forms regarding Compensation for Survivors of Those Killed during the "Cultural Revolution" in Our Region, with Sample Forms and Explanations). Guiban [1983] 43 hao. Zhonggong Guangxi zhuangzu zizhiquwei bangongting, September 15. https://www.maoistlegacy.de/db/items/show/829.

Guangxi Party Committee. 1987. *Guangxi 'wen'ge' dang'an ziliao* (Archival Materials on the Guangxi "Cultural Revolution"). 18 vols. Nanning: Zhonggong Guangxi zhuangzu zizhiqu weiyuanhui, zhengdang lingdao xiaozu bangongshi.

Guilin Municipal Party Committee. 1996. *Zhongguo gongchandang Guangxi zhuangzu zizhiqu Guilin shi zuzhishi ziliao* (Materials on the History of the Chinese Communist Party Organization in Guilin City, Guangxi Zhuang Autonomous Region). Guilin: Guangxi renmin chubanshe.

Hashimoto, Mantaro J. 1973. *The Hakka Dialect: A Linguistic Study of Its Phonology, Syntax and Lexicon*. Cambridge: Cambridge University Press.

Hua Linshan. 1987. *Les Années Rouges* (The Red Years). Paris: Le Seuil.

Hua Linshan. 1996. "Wen'ge qijian qunzhongxing paixi chengyin" (Causes of Mass Factionalism in the Cultural Revolution). Pp. 191–208 in *Wenhua da geming: shishi yu yanjiu* (The Cultural Revolution: Evidence and Analysis), ed. Liu Qingfeng. Hong Kong: Zhongwen daxue chubanshe.

Khan, Yasmin. 2007. *The Great Partition: The Making of India and Pakistan*. New Haven: Yale University Press.

Kuhn, Philip A. 1978. "The Taiping Rebellion." Pp. 264–317 in *Cambridge History of China: Volume 10: Late Ch'ing 1800–1911, Part 1*. Cambridge: Cambridge University Press.

Lary, Diana. 1972. "Communism and Ethnic Revolt: Some Notes on the Chuang Peasant Movement in Kwangsi, 1921–31." *China Quarterly* 49 (January–March): 126–35.

Lary, Diana. 1974. *Region and Nation: The Kwangsi Clique in Chinese Politics, 1925–1937*. Cambridge: Cambridge University Press.

Lee, Hong Yung. 1978. *The Politics of the Chinese Cultural Revolution: A Case Study*. Berkeley: University of California Press.

Leong, Sow-Theng. 1997. *Migration and Ethnicity in Chinese History: Hakkas, Pengmin and Their Neighbors*. Stanford: Stanford University Press.

Lewy, Guenter. 1978. *America in Vietnam*. Oxford: Oxford University Press.

Li Chuanjun. 2012. "Zai zhongyang wen'ge banshi jigou de jianwen" (A View onto the Administrative Staff of the Central Cultural Revolution Group). *Yanhuang chunqiu* 11 (November): 1–12.

Li, Fang-Kuei. 1960. "A Tentative Classification of Tai Dialects." Pp. 951–59 in *Culture in History: Essays in Honor of Paul Radin*, ed. Stanley Diamond. New York: Columbia University Press.

Li, Xiaobing. 2019. *Building Ho's Army: Chinese Military Assistance to North Vietnam*. Lexington: University Press of Kentucky.

Lingling Prefecture Annals. 2001. *Lingling diqu zhi* (Lingling Prefecture Annals). 2 vols. Changsha: Hunan renmin chubanshe.

Lingshan County Annals. 2000. *Lingshan xian zhi* (Lingshan County Annals). Nanning: Guangxi renmin chubanshe.

Lingui County Organization Department. 1996. *Zhongguo gongchandang Guangxi zhuangzu zizhiqu Lingui xian zuzhishi ziliao* (Materials on the History of the Chinese Communist Party Organization in Lingui County, Guangxi Zhuang Autonomous Region). Nanning: Guangxi renmin chubanshe.

Lingyun County Annals. 2007. *Lingyun xian zhi* (Lingyun County Annals). Nanning: Guangxi renmin chubanshe.

Lingyun County Organization Department. 1994. *Zhongguo gongchandang Guangxi zhuangzu zizhiqu Lingyun xian zuzhishi ziliao, 1929.11–1987.10* (Materials on the History of the Chinese Communist Party Organization in Lingyun County, Guangxi Zhuang Autonomous Region, November 1929–October 1987). Nanning: Guangxi renmin chubanshe.

Liu Guokai. 1987. *A Brief Analysis of the Cultural Revolution*. Ed. Anita Chan. Armonk, NY: M. E. Sharpe.

Luchuan County Organization Department. 1992. *Zhongguo gongchandang Guangxi zhuangzu zizhiqu Luchuan xian zuzhishi ziliao* (Materials on the History of the Chinese Communist Party Organization in Luchuan County, Guangxi Zhuang Autonomous Region). Nanning: Guangxi renmin chubanshe.

Lüthi, Lorenz M. 2008. *The Sino-Soviet Split: Cold War in the Communist World*. Princeton: Princeton University Press.

Luzhou City Annals. 1998. *Luzhou shi zhi* (Luzhou City Annals). Beijing: Fangzhi chubanshe.

MacFarquhar, Roderick, and Michael Schoenhals. 2006. *Mao's Last Revolution*. Cambridge, MA: Harvard University Press.

Mackerras, Colin. 1994. *China's Minorities: Integration and Modernization in the Twentieth Century*. Hong Kong: Oxford University Press.

Mao Zedong Chronology. 2013. *Mao Zedong nianpu, yijiusijiu-yijiuqiliu, di liu juan* (Mao Zedong Chronology, 1949–76, Vol. 6). Beijing: Zhongyang wenxian chubanshe.

Marks, Robert B. 1998. *Tigers, Rice, Silk and Silt: Environment and Economy in Late Imperial China*. Cambridge: Cambridge University Press.

Mullaney, Thomas. 2010. *Coming to Terms with the Nation: Ethnic Classification in Modern China*. Berkeley: University of California Press.

Naimark, Norman. 2001. *Fires of Hatred: Ethnic Cleansing in 20th Century Europe*. Cambridge, MA: Harvard University Press.

Nelsen, Harvey W. 1972. "Military Forces in the Cultural Revolution." *China Quarterly* 51 (July–September): 444–74.

Nelsen, Harvey W. 1981. *The Chinese Military System: An Organizational Study of the Chinese People's Liberation Army*. 2nd rev. ed. Boulder, CO: Westview Press.

Ngagpo, Jigme. 1988. "Behind the Unrest in Tibet." *China Spring Digest* (January–February): 22–32.

Organization Department, CCP Central Committee. 2000. *Zhongguo gongchandang zuzhishi ziliao 1921–1997* (Materials on the History of the Chinese Communist Party Organization, 1921–97). 19 vols. Beijing: Zhonggong dangshi chubanshe.

Organization Department, CCP Central Committee. 2004. *Zhongguo gongchandang lijie zhongyang weiyuan da cidian* (Historical Dictionary of Members of the Central Committee of the Chinese Communist Party). Beijing: Zhonggong dangshi chubanshe.

Pingle County Annals. 1995. *Pingle xian zhi* (Pingle County Annals). Beijing: Fangzhi chubanshe.

Qinzhou Prefecture Organization Department. 1996. *Zhongguo gongchandang Guangxi zhuangzu zizhiqu Qinzhou diqu zuzhishi ziliao, 1926–1987* (Materials on the History of the Chinese Communist Party Organization in Qinzhou Prefecture, Guangxi Zhuang Autonomous Region, 1926–1987). Nanning: Guangxi renmin chubanshe.

Roberts, J. A. G. 1969. "The Hakka-Punti War." Diss., Oxford University.

Robinson, Geoffrey B. 2018. *The Killing Season: A History of the Indonesian Massacres, 1965–66*. Princeton: Princeton University Press.

Rosen, Stanley. 1982. *Red Guard Factionalism and the Cultural Revolution in Guangzhou (Canton)*. Boulder, CO: Westview Press.

Ryan, William, Ellen R. K. Evers, and Don A. Moore. 2018. "False Positive Poisson." https://www.researchgate.net/publication/328399873.

Schafer, Edward H. 1967. *The Vermilion Bird: Tang Images of the South*. Berkeley: University of California Press.

Schoenhals, Michael. 2005. "'Why Don't We Arm the Left?' Mao's Culpability for the Cultural Revolution's 'Great Chaos' of 1967." *China Quarterly* 182 (June): 277–300.

Shin, Leo K. 2006. *The Making of the Chinese State: Ethnicity and Expansion on the Ming Borderlands*. Cambridge: Cambridge University Press.

Sichuan Province Annals. 1999. *Sichuan sheng zhi: dashi jishu (xia juan)* (Sichuan Province Annals: Narrative of Major Events [vol. 3]). Chengdu: Sichuan kexue jishu chubanshe.

Silber, Laura, and Allan Little. 1997. *Yugoslavia: Death of a Nation*. New York: Penguin.

Smith, Warren. 1996. *Tibetan Nation: A History of Tibetan Nationalism and Sino-Tibetan Relations*. Boulder, CO: Westview Press.

Song, Guoqing. 2020. "'Healing the Wounds?' Redressing State Crimes in Guangxi after the Cultural Revolution." Diss., Albert-Ludwigs University, Freiburg.

Song Yongyi, ed. 2002. *Wen'ge da tusha* (Cultural Revolution Massacres). Hong Kong: Kaifang zazhi she.

Song Yongyi, ed. 2016. *Guangxi wen'ge jimi dang'an ziliao* (Top Secret Archival Materials on the Cultural Revolution in Guangxi). 36 vols. New York: Guoshi chubanshe.

Spence, Jonathan D. 1996. *God's Chinese Son: The Taiping Heavenly Kingdom of Hong Xiuquan.* New York: Norton.

Strauss, Scott. 2006. *The Order of Genocide: Race, Power, and War in Rwanda.* Ithaca: Cornell University Press.

Su, Yang. 2006. "Mass Killings in the Cultural Revolution: A Study of Three Provinces." Pp. 96–123 in *The Chinese Cultural Revolution as History,* ed. Joseph W. Esherick, Paul G. Pickowicz, and Andrew G. Walder. Stanford: Stanford University Press.

Su, Yang. 2011. *Collective Killings in China during the Cultural Revolution.* New York: Cambridge University Press.

Sutton, Donald S. 1995. "Consuming Counterrevolution: The Ritual and Culture of Cannibalism in Guangxi, China, May to July 1968." *Comparative Studies in Society and History* 37, no. 1 (January): 136–72.

Tan Hecheng. 2010. *Xue de shenhua: gongyuan 1967 Hunan Daoxian wen'ge da tusha jishi* (Mythology of Blood: An Account of Hunan's 1967 Dao County Mass Killings). Hong Kong: Tianxingjian chubanshe.

Tan Hecheng. 2017. *The Killing Wind: A Chinese County's Descent into Madness during the Cultural Revolution.* Trans. Stacey Mosher and Guo Jian. New York: Oxford University Press.

Unger, Jonathan. 1984. "The Class System in Rural China: A Case Study." Pp. 121–41 in *Class and Social Stratification in Post-Revolution China,* ed. James L. Watson. Cambridge: Cambridge University Press.

Vogel, Ezra F. 1969. *Canton under Communism: Programs and Politics in a Provincial Capital, 1949–1968.* Cambridge, MA: Harvard University Press.

Walder, Andrew G. 2009. *Fractured Rebellion: The Beijing Red Guard Movement.* Cambridge, MA: Harvard University Press.

Walder, Andrew G. 2014. "Rebellion and Repression in China, 1966–1971." *Social Science History* 38, nos. 3–4 (Fall–Winter): 513–39.

Walder, Andrew G. 2015. *China Under Mao: A Revolution Derailed.* Cambridge, MA: Harvard University Press.

Walder, Andrew G. 2016. "Rebellion of the Cadres: The 1967 Implosion of the Chinese Party-State." *China Journal* 75 (January): 102–20.

Walder, Andrew G. 2019. *Agents of Disorder: Inside China's Cultural Revolution.* Cambridge, MA: Harvard University Press.

Walder, Andrew G., and James Chu. 2020. "Generating a Violent Insurgency: China's Factional Warfare of 1967–1968." *American Journal of Sociology* 126, no. 1 (July): 1–37.

Walder, Andrew G., and Yang Su. 2003. "The Cultural Revolution in the Countryside: Scope, Timing, and Human Impact." *China Quarterly* 173 (March): 82–107.

Walder, Andrew G., and Qinglian Lu. 2017. "The Dynamics of Collapse in an Authoritarian Regime: China in 1967." *American Journal of Sociology* 122, no. 4 (January): 1144–82.

Wang, Fahui, Guanxiong Wang, John Hartmann, and Wei Luo. 2012. "Sinification of Zhuang Place Names in Guangxi, China: A GIS-based Spatial Analysis Approach." *Transactions of the Institute of British Geographers* 37, no. 2: 317–333.

Weiner, Benno. 2020. *The Chinese Revolution on the Tibetan Frontier*. Ithaca: Cornell University Press.

Wu Di. 2010. *Neimeng wen'ge shilu: "Minzu fenlie" yu "wasu yundong"* (The Cultural Revolution in Inner Mongolia: "Ethnic Divisions" and "Elimination Campaigns"). Hong Kong: Tianxing jian chubanshe.

Yan Lebin. 2012. "Wo canyu chuli Guangxi wen'ge yiliu wenti" (I Participated in the Handling of Problems Left Over from the Cultural Revolution in Guangxi). *Yanhuang chunqiu* 11 (November): 13–20.

Yang Haiying. 2014. *Mei you mubei de caoyuan: Menggu ren yu wen'ge da tusha* (Grasslands without Tombstones: Massacres of Mongols during the Cultural Revolution). Xin Taibei: Baqi wenhua chubanshe.

Yang Jisheng. 2012. *Tombstone: The Great Chinese Famine*. Trans. Stacey Mosher and Guo Jian. New York: Farrar, Straus and Giroux.

Yang Jisheng. 2021. *The World Turned Upside Down: A History of the Chinese Cultural Revolution*. Trans. and ed. Stacy Mosher and Guo Jian. New York: Farrar, Straus and Giroux.

Yang Junge. 2004. "Wen'ge gaochao zhong de jingxi binguan" (The Jingxi Hotel during the High Tide of the Cultural Revolution). *Yanhuang chunqiu* 12 (December): 18–24.

Zhai, Qiang. 2000. *China and the Vietnam Wars, 1950–1975*. Chapel Hill: University of North Carolina Press.

Zheng Yi. 1996. *Scarlet Memorial: Tales of Cannibalism in Modern China*. Trans. and ed. T.P. Sym. Boulder, CO: Westview Press.

Zhou Enlai. 1967a. "Zhou Enlai di yici jiejian Guangxi liangpai daibiao tanhua jiyao" (Summary of Zhou Enlai's First Meeting with Representatives of the Two Guangxi Factions), June 1. In Chinese Cultural Revolution Database (2013).

Zhou Enlai. 1967b. "Zhou Enlai di erci jiejian Guangxi liangpai daibiao tanhua ji-yao" (Summary of Zhou Enlai's Second Meeting with Representatives of the Two Guangxi Factions), June 14. In Chinese Cultural Revolution Database (2013).

Zhou Enlai. 1967c. "Zhou Enlai di sanci jiejian Guangxi liangpai daibiao tanhua jiyao" (Summary of Zhou Enlai's Third Meeting with Representatives of the Two Guangxi Factions), June 15. In Chinese Cultural Revolution Database (2013).

Zhou Enlai. 1967d. "Zhou Enlai di sici jiejian Guangxi liangpai daibiao tanhua ji-yao" (Summary of Zhou Enlai's Fourth Meeting with Representatives of the Two Guangxi Factions), June 30. In Chinese Cultural Revolution Database (2013).

Zhou Enlai. 1967e. "Zhou Enlai di wuci jiejian Guangxi liangpai tanhua jiyao" (Summary of Zhou Enlai's Fifth Meeting with the Two Guangxi Factions), August 24. In Chinese Cultural Revolution Database (2013).

Zhou Enlai. 1967f. "Zhou Enlai di liuci jiejian Guangxi liangpai daibiao tanhua ji-yao" (Summary of Zhou Enlai's Sixth Meeting with Representatives of the Two Guangxi Factions), September 13. In Chinese Cultural Revolution Database (2013).

Zhou Enlai. 1967g. "Zhou Enlai di qici jiejian Guangxi liangpai daibiao tanhua ji-yao" (Summary of Zhou Enlai's Seventh Meeting with Representatives of the Two Guangxi Factions), September 22. In Chinese Cultural Revolution Database (2013).

Zhou Enlai. 1967h. "Zhou Enlai dui Liuzhou tielu ju liangpai daibiao de tanhua" (Zhou Enlai's Talks with Representatives of the Two Factions in the Liuzhou Railway Bureau), November 10. In Chinese Cultural Revolution Database (2013).

Zhou Enlai. 1967i. "Zhou Enlai jiejian 'lianzhi' fu jing daibiao tuan tanhua jiyao" (Summary of Zhou Enlai's Talks with the "Allied Command" Delegation to the Capital), November 16. In Chinese Cultural Revolution Database (2013).

Zhou Enlai. 1967j. "Zhou Enlai di baci jiejian Guangxi liangpai tanhua jiyao" (Summary of Zhou Enlai's Eighth Meeting with Representatives of the Two Guangxi Factions), November 19. In Chinese Cultural Revolution Database (2013).

Zhou Enlai. 1967k. "Zhou Enlai jiejian Guangxi liangpai hexin xiaozu de jianghua" (Zhou Enlai's Talks with the Core Leadership of the Two Guangxi Factions), November 23. In Chinese Cultural Revolution Database (2013).

Zhou Enlai Chronology. 1997. *Zhou Enlai nianpu, yijiusijiu-yijiuqiliu, xia juan* (Zhou Enlai Chronology, 1949–76, vol. 3). Beijing: Zhongyang wenxian chubanshe.

Zhou, Xun, ed. 2012. *The Great Chinese Famine, 1958–1962: A Documentary History.* New Haven: Yale University Press.

Zwierzchowski, Jan, and Ewa Tabeau. 2010. "The 1992–95 War in Bosnia and Herze-govina: Census-Based Multiple System Estimation of Casualties' Undercount." Berlin: Households in Conflict Network and Institute for Economic Research.

# INDEX

CPSIA information can be obtained
at www.ICGtesting.com
Printed in the USA
JSHW021441200123
36569JS00005B/5